KEEP YOU

Keep Your Pigeons Flying

by
LEON F. WHITNEY, D.V.M.

with drawings by
ERNEST H. HART

faber and faber

First published in 1961
by Faber and Faber Limited
3 Queen Square London W.C.1
Second edition 1968
First published in Faber Paperbacks 1983
Printed in Great Britain by
Redwood Burn Ltd, Trowbridge, Wiltshire

© *Leon F. Whitney 1961, 1968*

British Library Cataloguing in Publication Data

Whitney, Leon F.
Keep your pigeons flying.—2nd ed.
1. Homing pigeons
I. Title
636.5'96   SF469

ISBN 0–571–11541–1

To

MORRIS GORDON

that master of racing homing pigeons,
this book is affectionately dedicated.

Contents

Contents

Illustrations

9

Foreword

It is difficult to express my gratitude in a few words, but I cherish the opportunity to say a heartfelt thank you to the many friends who had a part in helping me with this book. Mr. Newton Brazier and Mr. Vincent Jorczyk first urged me to write it. Mr. Morris Gordon made suggestions for contents, Mr. H. J. Humphrey kindly read the manuscript and made helpful suggestions. M. Jef Van Riel of Belgium and Mr. John Reid of Scotland and several London fliers co-operated in the study of pigeon parasites. Dr. R. Arch co-operated in the Malucidin studies. M. Jan Aerts of Belgium has supplied much needed information. Especially helpful was the criticism and editing of Mr. Colin Osman. Dr. Everett Wehr supplied excellent and new information about parasites. Mr. R. G. Todd of the Pharmaceutical Society of Great Britain edited for the English market the information on drugs in Chapter 4. Mrs. Dorothy Livingston gave valued assistance in researching the material. Dr. Willard Hollander made suggestions for corrections of material which have been incorporated in this second edition. My secretary, Mrs. Margaret Berna, has been of great help in editing and typing. Brinkler, Osborne and Young kindly supplied the grains used in illustrations. To all of these friends, my deepest appreciation.

Introduction

This is not a book for the scientist. It was written for the pigeon fancier, as any scientist reading it will immediately deduce. I believe that those of us who make scientific findings available to the practical breeder are performing a service and are fulfilling a need widely felt by pigeon fanciers who have spent time, money and energy in their effort to keep our pigeons flying.

What good is derived from science if scientific information is not made available, but remains merely secluded and exclusive? Truth is for everybody. It is my belief that the time has come to make known the facts about pigeon diseases and parasites, so that the fancier can be made aware of trouble before disease destroys his flock.

Those of a more scientific nature are referred to the excellent books on the general subject of poultry diseases written for the scientist in his own language.

At the outset, I wish to make my position clear on the subject of treating sick pigeons: in the case of racing pigeons, treatment only pays in the early stages of any disease. In the case of fancy pigeons, it always pays. Once a serious disease attacks a racing homer, chances are he will never quite be the bird he might have been. But what about disease attacking a valuable stock bird? Indeed, it pays to attempt a cure.

For many years I have been racing homers and helping pigeon men with their problems. In addition, I have conducted research on pigeons and have published some of the results.

All of my experience convinces me that our first thought should be to keep them flying by prevention of disease. Our second consideration should be to keep our birds in the best health possible to promote endurance and speed, and lastly, we should try to cure sick pigeons at the first sign of sickness.

Introduction

To achieve these results, we must know something about how the body functions, about the causes of disease, about the symptoms of various diseases, whether germ-caused or parasite-caused, and we must know the latest scientific means not only of curing disease and eliminating parasites, but of preventing disease altogether.

There appears to be little use in publishing a book on cures of homing-pigeon diseases, because it has been common practice for the homing pigeon fancier to kill his sick birds.

When this book was almost complete, I wrote to a leading publisher about it. He naturally consulted some outstanding fliers, asking them if a book on curing pigeon diseases would sell. Every man consulted replied that it would not, because sick pigeons are always killed. So the publisher answered that he was not interested in the book. Had he written to those fliers asking whether a book on pigeon *health* would be acceptable, one which would help each man to win races, to raise every squeaker, to insure a good moult, to make and save him money, in short to keep the birds flying, every fancier would have said, 'It's a natural.' That's why this book bears the name '*Keep Your Pigeons Flying*'.

At this point, I want to make one point clear. I disagree with those who destroy every sick pigeon. Who knows for certain that an illness permanently cripples a pigeon? Does illness cripple a human being? Even severe injuries have failed to do so. Glenn Cunningham, one of the world's greatest milers, was once a cripple. Many a great race-horse had been sick many times as a colt. I have operated on race-horses with one side of their throats paralysed from disease and have brought them back to racing form. How many great greyhounds have survived attacks of hepatitis, Carre's disease (distemper), all kinds of intestinal parasites, including hookworms, and yet become top racers?

Consider the recent work conducted among various species of animals, studies made in an effort to determine whether the rapidly grown disease-free young lived as long or, were better specimens than the slowly grown young which had survived illnesses. All of this work seems to indicate that the latter group is healthier, longer-lived, and tougher.

Many writers on the subject of pigeon ailments express the common opinions of their time. Many a writer has not gone to the fountain of science, preferring rather to be content with discussion of diseases as he knows them. Thus, several otherwise excellent treatises on pigeons are handicapped by incomplete or even misleading chapters on diseases.

Introduction

One of my favourite books which imparts many excellent suggestions on rearing, training and racing, discusses the following pigeon ailments: going light, diarrhoea, stoppage of the crop, canker, roup, one-eye cold, wing disease, egg binding, fatty degeneration, feather rot. In that book we learn that human diphtheria and bird canker are caused by the same organism. When the book was written, this information was the best available.

When my father was a boy, chickens had very few diseases besides The Pip. Today, ailments formerly described as The Pip now encompass so many poultry diseases it takes a 2-in. thick book to describe them. As a matter of fact, The Pip is never mentioned. Indeed, there never was such a disease.

In 1912, one of the standard books published on animal diseases listed only the following *poultry* diseases: roup, cholera, going light, chicken pox, leukemia, gapes, scaly legs, favus, air sac mite, catarrh, pip, and simple diarrhoea. The section on pigeon diseases was contained in a mere 6-in. column of 600 words.

Even by 1920 human beings had a disease which physicians called *jaundice*. Nobody has jaundice any more. Jaundice, that is, as a disease. Jaundice is only a sign or symptom that something is amiss with one's liver. Pigeons rarely show the symptom of jaundice.

Today most pigeon fanciers seem to think that birds have a disease called *going light* and not too many other diseases. I hope, if it does nothing else, this book will convince you that there is no such disease. *Going light*—loss of substance—is, like jaundice, a symptom of many diseases.

Our present-day fountain of science pours forth rich knowledge. It does not consider opinion as truth. It asks: 'Has that opinion been tested to see if it conforms with nature?' Then, if not, science tests it to find out. The old books were interested in opinion. When the opinion said that canker and diphtheria were caused by the same organism, opinion was found to be wrong. And science leaves us a free record of such tests. Therefore, it is more difficult today to write a book on pigeon diseases than it was when opinion was accepted as fact.

Readers ask: 'Why?' 'How do you know?' Science is not interested in *authority* because *authority* can be wrong, and often is.

The books I mentioned above were written by authorities and most of them were as wrong as they could be, often, as we have seen, calling a symptom a disease.

We should all be doubters of authority until the opinion expressed

15

Introduction

has been tested to see if it conforms with nature. I hope you will doubt every sentence in this book and ask yourself: 'How does he know this?' If I have not gone to the source, which is science, then my writing is merely opinion. And while upon test it may conform with nature, until it does meet such requirements, it is merely opinion.

Clients have often said to me: 'The doctor has it easy compared with you veterinarians; his patients tell him where they ache, how they feel, how long they've been sick, but your patients can't talk.' That's true, they can't talk. But if the vet has a discriminating eye, the patients have ways of telling him.

Through my experience in studying pigeons, I must say that ailments in pigeons are more difficult to diagnose than those of dogs, cats, monkeys, and four-legged animals in general. The symptoms of so many ailments are so similar that even the long experienced student generally makes no claim as to his absolute diagnosis of a live bird. Poultry pathologists, asked to determine what disease is going through a flock of hens, generally ask to examine from four to a dozen birds in the last stages. They judge from the effects of the disease on the internal organs.

Although the field of pigeon diseases has not yet been adequately studied, enough is known about causes, symptoms, and cures to enable us to care for our birds much more wisely than we once could. That does not mean it is easy to recognize all the diseases of birds. Frequently you can't tell by looking at the outside of an individual sick bird what its trouble is. It sits hunched up, droops, refuses food, has diarrhoea—it looks and is sick. Probably no one can look at that pigeon and determine at a glance that it has, let us say, Paratyphoid. Symptoms of a number of other diseases are too similar for quick and easy diagnosis. If you remember this you won't blame yourself when you fail to detect the first signs of disease in your bird, and you will understand that your veterinarian also may run up against difficulty in immediate diagnosis, where outward symptoms are so much alike.

I completely disagree with those who say 'Kill them' at the first signs of illness: I have cured too many. If they were worth raising, they are worth curing, and just because our fathers didn't know how to cure canker, in fact didn't even know pigeons had intestinal parasites, it doesn't mean that we have to be ignorant and not even try. We are often royally rewarded when we do.

What is the reason, do you suppose, which lies behind the fact that a loft which has been high in ratings, suddenly or gradually drops to mediocrity? We all know of such lofts.

Introduction

Here, for example, are some of the experiences noted by various lofts in the United States. A well-known Boston area loft which had been the top loft for many years, struck three years when their birds rated toward the bottom of the list. Then they came back to the top again.

A Connecticut loft won the O.B. and Y.B. combined averages. The following year no bird was placed above fifteenth in the O.B. races. Training, food, and all other factors were the same so far as the owner knew.

A New Jersey loft bought some outstanding birds which had won many honours in California. In New Jersey they seemed to be third rate; nevertheless the owner persisted with the same birds, and during the third year he won top honours.

Another good illustration of what I mean is an article in the September, 1957, *American Racing Pigeon News*. A Californian who gives me permission to quote from his article states as follows: 'With 16 years' experience breeding and flying racing pigeons, it is a discouraging sight to find your young birds vomiting their feed for no apparent reason; going light, and dying. The infection became apparent in the loft in the latter part of May, and to date has not been definitely brought under control despite the great expense which has been involved plus the time consumed (which, incidentally, cost the writer his job).'

He goes on to tell how the trouble was diagnosed by his state pathology department and how all suggested treatments failed.

Another illustration is the experience of a fancier who imported Eu opean birds for which he made himself poor, and then was unable to raise more than 1 out of 3 youngsters because of Paratyphoid which he could not cure. Those birds which recovered spontaneously were all lost in flying because, as the owner believes, the disease had weakened them constitutionally. He says he understands that 'recovered birds are carriers', and wonders whether he will always have this trouble as long as he breeds pigeons.

Similar examples could be multiplied to fill this book. The owners whose birds failed to respond to their excellent care, in every case I have known, blamed the difficulty on the wrong cause. Surely it was not disease because there were few signs of sickness. What was it? In almost all cases, internal parasites.

To summarize, although diagnosis is not a simple matter, the owner can recognize and treat various common ailments. It is essential for all of us to know what pigeon diseases are; the particular outward signs,

Introduction

if any, which are characteristic; what causes these symptoms; what to do about effecting cures and, most important, how to prevent disease whenever possible.

This book, I hope, shows the pigeon fancier how to prevent disease, how to rid his birds of parasites and keep them flying. If we can keep disease out of our lofts, if we can keep parasites to a minimum, if we can protect our birds by immunization so they will not be able to contract diseases in the shipping crates, we shall keep 'em flying and doing their best. That is our goal and to help you reach that goal is the aim of this book.

This book is designed to be read in many countries and therefore I have mentioned drugs which may not be freely available in all countries. Wherever possible I have indicated the source of the drugs and of the method of obtaining them. The information was as near accurate as possible in 1967, but the various governments' regulations may have changed since then.

I

The Pigeon's Body and How
it Functions

So many grammar school and college graduates have managed to escape courses in even human physiology and anatomy that I have long ceased to be surprised by the fact, that few pigeon owners have any conception at all of bird physiology. If you are to get the most out of this book, it will be necessary to review briefly both structure and function as they are related to our pigeons. Even though the study of the mechanism of the living body is to me one of the most fascinating subjects in the world, the general attitude is such that I feel I must warn you that you are not in for an 'organ recital'. All that will be necessary here is to learn enough about your birds' bodies so that you may treat them sensibly.

The science which treats of the functions of living things or of their parts is called *physiology*. That which treats of the structure of the body and the relationships of its parts is called *anatomy*. Let us consider the two and see how the body is formed and how its components function.

The body of every animal grows from a single cell. What is a cell? It is a unit of life smaller than our eyes can see. The whole body of some tiny animals is a single cell, the *amoeba* and *paramœcium*, for example· Other animals consist of whole colonies of cells. All the visible animate creatures are immense colonies of cells, and each cell has some special function. Every one of these cells is composed of a covering within which is some *protoplasm*, a substance not unlike egg white, and a *nucleus*, which is its business part.

The first cell, which resulted from the uniting of a male cell (sperm) and a female cell (ovum), and thus started the bird, is complete in every detail. It is a favourite academic paradox to say that a cell multiplies by

19

dividing, and quite true, of course. If one cell divides into two cells, it has divided, but because it is two, it has multiplied. The two become four; the four, eight. As they go on dividing and thus increasing, different cells become specialized at certain stages.

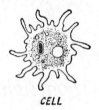

CELL

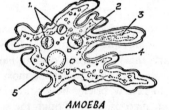

PARAMŒCIUM

AMOEBA
1. Food vacuoles 2. Nucleus 3. Endoplasm
4. Ectoplasm 5. Contractile vacuole

Some may become skin, some liver, some heart, some germ plasm, some feathers, some beak, and so forth. There are cells which never renew themselves; brain cells for example. Then there are other very much specialized cells, like those in the feathers and nails, which constantly renew themselves. They all live together in a happy community or colony, doing their work unless hindered by improper nourishment or crowding (from overfatness), or disease. That's what our pigeons are—big colonies of cells.

THE BODY'S COVERING

The skin is composed of several layers, each made up of innumerable cells. Two main layers are recognized: the outer layer, *epidermis*, and the lower layer or true skin, the *dermis*. Sometimes we hear the epidermis called the cuticle or the scarfskin, and colloquially the scurfskin. The true skin, in turn, consists of two layers. The skin is constantly shedding and renewing itself.

The Pigeon's Body and How it Functions

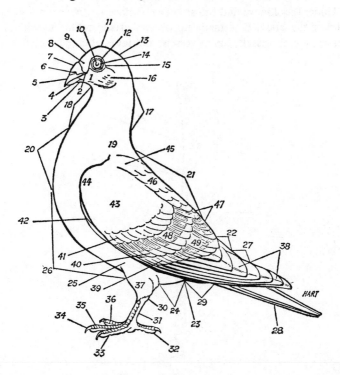

EXTERNAL ANATOMY

HEAD: (1) Cheek, (2) Angle of lips, (3) Chin, (4) Lower beak, (5) Upper beak, (6) Nostril, (7) Cere or wattle, (8) Lores, (9) Frontal or forehead, (10) Pupil, (11) Crown or topskull, (12) Fringe of eyelid, (13) Backskull, (14) Iris, (15) Eye cere or Orbital skin, (16) Ear feathers or Auriculars.

NECK: (17) Nape, (18) Throat or bib, (19) Neck blend or hackle.

BODY: (20) Crop, (21) Back, (22) Rump, (23) Vent, (24) Abdomen, (25) Flank, (26) Breast.

TAIL: (27) Upper or dorsal tail coverts, (28) Retrices, or main tail feathers, (29) Under or ventral tail coverts or fluff.

FOOT: (30) Hock, (31) Tarsus or shank, (32) Hind or first toe, (33) Outer or fourth toe, (34) Claw, (35) Middle or third toe, (36) Inner or second toe, (37) Leg or tibia.

WING: (38) Primary remiges or wing flights, (39) Secondary remiges or wing flights, (40) Secondary or greater wing coverts, (41) Median or middle coverts, (42) Spurious wing of thumb feathers, (43) Lesser coverts, (44) Wrist, or wing butt, (45) Shoulder, (46) Scapulars or 'heart', or saddle, (47) Tertials, (48) Second wing bar, (49) First wing bar.

21

The Pigeon's Body and How it Functions

Under the skin we find subcutaneous connective tissue, an interesting part of the body. It is made up of very elastic cells. Through it run nerves, lymph vessels, blood vessels, and fat is often deposited in it.

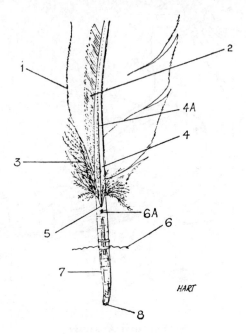

STRUCTURE OF CONTOUR FEATHER

(1) Outer web of vane, (2) Vane or Vexillum, (3) Fluff, (4) Rachis or shaft, (5) Hyporachis, (6) Skin level, (7) Quill or calamus, (8) Proximal umbilicus. (4A) Shaft groove, (6A) Distal umbilicus.

Out of the skin grow the appendages we call feathers in birds. Feathers are modifications of hairs. They grow out of the skin from *follicles*. In the follicles (sacs or sheaths) are little muscles which, for example, cause a bird's feathers to fluff out.

The intricate and beautiful feather coats of birds are actually complex adaptations of hairs which the mammals grow in simple form. These feathers, which are arranged in patterns, grow from the inner layer of the skin.

There is, of course, an extraordinary variety in plumage and colours in birds of various species. There are three general kinds of colours. One type is called chemical-absorption colours. Feathers with these

The Pigeon's Body and How it Functions

colours absorb chemicals which, in some species of birds, actually wash out in rain or when the bird takes a bath. Such colours are black, red, brown, orange, green, but never blue. A second kind of colour is produced by pigment combined with the actual structure, in the furrows and ridges of the feathers' surface. Here we find blue, green, and yellow and combinations of these. The third type of colouration is the iridescence one sees on a pigeon's neck, for instance. It is metallic and is produced by granules of pigment confined to the thin transparent covering of feathers.

LARGER FEATHERS OF THE WING

The primaries are replaced starting with 1 and progressing to 10. Secondaries usually moult from the outside inward, i.e., 1 and 10, 2 and 9, 3 and 8, etc

Although it may seem different to the casual observer, the moulting of birds is analogous to the shedding of hair on the part of mammals. It is controlled by similar influences: the number of hours of daylight, hormones, and, to some extent, the temperature. In the case of birds, it is believed that the amount of fat which they accumulate may also have something to do with moulting.

If one looks carefully, one will see an occasional pigeon with wing feathers of unequal length. There may be three short flight feathers, then one or two half an inch longer, the next short, and so on. Yet how few persons observing such a wing realize what it means? Many fanciers examine the wing of a flier to judge its value. Irregular wings disqualify a flier but they should not disqualify a bird for breeding.

The irregular feather length is simply a map of the bird's treatment or health during the time the feathers were growing during the moult. The longest feathers represent the potential wing. If feathers are short

23

they signify that the bird was either sick or undernourished during the time the short feathers were growing.

The growing primaries do not increase in length at the same rate, If the outside or end primary is called No. 10, then No. 6, No. 5, No. 4, No. 3 grow faster than any others. Thus No. 6 grows faster than No. 7, No. 7 faster than No. 8, which in turn exceeds No. 9, and No. 10 grows slowest of all. The No. 3 grows faster than No. 2, which grows faster than No. 1. These are relative speeds of juvenile feathers. Those growing in after the first moult were also measured and it was found that the rate and duration of growth were responsible for any increase in the feather length. Under excellent conditions during the moult, the second feathers are a little longer than the first lot.

Under the feathers, the skin of birds is in general like that of mammals, except that it emits more oil. Pigeons possess an oil gland at the base of the tail, from which oil is spread to the feathers by the actions of the bird. If you have watched a bird preening itself, you will have seen that it first reaches around to the middle of its back at the base of the tail and then preens its feathers with its bill. It is thought to obtain the oil from the gland by pinching it. The motion is made very rapidly. Spreading the oil over the feathers makes them water-resistant.

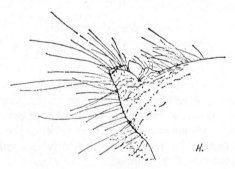

OIL GLANDS AND FILOPLUMES OF TAIL

These protective coats, plus its natural resistance to water, make the skin waterproof. It is not, however, resistant to all oils, some of which can soak through it. In fact, the skin can absorb a good many drugs and substances which can be toxic (poisonous) to the bird.

In addition to its function as a protective covering, the skin is also an organ of touch. Some parts are extremely sensitive. Through it, too, the bird responds to variations in heat and cold outside.

The Pigeon's Body and How it Functions

The skin heals by growing outward from the lower layers if it is not wholly destroyed by a gash, scald, or other injury. (Blisters usually are pockets of fluid between layers of skin.) It is for this reason that you should, in the case of an injury to a pigeon, bring the sides of the destroyed area as closely together as possible, so that the space to be covered over will be as narrow as you can make it. Moreover, if left open, the newly generated skin will be devoid of glands and feathers. Great bare areas become covered with skin, but not skin with the usual accessories.

Do pigeons sweat? The fact that they do is shown by a study of their water losses. Indeed, as in the case of many mammals, pigeons control their temperatures by sweating. The heat loss effected by water vaporization is considerable. One of the principles of refrigeration is water evaporation which, when it occurs, reduces the temperature at the point of evaporation to close to freezing. This accounts for the fact that a breeze evaporating even a tiny film of perspiration from our own exposed skin brings about a welcome chilling effect. Everyone knows how cold the skin feels when it has been touched with ether which evaporates. This is also true with water evaporation. The same thing goes on in the pigeon's lungs, thus helping regulate the bird's temperature. Pigeons in fact mostly sweat internally, releasing water vapour into the the lungs and air sacs. About one-third of the total water loss comes from the skin, lungs, air sacs, liver, muscles; two-thirds from the intestinal tract. Only that part which is evaporated from the skin and lungs reduces the body's temperature. The water loss from the kidneys and intestines has little effect. In diarrhoea, pigeons need more water to make up for the loss, and when flying they also need more water. Just how much water is lost for each 100 miles of flying should be studied. Our pigeons may not show abnormal thirst after a 100-mile flight, but does anyone actually know whether the loss is so slight that a bird in flying 500 miles need not stop for a drink? The fact that many do stop, even winning birds, is attested to by our occasionally finding mud on their feet.

THE BODY'S FRAMEWORK

The Skeleton. The skeleton is the framework of the body and protection for the organs. The ribs cover the lungs, heart, liver, stomach, kidneys and pancreas; the skull covers the brain and such delicate organs as the hearing mechanism. These services which bones perform are not

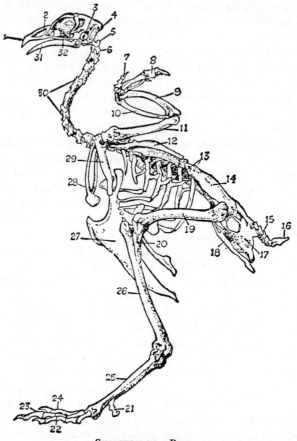

SKELETON OF A BIRD

(1) Premaxilla, (2) Nasal, (3) Ear opening, (4) Occipital, (5) Atlas, (6) Axis, (7) First digit, (8) Second digit, (9) Ulna, (10) Radius, (11) Humerus, (12) Scapula, (13) Ribs, (14) Ilium, (15) Tail vertebra, (16) Pygostyle, (17) Ischium, (18) Pubis, (19) Femur, (20) Fibula, (21) First toe, (22) Fourth toe, (23) Third toe, (24) Second toe, (25) Metatarsus, (26) Tibia, (27) Sternum, (28) Clavicle, (29) Coracoid, (30) Cervical vertebra, (31) Mandible, (32) Maxilla.

always fully appreciated because we think of them primarily in their role of support.

Each species differs from the next in form; breeds within species differ from other breeds, and individuals vary in some respects. The skeleton on which the soft tissue of the body hangs is the basic cause of

The Pigeon's Body and How it Functions

these form differences. In some breeds of pigeons, for example, the mere shortness of certain leg bones can cause a startling difference in appearance.

Some bones are solid, others hollow or filled with marrow in which white blood-cells may be generated. Some are mere beads and others long and strong. The way they are joined is an interesting study in itself. There are ball-and-socket joints (hips), hinge joints (knees), others made by one bone abutting another with a cushion between (vertebrae) and modifications of all three kinds.

The skeleton is a marvellous framework, replete with strength where strength is needed, rigidity where rigidity is needed, flexibility, swivels, and hinges where stretching, bending and rotating are required.

Each long bone is made up of a shaft of hard, brittle material with a covering of dense, hard bone. Around the whole is a sort of skin called the *periosteum*. On top or on the bottom of the spongy end, if the bone terminates at a joint, is a springy, cartilaginous pad, called the *epi-physeal* cartilage, which takes the shocks. All through the bone small spaces form tunnels, which carry blood and nerves; nourishment is also furnished by the periosteum.

Some bones are flat: ribs, head bones, and shoulder blades are examples. They are not so solid as they seem, but are well fortified with nourishment. The ribs join at the lower extremities with cartilage. These look like true ribs but are only extensions upward from a flat 'bone'—the *sternum* or breastbone. The sternum is not actually a bone, but is composed of cartilage of a springy, tough nature, which is fortunate as it needs to be flexible, considering all the strains it undergoes.

At the points where ribs and these tough, elastic extensions of the breastbone meet, one sometimes finds enlargements which may stay throughout life. These enlargements are an indication of rickets or, in other words, evidence that the bird was inadequately fed or was sick for a considerable part of his growing period.

The pigeon's wings are clearly analogous to the front legs of a dog, or arms of a man, but the skeletal structure has been altered in a number of ways and in the case of man and bird, only the hind legs support the body. A most striking difference is in the formation of the breastbone, which in the bird is deep like a keel instead of flat. The differences in the head, and the beak, are familiar to everyone. Birds have 'wishbones'—*clavicles* (collar-bones), like a human being.

The process of bone healing is most interesting, and it is worth while

27

to understand it in case you have to manage a bird, one or both of whose legs or wings are fractured.

Let us suppose that a break occurs in the bones of the leg. The break is a simple one, and when our bird returns home after his accident, the broken leg is obvious. Considerable traction—force in drawing—is required to pull the leg out so that the ends of the bone may be brought together—*in apposition*, your doctor calls it—and set.

Now the ends of the bone must knit. Here is where it is worth while for the owner to know what happens, so that he can give the bird the attention and care required.

For several days the body withdraws lime and other minerals from the bone ends. Gradually they become soft, like cartilage. Up to the end of this period it doesn't make much difference if the bones are not perfectly matched at the break. The second step, after the softening process, is the growth from each end of connective fibres which join the bone ends together, whereupon it shrinks, pulling the ends closer. This process is completed in 6 to 7 days. Up to this time, it doesn't make much difference how straight the bone is kept, so long as the ends are in apposition. At any time during this interval it is possible to bend it at the break.

Next comes a stage when the junction or *callus* becomes impregnated with mineral salts of calcium and phosphorus—in other words, it hardens. From this point on, it is essential that the bone be kept straight, and meticulous care must be given to seeing that it is. Once the callus is strong enough so that the bone will not bend, the splint or cast can be removed.

The last period involves the shrinking of the callus. Some bones will set with what appears to be a disfiguring bulge about the break, but in time this largely disappears, leaving a well-repaired bone even stronger than the adjacent unbroken parts.

Many injured bones can't be set properly. Some are so badly shattered that chips must be removed and nature be trusted to pull the pieces together. There are breaks of such a nature that the bone breaks but stays in place; others where part of the bone breaks and part does not. These are called greenstick fractures. Compound fractures are those in which the broken bone protrudes through the skin.

The Muscles. Skeletal muscles help hold the framework together and co-operate with it in walking, flying and so forth. But there are two kinds of muscles, the skeletal being obvious, while the others, not seen from outside the body, are called the *smooth* muscles. Under a micro-

The Pigeon's Body and How it Functions

scope, fibres of a skeletal muscle appear to have bands or striations, which do not exist on the smooth muscles. The striated muscles are under voluntary control. The duties of the smooth muscles are generally restricted to the functioning of organs and digestive tract. The gullet, intestines, bladder, blood vessels, and sphincter muscles, which act more or less involuntarily, are all smooth.

The food of muscles is blood sugar which is broken down into usable substances. The wastes are removed by the blood and leave the body by the lungs and other avenues of excretion.

THE CIRCULATORY SYSTEM

Heart and Vessels. The body is nourished by the blood. It delivers to the cells the substances they need, picks up the bad and useless, and delivers waste to the organs of excretion. At the centre of this marvellous system is a pump, the heart, an organ situated in the chest, as we know, and which for efficiency is not excelled by any man-made device.

The heart receives blood into two sides, then squeezes or contracts, so that the blood is driven into two large tubes (vessels). One leads to the lungs; the other divides and carries blood fore and aft into smaller vessels which, in turn, carry it about the body. In the lungs the blood liberates a gas, *carbon dioxide*, takes up another gas, *oxygen*, and is hustled back to the heart to be pumped around the body to distribute the oxygen and pick up cell waste.

The great arteries which carry the blood from the heart start dividing into smaller arteries, these into other smaller and smaller ones, called *arterioles*, and thence into *capillaries*. From the capillaries the blood returns to the heart via *venules*, *veins*, and finally large veins. It also returns in *lymph tubes* or *vessels*. (The lymph is blood without red cells.) A most interesting feature of the blood supply of the bird is a transverse vein in the neck connecting the two jugular veins. If you watch a bird you will see that his head can turn almost completely around. This twisting, of course, shuts off the flow of blood through one jugular vein, but the blood starts from the brain in both jugulars and flows across from the constricted vein into the functioning one via this short circuit or transverse vein.

The pump keeps up its contracting squeezes and relaxations rhythmically for the life of the pigeon. It says, lubb, dubb, lubb, dubb, and in a 1 pound bird pumps about 4 ounces of blood every minute. Everything about it is wonderful: the delicate valves, the strength, its four chambers,

The Pigeon's Body and How it Functions

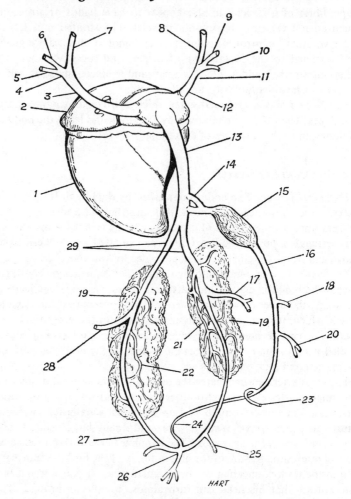

DIAGRAMMATIC DRAWING OF HEART AND VEINS

(1) Left ventricle (heart), (2) Left atrium (heart), (3) Left anterior vena cava, (4) Left subclavian vein, (5) Left pectoral vein, (6) Left brachial vein, (7) Left jugular vein, (8) Right jugular vein, (9) Right brachial vein, (10) Right pectoral vein, (11) Right subclavian vein, (12) Right anterior vena cava, (13) Posterior vena cava, (14) Hepatic vein, (15) Liver, (16) Portal vein, (17) Right femoral vein, (18) Gastro-duodenal vein, (19) Kidneys, (20) Anterior mesenteric vein, (21) Right renal vein, (22) Left renal vein, (24) Coccygeo-mesenteric vein, (25) Right internal iliac vein, (26) Cocygeal vein, (27) Left internal iliac vein, (28) Left femoral vein, (29) Common iliac veins.

The Pigeon's Body and How it Functions

the skin around it, called the *pericardium*, the nervous mechanism which causes it to beat.

The Blood. The blood is an organ. Even though it is fluid, it is a colony of specialized cells in a specialized fluid which, as we have seen, discharges carbon dioxide and picks up oxygen and nourishment, which it transports.

The liquid part is called *plasma*. In the plasma float *red cells*, whose job it is to handle the oxygen, as mentioned above. When arterial blood gushes from a cut it is bright red, the *haemoglobin* being rich in oxygen; when it runs from a vein it is darker and almost bluish, because the haemoglobin has given up its oxygen.

Another difference that is in no way obvious from the outside is in the composition of the blood. Pigeons have only 2/5ths as many red blood cells to any given quantity of blood as the dog.

One of the amazing facts about poultry blood is the way the haemoglobin increases during broodiness. I can find no study of the phenomenon in the pigeon, but in hens the haemoglobin increases as much as 50 per cent. If it occurs in pigeons, and it probably does, this furnishes an explanation of why they fly long-distance races better when sitting or driving. The haemoglobin which carries the oxygen to the tissues, being more abundant, can transport far more of this essential gas.

Then there are *white blood corpuscles* of various sizes. Usually they appear spherical, but because of their softness and elasticity they can move through small openings, changing shape to do so. Moreover, they can engulf impurities and germs.

Platelets, oval or circular discs which help blood to coagulate or to clot, are other tiny components of blood.

Besides these visible entities, there are chemicals such as *fibrin*. Fibrin stays in solution until an injury allows blood to escape; then a ferment called *thrombin* causes the fibrin to clot.

Spleen and Lymph Nodes. All along the path of the blood and lymph are filter organs, chief of which is the spleen. It is an ovoid, long, narrow organ, more purplish than red, which lies close to the stomach. The spleen's function is chiefly that of an organ of blood purification. Great numbers of bacteria are destroyed by it. When red blood cells become aged, the spleen breaks many of them down into liquid; but in addition, red cells as well as white are made in its tissue. The blood spaces in the spleen are very large compared with ordinary capillaries; and when the organ is ruptured in an accident, haemorrhage into the abdomen may result in death, though not necessarily.

31

The Pigeon's Body and How it Functions

While the spleen is the principal filter organ of the blood, other smaller glands may be found along the lymph vessels and, by their construction, remove solid impurities, such as bacteria, from the blood fluids. Lymph does not move about by blood pressure, but rather by the body's movements: muscle movement, breathing and the consequent expansion and the nodes along its course. Valves in the lymph vessels permit flow in but one direction, which is also true of veins.

THE RESPIRATORY SYSTEM

A pair of organs situated in the chest, one on each side, the *lungs*, function in co-operation with the blood in the oxygen to carbon

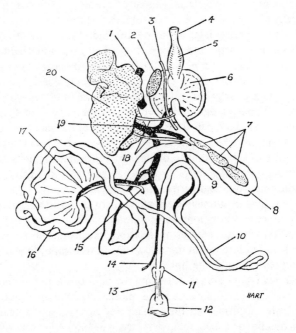

DIGESTIVE TRACT

(1) Post-caval vein, (2) Spleen, (3) Coeliac artery, (4) Esophagus, (5) Proventriculus or glandular stomach, (6) Gizzard, (7) Pancreas, (8) Duodenum or first loop of small intestine, (9) Mesenteric vein, (10) Ileum, or last loop of small intestine, (11) Caecum, (12) Cloaca, (13) Rectum, (14) Inferior or posterior mesenteric vein, (15) Superior or anterior mesenteric vein, (16) Middle loop of small intestine, (17) Superior or anterior mesenteric vein, (18) Bile ducts, (19) Hepatic portal vein (20) Liver.

dioxide transfer and, to a certain extent, in body temperature control as well.

From the throat a tube made up of many bands of tough cartilage runs down into the chest and branches into two *bronchial tubes*, one for each lung. (Bronchitis is inflammation in these tubes.) They, in turn, branch and subdivide into *bronchioles*, and finally into air sacs, each of which is surrounded by a network of blood capillaries so thin that gases can be absorbed or escape through them.

There are interesting differences between birds and other pets which very few laymen know about, though to me they are important as well as fascinating. A significant formation which is found only in birds and which has to do with breathing is the remarkable ramification of open passages, called air sacs, throughout the body. The homing-pigeon fancier sometimes judges a bird's condition by how light it feels when it comes in from a training fly. If the bird seems very light, he judges it to be in excellent flying condition so long as the muscles are hard and firm. But if the bird feels lead-like and heavy in his hand, the judge may eliminate it temporarily from his racing birds.

There may be nothing whatever to this old belief of homing-pigeon fanciers, but it illustrates the fact that something is known about these air sacs by practical fanciers. Air sacs are found in various parts of the body, and, in some species, even in the bones, which are hollow. Birds have been known to drop straight down into water with only a broken leg sticking out and live there for some time, breathing through the bone. Pigeons have solid bones and cannot do this.

THE DIGESTIVE SYSTEM

As we have seen, one of the functions of the blood is to transport nourishment to the body's cells. The nutrients are made ready for the blood by the digestive system.

The Tongue. The tongue is the principal organ for moving food in the mouth and for taste, although pigeons rate low in this capacity. Taste is experienced by the reaction to chemical stimuli of 'buds' or sensitive areas, which stud this organ and produce the sensations of saltiness, sweetness, bitterness, and acidity.

It is generally held that all species of poultry have very low-grade taste and scenting ability. Some recent studies, however, indicate that this view is only opinion with but little study to back it up. Work now being done with chickens indicates that these birds, at least, can taste

The Pigeon's Body and How it Functions

certain substances quite well as shown by preferences or rejection of these substances in solution.

Moreover, birds, it now appears, have nerves in their beaks which are quite sensitive, enabling the birds to distinguish between objects which look alike but have different weights or surface textures, e.g. pebbles and grains.

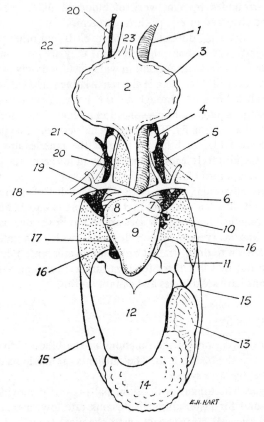

INTERNAL ANATOMY (DIAGRAMMATIC)

(1) Trachea, (2) Crop, (3) Lobe of crop, (4) Thyroid gland, (5) Brachial nerve plexus, (6) Lung artery, (7) Left auricle (heart), (8) Right auricle, (9) Ventricle of heart, (10) Lung vein, (11) Left lobe of liver, (12) Liver, (13) Gizzard, (14) Great omentum membrane, (15) Air sac, (16) Lung, (17) Post-caval vein, (18) Pectoral artery, (19) Dorsal artery, (20) Jugular vein, (21) Carotid artery, (22) Thymus gland, (23) Esophagus (gullet).

The Pigeon's Body and How it Functions

What part sight plays in choice of food and what part taste plays remain to be determined. Those of us who have tried feeding pellets to pigeons know that there often is considerable reluctance to eating them. Pigeons eat smooth peas and leave wrinkled peas. And we all know with what gusto pigeons will eat hemp seeds even when they have never seen or tasted them before. To my taste, there is little difference between hemp and kafir corn or dari as it is sometimes called, unless I crush them with my teeth. The pigeon does not crush them, yet one will eat every hemp seed out of a mixture before it touches a single kafir grain.

Now all this, which needs much investigation, is of practical interest, especially in medication. There are many drugs which, if mixed with some preferred flavour, will be readily drunk when by themselves, in solution, they are rejected.

The Throat. In the throat the delicate business of getting food properly started down the gullet instead of down the windpipe is accomplished by the *pharynx* and *larynx* (pronounced larinks, not larnicks). The gullet and windpipe are located one in front of the other, with the gullet behind.

The windpipe starts as what appears to be a slit in the back of the tongue, but this orifice can widen with the need for more air and close when the pigeon swallows.

Birds swallow by stretching the neck and jerking the head, and by tongue pressure. As the food goes down the gullet, it is mixed with saliva and then comes to an enlargement called the *crop*, where it soaks and softens but is not digested.

In the pigeon and dove the crop produces 'milk'. The male as well as the female has this unique ability, making it the only male in any known species, except some species of the parrot family, which usurps this characteristically female function. The external layer becomes laden with fat. These cells are shed into the crop and become milk. But it hardly resembles mammalian milk, for it is lumpy and of a different consistency, and contains no milk sugar but only protein and fat.

One day after the beginning of a sitting, the normal rate of cell division in the crop sac increases 600 per cent. During the first half of the incubation period this rate persists. During the last 7 or 8 days the rate increases even more.

A great deal of study has been given to crop milk, to the hormones responsible, to the effect of castrating the hens and cocks, to the psycho-

35

The Pigeon's Body and How it Functions

logical influences. These are artificial and interesting studies, but only for the specialists who already have a bibliography on the subject.

Crop milk is of interest to the scientist who wants to know why the day-old pigeon weighs twice as much as it did at hatching and why it continues its surprisingly rapid growth.

Pigeon milk, or crop milk, is actually masses of cells containing fat droplets. There is no sugar in the crop lining from which this 'milk' sloughs off. Therefore there is no sugar (lactose) in the milk as there is in that of mammals.

The fat analyses much like butter-fat from cows. Many analyses have been made and there is some variation from pigeon to pigeon. In general, the milk contains about 30 per cent dry matter and 70 per cent water. Of the dry matter, about 58 per cent is protein, 94 per cent of which is true protein. Fat constitutes 33·8 per cent. On one point, the several analyses I have been able to find vary considerably, namely concerning the amount of ash. This is composed principally of phosphorus, calcium, sodium and potassium, and the total varies anywhere from 3·6 per cent to 4·6 per cent of the dry milk. A fat-like substance called *lecithin* is found in a loose combination with the protein.

Crop milk is rich in some vitamins. A teaspoonful contains as much vitamin A as a drop of standard cod-liver oil. All of the common B vitamins have been found.

There is a growth-promoting factor about crop milk which has not as yet been fully understood. This was determined by a simple clear-cut study of withdrawing the pigeon milk from squeakers right after they had been fed by their parents. This was stored until enough was collected. Then it was fed to day-old White Rock chicks (5 grams per day per chick) along with the usual basic ration. Controls were kept which received only the basic ration.

The crop milk-fed chicks grew faster, their feathers appeared earlier, and their combs were larger than those of the controls. After 6 weeks their weight was 38 per cent greater than that of the controls.

Below the crop is more gullet, down which the food descends until it reaches the part corresponding to the mammalian stomach with its glandular walls capable of secreting digestive juices. From there the food slides into the gizzard. Here is an organ worthy of admiration—a natural grist-mill with walls so tough that they don't wear out even with grit and gravel inside rubbing grain until it is powdered and soaked into a mush.

Peristalsis. In order to understand how food moves along through the

The Pigeon's Body and How it Functions

body, one must realize that the smooth muscles we mentioned earlier are at work carrying out this function. The only so-called voluntary muscles concerned are in the beak, the throat and the anus, and these are partly involuntary. Physiologists regard the inside of the alimentary tract as continuous with the skin on the outside of the body. Actually, the lining is of the same origin as the skin. The tract constitutes a tube with valves and enlargements. The food is swallowed. At once a constriction in the gullet starts behind it and, as it progresses, forces the food into the crop. The progress may be upward. A pigeon drinks with his head downward, and the water is moved upward for some distance before it drops downward into the crop. The contraction which passes along the tube is called *peristalsis*.

In the glandular stomach this wavelike movement continues. It mixes the stomach juices with the food. The exit valve of the stomach, the *pylorus*, opens and lets the food out into the intestine in sausage-like gobs into which constrictions have divided it. Soon other constrictions may start which cut the sausages in half, but all the time this marvellous process pushes the intestinal contents along through the whole length of the intestines as digestion continues.

The Gizzard. Food is ground finer in a tough organ called the gizzard which contains many small stones to assist in the grinding process.

The Stomach. In the stomach some digestion of food takes place, for it is a reservoir into which glands pour an acid liquid that helps digest proteins and fats. It contains pepsin for protein digestion. Starch digestion stops when the food in the stomach becomes acid.

The Intestines. The *duodenum* is a thickened area of intestine between the gizzard and small intestine. It is important because into it two ducts or tubes discharge their contents. One is *bile*, which is made in the liver. Bile splits fat up into tiny globules so small they are invisible and at the same time affords a laxative effect to the food.

The second duct conducts from the *pancreas* more starch-digesting substance (*amylase*) which the pancreas, as one of its duties, manufactures. Starches are turned into *dextrin*, and then, as the food is pushing along, it is broken down into *glucose* by another substance excreted by the small intestine and thence absorbed through the intestine. Glucose is blood sugar. It is also the sugar of grapes and an article of commerce known as corn syrup. And so in this way digestion transforms the carbohydrates in the food into a form in which they may be transported by the blood. Proteins and fats are also reduced to their component parts: *amino acids* and fatty acids into forms by which

37

they, too, can pass through the intestinal walls and into the lymph and blood.

The pancreas handles another important function besides that of furnishing enzymes (digestive ferments). That is the regulation of the power of the body to handle blood sugar. In this task, the pancreas functions with the liver, which, as we shall see, stores up or liberates the sugar (glucose). In the pancreas are tiny islands which manufacture *insulin*, and it is insulin which in some way regulates the percentage of glucose in the blood. If there is too much, it sees that the liver stores it; if too little, the pancreas sees to it that the glucose is called out. A lack of insulin causes *diabetes mellitus*, or sugar (or honey) diabetes. The excess sugar escapes into the urine and may be measured. The disease also causes an increase in thirst and amount of urine excreted. During egg-laying the size and number of these islands increases markedly.

Absorption of materials from the intestine is increased by a unique arrangement. The inner surface feels, and indeed is, almost like velvet, being studded with microscopic, short, hairlike projections called *villi*. Each one, while minute in itself, increases the surface of the intestine by a little, and in the aggregate, these tiny projections increase the area of the intestines immensely.

The Liver. The liver is the largest organ of the body. It lies in front of the stomach and just behind the diaphragm, and is constantly massaged by the regular inhalations and exhalations caused by breathing. In colour, the healthy liver is a dark red with a glistening surface and several lobes, the number differing among the species.

All its activities are not concerned with digestion. Besides turning old red blood cells into bile pigment, it is a prime organ of regulation and manufacture. Bile, as we have said, comes from the liver. *Urea* is made in the liver by converting ammonia left over from protein *metabolism* (chemical changes). Bacteria are destroyed in the liver to some extent, too, as they are in the lymphatic system and spleen.

As a sugar regulator for the body, the liver is essential. Suppose glucose is absorbed from the intestine in greater quantities than the body can use. The liver then changes it into *glycogen* (actually animal starch) and stores it. When the blood-sugar level gets too low, the liver obliges by releasing glucose from the conversion of the glycogen. Along with fat storage, this store-house in the pigeon makes possible the long-distance racing.

Blood-sugar glycogen is food, but food-in-storage. The liver—being the principal storage reservoir, when food for energy is needed—con-

The Pigeon's Body and How it Functions

verts the glycogen into dextrose and sends it into the blood. The ultimate control is believed to be under hormones. Insulin affects the storage in the liver, whereas adrenalin (epinephrin) affects the output.

A frightened pigeon probably has a much larger sugar supply in its blood than a calm bird. In chickens, the normal percentage of blood sugar is 0·139. The liver may contain 1·0 per cent of its weight as sugar. Glycogen is also stored in the muscles to the extent of 0·9 per cent of their weight, when resting. Sickness upsets these balances—a good argument never to ship a sick bird for either training or racing.

Fats are absorbed and not acted upon in the liver. Fat is deposited in the tissues of the body to be used when called upon, or it may be used at once for energy if needed. How much fat conversion occurs during long races we do not know, but it must be considerable.

Final Steps in Digestion. What is left of the food after it has travelled through the small intestine is deposited through a valve into the *cloaca*. The *ceca* are a pair of blind guts which are attached to the cloaca.

The more faeces there are, the more there is for bacteria to work on, and the more products of bacteria there are to be absorbed by the body along with the surplus water. This is another good reason for not over-feeding or under-exercising pigeons.

This efficient 'factory' of the digestive system is like an automobile assembly line running backward, with the cars being taken apart bit by bit instead of being assembled. As it passes through the digestive system, the whole mass of food which entered the mouth is reduced to its essential parts, fatty acids, glucose, and amino acids, and these disassembled products are absorbed into the blood.

THE EXCRETORY SYSTEM

The Kidneys. Blood disposes of certain chemical substances, other than gases, through the kidneys. All the blood travels through their intricate mechanism, disposing of waste. These wastes are principally urea, sugar, poisons, and substances such as carbonates, which can be expelled in no other way.

Urea is the end product of the breakdown of the proteins in the body. The *nitrogen*, which is the principal constituent of protein, is also the principal component of urea. Everyone knows how urine gives off ammonia when hot. Ammonia also contains nitrogen.

In pigeons, kidneys are located under the protection of the pelvis and on either side of the body close to the backbone. They constitute

The Pigeon's Body and How it Functions

one of the most delicate and ingenious filter plants possible to imagine. Everyone who has eaten kidneys or fed them to animals knows in general what they look like. But few have observed, microscopically, the minute inner workings, or even wondered at their marvellous construction. If one slices a kidney lengthwise, one sees a 'pelvis', so called, which constitutes a pocket for collecting urine, from whence it is conducted via a tube, the *ureter*, to the bladder.

That is about all one does see of the mechanism with the naked eye. The microscope reveals the most interesting features: the blood vessels, which divide to become capillaries, in tiny containers called *glomeruli*, and minute collecting tubules into which the urine filters and is conveyed to the pelvis. There are beautiful and ingenious arrangements to effect the transfer and reabsorption into the blood of certain useful substances and rejection of the useless, all of which is accomplished while the blood is passing through the kidney, entering under high pressure and coming out under much lower pressure.

Diseases can easily upset the normal function of the kidneys so that they cannot retain the useful nitrogenous substances like *albumin*, or may lack absorptive capacity, so that too much water is secreted from the blood causing great thirst. Albumen found in urine and excessive thirst are both indications of kidney disease. In the pigeon, the urine is mixed with faecal matter in the cloaca, so urine analysis is difficult.

Kidneys that function properly regulate the amounts of blood ingredients in considerable degree. If too much sugar is present, some will be found in the droppings. The same may be said of salt.

Other Excretory Means. Other impurities and surpluses from the blood—some mineral salts, for instance—are also excreted into the intestines; some gases are excreted by the lungs. The excretory system actually is composed of three parts, not of the kidneys alone, as the average layman thinks.

THE GLANDULAR SYSTEM AND REGULATION OF BODY FUNCTIONS

Ductless Glands. The blood acts also as a vehicle for transporting the products of the body regulators, the hormones, only one source of which has thus far been considered, the pancreas. The spleen and lymph glands are also ductless glands but, as far as we know, do not secrete hormones. A ductless gland is one which does not have an outlet except back into the blood.

Some glands, like the pancreas, are mixed ductless and ordinary

The Pigeon's Body and How it Functions

glands. Salivary glands are good examples of ordinary glands, because they have ducts which lead their products away from the glands, secreting saliva in the mouth. The important, strictly ductless glands, are the *pituitary*, the *adrenal*, *thyroid*, and *parathyroid*. The important mixed ductless and ordinary glands are *pancreas*, *ovaries*, and *testicles*.

The Pituitary. Probably most important as a body regulator is the pituitary gland, located at the base of the brain, to which it is attached by a stalk. It has a front and rear lobe. It seems incredible that such a tiny organ could be capable of performing such feats as it performs. Yet its direct and indirect chemical influence on other glands and organs persuade them to extraordinary accomplishments. Here are a few of its capacities. It can:

Cause a pigeon to want to mate;
affect the moulting of the feathers;
cause a pair to become broody;
cause stunted growth if under-active;
cause sexual development;
help regulate metabolism of carbohydrates;
cause overfatness if under-active;
raise blood pressure;
cause production of pigeon milk by the crop in both sexes.

Because it is so potent the amount of chemical required for these tasks is very small.

Prolactin, one of the pituitary hormones, the one which causes the production of pigeon milk if injected into any pigeon, even an immature bird, will start crop sac increase within four days. That there is considerable co-operation among several glands in doing this job is shown by the fact that when the adrenals and pituitary are removed, prolactin by itself accomplishes results but only one-eighth as well as when the glands are present.

Prolactin also has a powerful effect on certain organs. The pancreas, the liver and the intestines increase in size and weight 26 per cent, 29 per cent and 36 per cent respectively, and the pigeon's digestive capacity and general vitality are therefore increased. This all helps to give a greater appetite which persists so that the squabs are well fed. It also explains why sitting pigeons fly better in races.

The Adrenal Glands. These glands, situated near the kidneys, are also known as the *suprarenal* glands. They produce *epinephrine*, also called *adrenalin*, a potent chemical concerned with blood pressure by its effect on the heart and vessels right down to the capillaries. They also

41

determine in some manner the amount of salt in the urine and affect the use of fat and sugar. Their outer layers secrete *cortisone*, now being used in the treatment of arthritis.

Any reader interested in delving into the glandular basis of the control of a pigeon's, male or female, reproductive behaviour would do well to study the work of students on the adrenal glands, which co-operate with the pituitary and the sex glands. The study uncovers many interesting facts. The gland changes radically and corresponds with the changes every fancier has observed in the actions of his birds. A bird which has only just obtained sexual maturity shows the same eagerness in mating behaviour, the clear-cut changes in pattern which older birds exhibit, and these changes correspond to the changes in the adrenals.

The Thyroid. This gland lies in the neck on either side of the windpipe, the two parts not being connected as is the case with many other species, so that with every swallowing movement, the thyroid is moved too. An important chemical regulator, *thyroxin*, is secreted by it, and this is known to contain about 60 per cent iodine. Pigeons whose diets are low in iodine content become sick, and some grow into *cretins*, peculiar abnormalities not often seen among pigeons. A cretin is a dwarf, stupid, slow, dull, gross in appearance.

Thyroxin regulates the speed of living in any animal. Slow, poky animals, overweight and phlegmatic, respond by quicker actions, more rapid pulse, restlessness and sleeplessness when given the drug. When the gland secretes too much of its regulating substance, the bird becomes nervous, develops a ravenous appetite, wastes away, and develops an increase in the size of the gland itself. Such increase is called goitre in man or in animals. It is seldom seen in birds because their grain is seldom grown in iodine-deficient soils.

Metabolism. We hear much about *metabolism*, which is the burning of food and its utilization by the body. Metabolism is regulated by glands and the thyroid is probably most important in this process.

Whether a pigeon is well fed or fasting, old, middle aged, or young, its metabolism has two peaks during the day. One is early morning, the other late afternoon. During the night and middle of the day its rate of metabolism is less.

Body temperature in the pigeon varies during the day, being highest when the metabolic rate is highest. Temperatures may vary from 105 to 109 degrees.

Among birds, pigeons are remarkable for their low heat production, hunger resistance, low calorie and food utilization. Contrasted with the

The Pigeon's Body and How it Functions

robin, thrush, and blackbird, there is a great difference. Many birds must be fed much more and frequently in order to live. A pigeon's crop stores food for several hours and even with no food he can live for many days.

Anyone who has bred pigeons has remarked on the extremely rapid growth of the squeakers. It is fast, but when a curve is made showing the rate by age, there is but little difference between that curve and the curves of human beings, pigs, calves and fowl. The curves are all the same shape, but the speed of growing is different.

Three days after hatching, the squeaker adds 38 per cent of its weight daily; at 11 days the rate is 14 per cent, although the actual daily weight additions are greater and the bird is burning energy at a rate twice as fast in proportion to his weight as he does at maturity. Even at 25 days, when we think his growth is finished, he is still using 50 per cent more energy than he will when grown. This explains why the food consumption of the old birds during breeding season becomes so greatly increased.

Parathyroids. Located usually close to the heart, are two small glands whose concern is with the regulation of calcium metabolism. If they are removed a condition known as *tetany* develops, involving violent trembling and death ensues.

The Ovaries. Near the backbone, against the ribs, are small organs, the *ovaries*, only one of which develops in the pigeon. The ovary has several functions. The first and most important task, of course, is that of perpetuating the bird.

The female pigeon has only the left ovary. From it an *oviduct* runs in a wiggling fashion to the cloaca. The fertilized *ovum*, with the yolk, leaves the ovary, starts down the oviduct, where it accumulates the egg-white (albumen) secreted in the upper part of the oviduct. As it moves farther along, it is coated by special glands with a membrane, and still later with a shell. The egg is laid through the cloaca.

That the ovaries, even before reproduction functions begin, are concerned with body development, no one can doubt. Even such a thing as mental interest is controlled by them. If the ovaries are removed before puberty (sexual maturity), the pigeon grows somewhat ungainly and tends to put on fat more than a twin whose ovaries have not been removed. This propensity continues through life. The bird is an intersex in appearance.

The presence of a mate or an open nest box and nest bowl or even the pigeon's own image in a mirror can start a sequence of hormone-

The Pigeon's Body and How it Functions

produced events. The acts of billing, treading, driving, nest building, laying and sitting are all part of that chain. Even the appetite is stimulated in birds of both sexes. So is the development of the *incubation patch*. This is the conditioning of the breast skin and feathers in both sexes so that they can successfully incubate the eggs.

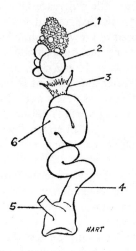

REPRODUCTIVE SYSTEM OF HEN
(1) Ovary, (2) Ripening follicle, (3) Ostrum (mouth of oviduct), (4) Uterus, (5) Rectum, (6) Oviduct (albumen secreting section).

If we could observe an ovary through a window in the pigeon's side, we would see some interesting changes take place. The resting ovary is about the size and shape of a tic bean. The ovary contains the germ plasm of the pigeon—its heredity. Some of its cells grow towards the surface very slowly at first. But when the birds are mated, and driving occurs, the rate of growth of the cells is speeded up at a rate eight to twenty times of normal, and they become follicles which protrude out of the ovary until one bursts. The ovarian follicles grow because of the influence of a hormone—the *gonadotrophic*—from the pituitary gland. A second ovum leaves the ovary about two days later. What leaves the ovary is actually the germ cell plus the egg yolk.

As the follicle grows, it secretes a hormone—*estrogenic*—which stimulates the growth of the oviduct. This, as we saw, is the tube down

44

which the ova and yolk pass. An ovarian hormone—*progesterone*—induces the formation of albumen (egg white) in the oviduct.

As we saw, prolactin causes increase in some organs. The ovaries also play some part. The liver undergoes changes which correlate with the activity of the ovaries. During the early activity of the ovary, liver cells are stimulated and again when prolactin causes the crop to produce milk.

At the time of laying there is a corresponding change in the bird's bone marrow. From the bones, calcium is removed and transported to the oviduct. After laying, calcium is taken from the food and transported back to be deposited in the bones. These facts emphasize the need for digestible calcium in the food or grit box of every pigeon, especially before and during breeding time.

Abnormal sex behaviour is occasionally found in pigeons. There are intersexes and true hermaphrodites. These birds may have both testes and ovaries and be able to fertilize hens or act as hens but not lay eggs. The characteristic is sometimes inherited. One study with tipplers established the fact which accounts for similar observations with other breeds.

The Testicles. The male pigeon has two testicles inside the body, located against the top of the abdominal cavity. They enlarge during breeding seasons.

Pigeons copulate by matching the cloaca of the male with that of the female.

Besides producing sperm, the testicles secrete the male hormone, androgen. The natural secretion affects the male animal profoundly, and without it, he would be little good as a sire.

Mating, Nesting, Raising Young. Old theories concerning mating, nesting, and brooding in birds emphasized temperature, feeding, and the moult. However, in all probability, these functions are influenced almost entirely by the length of the day—a fact only recently discovered. Pigeons respond to this influence as do all other creatures. Towards autumn, when the days begin to get noticeably shorter, pigeons moult and a new set of feathers grows in. When the days start to grow longer in the spring, mating, laying and rearing young occur naturally.

Electric light has the same effect as natural daylight in regulating the changes in a bird's body—a fact that has not been used to any extent in pigeon breeding.

Failure of Eggs to Hatch. Infertility of either parent is the most common cause of failure of the eggs to hatch. However, there are other causes with which the owner should be familiar. Disturbing the bird so that she sits erratically, careless handling of the eggs, soggy nests, vermin in the nests or on the birds, canker infection, paratyphoid—all may result in failures. An incomplete diet, or insufficient food for the mating birds, may be a contributing factor.

It is advisable to candle eggs, but when this is done, they should be touched as little as possible. Holding them over a bright light while they are lying over a small hole in a piece of black cloth, or at night over a flashlight, makes it easy to distinguish the fertile from the sterile eggs.

If a number of birds are mated, it is advisable to keep an accurate record of each setting. There are often opportunities to switch eggs or to combine two clutches when something unforeseen occurs. If this is done, eggs of the same age must be placed together.

Chilling. If a nestling falls out, or is pushed out of the nest by a fight and lies for some time on the nest-box bottom, you may find it so cold that it seems nearly lifeless. Is there hope for it? Yes. When replaced in the nest it will usually revive in a surprisingly short time. Some hen pigeons refuse to sit on chilled youngsters but will sit if the youngsters are warmed before they are placed in the nest.

There are occasions when it is necessary to use foster parents. If one has several pairs sitting at once, it makes very little difference if a young one is transferred to a nest in which there is only one squeaker. Usually the pair will readily accept the new baby.

The Nervous System and Organs of Perception

The nerves are the telegraph wires of the body. Thousands of miles of these fibres control the body's activities. They stimulate the muscles to contract, and each of even the tiniest muscles has its nerve supply. The brain is the central station from which the nerves radiate through several pathways, the principal one being the spinal cord. Most of the conscious body movements are regulated by the brain and spinal cord. These two wonderful organs are exceedingly well protected, entirely enclosed in bones—the skull and spine.

Nerves carry impulses to the brain from distant parts of the body. Organs of sense, such as the delicate nerves in the skin, may telegraph to the brain. For example, *feeling* is a function of these nerves of the skin—sensitivity to temperature, to electrical stimuli, to wetness or dryness, to sharpness, as in the case of a pin prick.

The Pigeon's Body and How it Functions

Whereas telegraph wires carry messages both ways, nerves conduct impulses in only one direction, some to the brain and some away from it. Suppose a pigeon touches a hot object, its sense organs tell the brain with the speed of electricity, and instantly the muscles are given an impulse which pulls them away from the hot object.

We used to talk about the five senses, but today, besides the ordinary five, psychologists recognize many more: the kinesthetic sense or muscle sense, the sense of balance, which can be demonstrated even while birds are embryos, the sex sense, to mention only a few.

The Brain and Spinal Cord. The nerves are unlike other cells in that they are long, thin fibres. Many fibres may be associated in bundles, and the largest bundle of all is the spinal cord, which gives out and takes in pairs of nerves between every vertebra of the backbone. The bundles of fibres branch here and there (the trunk divides into branches), until the final divisions are tiny individual fibres en-nervating some small area of the body.

Besides the cord there are other nerves which leave the brain, running to organs and other parts of the body. All of the body—organs, muscles, glands, intestines—is controlled by the cord and by these 'cranial' nerves.

For every sensitive area in the bird, there is a corresponding centre in the brain. When we see a pigeon scratch, do we think that a nerve somewhere in the skin telegraphed the brain which set in motion the bird's leg?

This is due to the so-called reflex action; a human knee jerk is a reflex, and pigeons are like us in having such areas.

When compared with our own, the brain itself is small in pigeons, chiefly because the fore part, called the *cerebrum*, is so much smaller in lower animals. The positive, willing, conscious actions are involved in this portion of the brain. Ordinary living is a concern of the lower part, called the cerebellum. There are other parts, most of which, like the two mentioned, are in pairs.

Birds can function mechanically without the cerebrum, but have no memory, can't learn or don't have the will to do anything. Their existence is almost like that of a vegetable. They can breathe, eat if their faces are held over the pan, defecate, urinate, sleep, wander aimlessly around and peck when hurt.

The cerebrum is the part of the brain which responds most to training.

Let no one think a pigeon can have its brain 'cluttered up' by the

The Pigeon's Body and How it Functions

training. Once it learns what is wanted of it and is properly rewarded, each succeeding act of habit taught is easier to teach than the acts before. Those most highly educated of all pigeons find learning easier and easier.

The Eye. Many misconceptions exist about the eye. It is not so complicated as many think and is much tougher than most people believe it to be. Looking at the eye one sees a big, round, transparent part of a globe, the *cornea*. Surrounding it one sees a ring of clear white glistening tissue, the *sclera*. The tissue immediately surrounding the eye is the *conjunctiva*. Outside of this is the lid surrounded by *cere*, the amount of which varies according to the breed and strains within breeds.

In the middle of the eye we see the pupil. This really is only a name of an opening within the circle of the iris. The pupils get larger or smaller, depending on the amount of light the eye needs for vision, or on drug action, or on brain disease or concussion. A bird looking at a bright light shows a very small pupil. When it gets dark, the pupil enlarges. The coloured tissue we see around the pupil is called the *iris*. It ranges from pearl in some pigeons, yellow, greenish in others, to blood colour in albinos and dark brown or red, orange and variations in still others.

Behind the pupil lies the *lens*. It is tough, crystalline, and fibrous. Through it light rays are bent so that the image comes to rest on a sensitive area behind the lens, known as the *retina*.

The fluid in front of the iris and pupil is a thin liquid called *aqueous* (watery) *humour*; the fluid behind is called the *vitreous humour*. It is much thicker and cloying.

The retina is the part of the eye which receives the light impressions on nerves embedded in it, which in turn transmit those impressions via the optic nerve to the brain.

A controversy rages as to what the eye holds as a basis for prediction of homing ability or of some quality which enables one bird to surpass another in the capacity to reach home. There are those who breed their birds entirely using 'eye sign' as their basis. This is outside the realm of this book, but that the eye is of tremendous importance to a pigeon cannot be doubted, when one realizes how huge the eyes are compared with the bird's brain. In volume, both eyes together are larger than the brain. Even the retina of the eyes is large compared with retinas of other species.

How important the eye is to the brain of animals has been shown by Dr. Leon Stone of Yale University. He used salamanders in his studies.

48

The Pigeon's Body and How it Functions

There is one species with a small eye and a small brain; another with a large eye and a large brain. When he transplanted embryonic eyes from the large-eyed species in place of eyes in the small-eyed species, the eyes grew large and the brain increased greatly, too, in keeping with the large eyes.

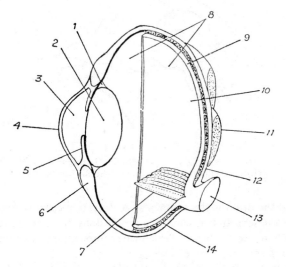

BISECTED PIGEON EYE

(1) Ciliary body, (2) Lens, (3) Chamber of aqueous humor, (4) Cornea, (5) Iris, (6) Sclerotic plate, (7) Pecten, (8) Chamber of vitreous humor, (9) Retina, (10) Foveal region of retina, (11) Eyeball muscle, (12) Sclerotic coat, (13) Optic nerve, (14) Pigment layer.

We may suppose that the eye is correlated with the brain in size, but what correlation there is between colour and homing ability has not been determined. Although we are told it has been studied, I can find no published data on it, only books full of opinion and advice; not tables of studies made. So we can regard it still in the realm of opinion. If it has been tested to determine whether it conforms with nature, I cannot find the evidence.

The Ear. Although the eye is a marvellous organ, the ear excites even more wonder. Here is a truly wonderful device for catching sounds and carrying the impressions to the brain on nerves. In pigeons, the ear begins with a hole in the head. By turning the head, the sounds can be captured. The sounds are conducted inward through the external canal.

49

The Pigeon's Body and How it Functions

The tube becomes smaller at the bottom, then turns upward slightly and terminates in a very delicate membrane, the drum. All the rest of the ear is within the solid bone of the skull.

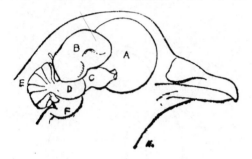

EYE AND BRAIN

(A) Eye, (B) Cerebral hemisphere, (C) Mid-brain (Diencephalon), (D) Optic lobe (E) Cerebellum, (F) Hind-brain (Medulla oblongata).

Behind the drum is the columella. A delicate mechanism communicates via the semicircular canal the impressions of vibration registered by these bones to the nerves, which carry impressions or stimuli to the brain via the auditory nerve.

The Nose. As far as we know, the pigeon's nose is one of his least developed sense organs. Besides breathing through it, we are not sure of just how much use it is to him. Actually, that part of the bird's face which we call the nose is only a small part of his smelling apparatus; all the important parts are out of sight. These consist of a complicated pair of cavities with a partition, *os septum*, between. The front part is called the *anterior nares*; the back part, the *posterior nares*. The first part of the cavity is called the *vestibule*.

As it is breathed in, the air passes through the vestibule and thence through a remarkable shelf-like arrangement made up of turbinate bones covered with erectile tissue which can become engorged with blood. A mucous membrane overlies this tissue.

When the air is cold, the erectile tissue fills with extra blood which helps to warm the air before it passes to the lungs. The arrangement of bones and erectile tissue also filters the air at all times, removing dust and bacteria from it.

Before pigeons can smell odours, the odours, which are gases, must be dissolved in the watery secretion which is present in the olfactory organs. A chemical stimulus received by large numbers of nerve fibres terminating in olfactory hairs in the mucous membrane goes to the brain via the olfactory nerve. At the first stimulus or acknowledgement of the new odour, most animals begin to sniff, which, of course, brings more of the odour into contact with the mucous membrane, where it dissolves and the stimulation is thereby increased. But birds do not use their noses in analysing odours, if we can judge by their actions. Vision plays a far more important part in their lives.

2

What You Should Know about Foods and Feeding

Pigeons are definitely vegetarians according to the definition of the word, but we know, on the basis of sound research, that they can digest animal protein well. They have been kept on goat's milk diet for many months, they often eat so many garden slugs that their beaks become slimy; they eat snails and some bugs, and they have been fed various kinds of dehydrated fish and animal tissue. But still by nature, their principal food is grain and some succulent plant tissue.

We have already seen how a pigeon digests its food, the mechanism for digestion, that is. Now we must see how the various food ingredients are set upon by enzymes and broken down into their component assimilable parts. And too, we must consider each of the various available food ingredients which pigeons can digest, and formulae for mixing them for special occasions and how to compound them. It is not as difficult as many think.

Nearly all the information about nutrition has been supplied by the great and small scientific laboratories of the world since 1900. Some of our knowledge of food values and human needs has come through feeding experiments with pigeons. I procured pigeons for Dr. G. R. Cowgill in 1925 who did fundamental research on vitamin B, as it was called then. Pigeons were used as the standard test bird for this vitamin in foods at that time. Yet, for all of our more recent knowledge, we have been extremely slow in applying it to our birds.

Suppose then we study the foods and the elements of which they are composed and then apply this knowledge to determine how the body makes use of them by the dis-assembly line process: Food goes into the mouth of the pigeon, and the workmen, consisting of chemicals and

What You Should Know about Foods and Feeding

grit, grind it until the elements of the food are taken apart and only the framework remains.

Foods are composed for the most part of proteins, fats, carbohydrates, minerals and water.

Carbohydrates. Pigeons eating seeds are consuming more carbohydrates than anything else. This is principally starch which is manufactured in the leaves of the plants which produced the seeds. In the plant leaf, there is *chlorophyll*, much like the haemoglobin in the pigeon's blood. In the presence of sunlight, the leaf takes carbon dioxide from the air (6 parts) and combines it with water (5 parts) and makes starch $6(CO_2)+5H_2O \rightarrow C_6H_{10}O_5+6O_2$. The oxygen is given out into the air, the starch is fluid and is deposited in the plant tissues as structure and seed.

Some of the structural part is indigestible and referred to as *fibre*. An analysis giving carbohydrates may call it carbohydrate or may say N.F.E., which means *nitrogen-free extract*, which is the combination of the digestible with the indigestible carbohydrates.

The plant does other wonderful things, too. It takes nitrogen from the soil and combines it with the starch to make protein. It also removes some of the oxygen and stores this product away as *fat*. Leguminous plants are able to fix nitrogen from the air on their roots and the seeds from these plants generally have more protein than other classes of plants.

When we compute the richness of a food—how much heat it contains in a canned form—we calculate that each gramme of carbohydrate or protein burns up, giving off four calories. The calorie is the unit of heat. Whether the food is burned in the open fire or burned by the body for fuel, carbohydrate still gives off four calories per gramme. A gramme of water is $\frac{1}{4}$ level teaspoonful.

Proteins. Proteins are of many kinds. The following table names them, gives rich sources and mentions certain properties.

Protein	Rich Sources	Properties
Albumin	Egg white Milk Meat Blood	Soluble in water Does not precipitate by dilute acids or salts Coagulates when boiled
Casein	Milk Cheese Cottage Cheese	Does not coagulate when boiled Coagulated by renin Coagulated by pepsin Coagulated by acids

53

Gelatine	Well distributed throughout animal body	Becomes solid on boiling Three per cent or more in a batch of food will solidify it Precipitated by tannic acid and alcohol
Keratin	Feathers, beak and nails	Tough fibrinous, indigestible, useless in pigeon feeding but sometimes found in foods Manufactured in feather follicles, etc. Contains much sulphur
Vegetable Proteins	All vegetable matter Richest in seeds, especially legumes	Very similar to animal proteins In legumes one protein is found like albumin in milk Some are like fibrinogen, some like albumin with similar properties

All of the above proteins are composed of integral parts called *amino acids*, each containing one or more (N H₂) group. There are over 50 different amino acids, and thus with all the combinations possible, proteins can and do exist in innumerable variety. No two proteins have the same amount of amino acids.

TABLE I

AMINO ACIDS

Essential	*Partly Dispensable*	*Non-Essential*
Tryptophan	Arginine	Alanine
Lysine	Cystine	Glutamic Acid
Phenylalanine	Tyrosine	Hydroxyglutamic Acid
Histidine	Glycine	Aspartic Acid
Threonine		Serine
Methionine		Proline
Leucine		Hydroxyproline
Isoleucine		Citrulline
Valine		Norleucine

While there are over 50 different ones, there are 9 known to be essential (*see* column 1 of Table I). We are not yet certain whether these 9 are essential to pigeons, but they are to growing chicks, and probably are to pigeons. It may well be that during the moult, pigeons need more

TABLE II

AMINO ACIDS IN CERTAIN PIGEON FOOD INGREDIENTS

	Arginine	Cystine	Glycine	Histidine	Leucine	Isoleucine	Lysine	Methionine	Phenyl-alanine	Threonine	Tryptophan	Tyrosine	Valine
Milk—Whole	3·6	0·8	1·9	2·8	10·1	6·5	8·4	2·1	5·3	4·8	1·1	5·6	6·7
Skim, Dry	—	—	—	2·5	10·9	5·1	8·7	2·2	4·5	4·7	1·5	5·3	5·9
Whey, Dry	—	1·4	—	1·3	7·7	6·4	5·8	0·6	1·9	12·2	0·6	2·5	4·5
Blood Meal	5·2	—	5·5	9·3	13·7	1·2	9·2	1·2	7·3	2·3	1·5	2·2	10·7
Meat Scraps	5·4	—	—	3·4	8·0	3·4	6·1	1·1	5·1	5·5	0·6	2·3	6·1
Feathers	8·0	8·7	—	0·4	8·5	6·4	1·4	0·5	5·5	4·7	—	3·2	8·9
Cod Meal	5·7	1·3	5·8	2·8	10·2	7·6	9·5	2·9	4·6	6·1	0·8	2·9	6·7
Herring Meal	8·1	0·9	7·4	2·8	7·8	5·6	9·5	3·1	4·1	4·3	0·9	3·1	7·0
Barley	4·8	2·5	4·3	2·0	6·7	3·3	3·4	1·6	4·9	3·7	1·0	4·1	4·8
Maize (Corn)	5·3	1·9	2·9	2·2	12·6	5·9	2·4	1·9	4·8	4·7	1·0	—	7·1
Millet	—	—	—	—	9·3	—	3·7	1·9	4·5	—	1·9	3·2	6·2
Oats	6·7	1·8	1·4	1·6	5·7	5·1	3·4	1·5	4·8	3·4	1·3	—	6·6
Oatmeal	6·7	—	—	1·5	7·7	4·3	4·2	1·7	5·3	3·2	1·6	—	5·8
Rice—Unpolished	8·4	—	—	2·1	8·0	4·4	4·4	2·2	4·8	3·4	1·5	—	6·2
Polished	—	—	—	2·2	8·0	6·0	3·8	2·2	4·6	—	1·2	—	6·2
Rye	—	—	—	1·6	6·0	3·9	4·0	1·6	4·6	3·3	1·3	—	5·0
Wheat	—	—	—	2·2	5·6	4·1	2·5	1·6	4·2	2·7	—	—	4·6
Rice Polishings	9·6	—	—	2·2	3·7	2·6	—	—	5·0	—	2·9	—	3·8
Wheat Germ	5·6	—	3·7	4·3	6·6	3·8	5·1	2·8	2·6	3·0	0·9	1·3	6·3
Middlings	7·3	—	—	2·6	5·6	4·8	2·6	0·9	4·1	2·6	0·8	—	5·2
Cabbage	5·2	—	—	2·1	3·7	3·1	3·9	1·3	4·3	2·8	0·9	—	4·0
Beans—Peas	5·9	0·7	3·7	2·5	6·2	6·2	6·9	1·9	1·9	3·8	0·6	3·1	4·5
Horse	6·8	1·1	—	2·9	7·6	5·5	5·5	0·5	5·0	2·6	0·3	—	5·1
Cow Peas	7·0	0·7	—	3·7	7·5	4·9	6·2	1·0	3·4	3·3	1·4	—	6·3
Lentil	11·5	0·8	1·0	2·1	5·8	5·5	5·8	0·8	5·2	2·9	0·5	—	5·3
Lupin	3·4	2·7	6·7	3·2	8·7	1·3	2·9	0·8	4·1	—	1·4	4·2	1·4
Soy bean	9·9	—	—	1·1	3·8	2·4	1·8	2·5	3·9	1·9	1·1	—	2·6
Linseed Meal	5·9	0·9	—	2·7	6·3	5·6	3·5	0·5	2·5	3·9	1·1	2·2	5·9
Soy bean Meal—Exp.	5·3	—	—	2·5	8·4	6·1	6·7	1·5	3·9	4·6	1·1	1·9	5·5
Ext.	6·7	—	—	3·0	7·9	6·2	5·3	0·8	4·6	3·7	2·1	2·1	5·3
Grass, Dry	6·7	—	—	3·1	13·4	9·3	7·2	2·1	8·8	6·7	1·1	3·1	10·3
Alfalfa	3·5	1·7	3·6	1·7	4·3	9·9	4·2	1·3	4·1	5·0	1·5	1·8	4·9

of one than of another. Pigeon feathers are rich in cystine. When feathers are growing rapidly, may not a change in diet be valuable, enriching it in cystine-rich food ingredients?

Table II on page 55 gives a good idea of the amino acids contained in several foods which shows the variation with the consequent difference in the foods.

As you will see, in compounding rations, it is highly important to know the amino acids as well as the protein analysis. For example, maize (American corn) which is high in *zein* is very low in *tryptophane* and *lysine*, so proteins which compensate for that lack must be added to a ration of which maize is an important ingredient. Soy beans contain almost all of the amino acids essential for growth, but are slightly low in *methionine* and *cystine*. Cereal grains are all deficient in lysine.

For fast-growing chicks—and they do not grow as rapidly as squabs —the following table shows the approximate minimum percentages of amino acids to support that growth.

TABLE III

AMINO-ACID REQUIREMENTS, PERCENT OF DIET, FOR
GROWING CHICKS

Argenine	1·2
Histidine	0·15
Leucine	1·4
Isoleucine	0·72
Methionine	0·7
Threonine	0·6
Phenylalanine	1·3
Valine	0·8
Glycine	1·5

Some vitamins are formed in a pigeon's system, but such small amounts of amino acids are formed, that the nine essential ones must all be supplied in food.

The percentage of complete protein needed to force rapid growth in chicks has been found to be in the neighbourhood of 20 per cent. This is more than has been found necessary for squabs. A food containing 15 per cent protein, all in grain form, has grown millions of pigeons satisfactorily but not necessarily as rapidly as possible. Some of the most successful squab raisers insist on 20 per cent protein in their rations and they are probably justified in demanding it.

What You Should Know about Foods and Feeding

Maintenance rations are a different matter. Taking our example from poultry again, laying hens need no more than 15 per cent; rations of 12 per cent protein have maintained pigeons in excellent condition.

Racing birds are working and using energy. They do not need high protein foods before a race; they do welcome it during recuperation for muscle building after a gruelling long fly. But more about this important aspect of feeding later.

An important point to remember is the relation of protein to one of the minerals (which we will consider soon), namely sulphur. Two of the amino acids, methionine and cystine, contain sulphur and are the principal means by which the body acquires it.

The National Research Council in the United States has a committee which studies poultry requirements and makes recommendations. They have made none for pigeons, but we can infer from their recommendations for growing chicks that the much faster growing squabs need at least as much protein and probably more than chicks. Think also of the natural food, crop milk, and you have some guide as to the proper amounts to feed the parent birds which will, in turn, feed it to their squeakers.

Crop milk contains 58 per cent of protein, figured on a dry basis. The National Research Council and many private investigators tell us a growing chick needs 20 to 24 per cent of protein and that this protein must be of good quality, by which they mean with adequate amounts of essential amino acids and of a digestible nature. (Hair and feathers, when tested, are high in protein but it is not utilized.)

As to the amino-acid requirements, it has been shown that they change with age, less of some being required as a chick grows older. Using all of the estimates which I have been able to collect, including those of the National Research Council, the amino-acid percentages found in Table IV, page 58, would appear to be safe in feeding breeding pigeons which are feeding nestlings.

Fats. As we have discussed, fat is carbohydrate with much of the oxygen removed. Seeds contain much of the fat which the plant stores. This gives the sprouting seed food for its sustenance until it can start to manufacture its substance from the air. Fat also makes food rich. Because of the lack of oxygen, when fat burns it gives off 9 calories per gramme or $2\frac{1}{4}$ times as much as protein or carbohydrate.

Therefore, when you look at the *fat* in a feed analysis, judge the seeds' richness by this yardstick because fat contains $2\frac{1}{4}$ times the 'mileage' that protein or carbohydrate can furnish.

What You Should Know about Foods and Feeding

Fats are composed of fatty acids, a wide variety of them. To name a few: oleic acid, stearic acid, palmitic, lauric, butyric acids. Only three fatty acids are known to be essential; linoleic, linolenic and arachidonic acids.

TABLE IV

PROBABLE MINIMUM SAFE AMINO-ACID PERCENTAGES FOR
NESTLING PIGEONS

Argenine	1·3	Phenylalanine	1·7
Cystine	0·5	or	
Glycine	1·5	Phenylalanine	1·0
Histidine	0·3	and Tyrosine	0·7
Isoleucine	0·6	Threonine	0·7
Leucine	1·5	Tryptophan	0·3
Methionine	1·0	Valine	0·8
or			
Methionine and			
Cystine	0·5		

Fats, depending on the fatty acids comprising them, melt at different temperatures but, regardless of melting point, they all supply the same amount of energy, unit for unit. The fat in peanuts is oily, a low-melting-point fat—that of corn (maize)—is a firmer fat.

When a pigeon, or any animal consumes fat, it is dispersed about the body and stored in its original form. In time the body converts it into pigeon fat. Butchers can often tell what grain a hog was fed, by the texture of the pork, maize-fattened pigs having firmer flesh than peanut-fattened. After a gruelling race, if a pigeon was to eat peanuts and fill its storage capacity with their fat, it would actually be part peanut until, in time, it became all pigeon by converting the peanut fat into pigeon fat.

If it is a fact that the pigeon digests food as it flies, then it would seem advisable to feed liberally on high-fat grains because they contain so much more energy than the low-fat foods.

Fats are vehicles for vitamins A, D, E, and K which are usually classed as *fat-soluble* vitamins.

How to Calculate the Calories in a Food. Here we come to an important bit of information which every pigeon fancier should have if he wants to calculate the number of calories in a food or mixture of foods; in short, to learn how 'rich' the food is. Already you have seen that the

58

What You Should Know about Foods and Feeding

percentage of protein is not the criterion of richness, rather the total calories which the food supplies.

Read the analyses of food. For example, here is one:

Protein	14·0
Fat	2·0
Carbohydrate	56·2
Ash	1·3
Water	4·1

There is no percentage of fibre given, which is often the case, so we read the list of ingredients: American corn, Canada peas, vetches, buckwheat, whole rice, millet, canary seed, maple peas, hemp seed, kafir corn. We refer to page 81 and study the percentages of fibre and fat. Since the fat is so low we realize there must be precious little hemp seed with its very high fat percentage. We see the average fibre runs about 5 per cent, so we subtract that figure from the 56 per cent given for total carbohydrate and get 51 per cent.

Now we add together the protein (14 per cent) and the carbohydrate without the fibre (51 per cent) and get 65. We multiply that by the number of calories which each unit of these two elements burns into: $65 \times 4 = 260$ calories. Next we multiply the fat (2 per cent) by 9: $2 \times 9 = 18$.

Now we add the 260 and 18 which equals 278, or the number of calories in 100 grammes of food.

We want to know how many calories there are in a pound, so we multiply by 4·5 because there are 450 grammes in a pound: $278 \times 4.5 = 1251$ calories per pound.

Minerals. Besides protein, carbohydrates and fat—all organic substances—we must consider certain inorganic chemicals without which our pigeons could not exist for long.

Some uncombined chemical elements are called minerals. You learned about the elements in your school chemistry course. A chemical element is a substance, made up of atoms, which cannot be decomposed by chemical means. Some of these elements are minerals, some gases. Most of the pigeon's nutrition is in combinations of elements, chemically very complicated combinations.

Minerals compose about 6 per cent of the pigeon's body in the following proportions:

59

Calcium	40
Phosphorus	22
Potassium	5
Sulphur	4
Chlorine	3
Sodium	2
Magnesium	0·7

with many minerals in lesser amounts. Among these are: iron, manganese, copper, iodine, zinc, cobalt, fluorine, boron.

The following table gives you briefly facts of interest about the essential minerals.

TABLE V

SOME ESSENTIAL MINERALS: THEIR FUNCTIONS AND SOURCES

	Functions in Body	*Principal Sources*
Calcium		
90% of body calcium is in the bones; 1% in circulation	Bone building	Oyster shells
	Rickets preventive	Snail shells
	Blood component	Certain grains
Stored in Body	Reproduction	Alfalfa-leaf meal
	Muscle function	Milk
	Nerve function	
	Heart function	
Phosphorus		
Bones, blood, muscles and feathers	Bone building	Grains
	Carbohydrate metabolism	Oyster shells
	Fat metabolism	Ground bone
	Blood component	So abundant in diet as to be of little concern
	Rickets preventive	
	Liquid content of tissues	
Iron		
Composes only 4/1000ths of the body weight	Component of red blood cells	Grains from iron-rich soils
Needed in minute quantities	Transports oxygen in blood	Iron salts
Is stored in body	65% is found in blood	
	30% is found in liver, bone marrow and spleen	
Potassium		
In blood and tissues	Body-fluid regulator	So abundant in pigeon food as to be of little concern
	Helps regulate blood	
	Muscular function	

60

What You Should Know about Foods and Feeding

	Functions in Body	Principal Sources
Sodium		
Found in body in combination with phosphorus, chlorine and sulphur	Regulates body fluids Blood regulator Component of gastric juice Component of urine	Ordinary salt
Chlorine		
Found combined with sodium and hydrogen	Component of gastric juice Blood regulator Regulates body fluids Component of urine	Ordinary salt
Iodine		
Most of iodine in body is found in thyroid gland	Thyroid health and normal growth Regulates metabolism Prevents goitre and cretinism In formation of thyroxine	Foods grown in iodine-rich soils Iodized salt Fish meal made from salt-water fish Shellfish
Magnesium		
Needed only in minute amounts	Muscle activity Bone building Normal growth Nerve function Blood function	Bones Vegetables Epsom salts Grains
Copper		
Needed only in minute amounts	Forms haemoglobin with iron	Copper sulphate Some grains
Sulphur		
Minute amounts required but needed regularly	Body regulation Combination in salts as sulphates	Any food with methonine and cystine in fair amounts
Cobalt		
A vitamin constituent	Concerned with growth	In grains and greens grown in cobalt-rich soils

As to total mineral requirements, the National Research Council's Committee on Animal Nutrition gives us the following table, which shows their recommendations for the amounts of minerals to be included

What You Should Know about Foods and Feeding

in a baby chick ration for the first eight weeks of its life. Since our squeakers grow so much more rapidly, these may need to be increased slightly for pigeon rations to be fed the old birds, to feed their nestlings.

Calcium	1·8%	Salt	0·5%
Phosphorus	0·6%	Manganese	25 milligrams per lb.
Potassium	0·2%	Iodine	0·5 milligrams per lb.

I find these minerals are included in the better grade pellets now available at food dealers. This is probably the easiest way to feed them. A mixture of ground bone, oyster shell, salt with potassium iodide included (iodized salt) will include all.

Vitamins. Another class of essential elements in food is vitamins. It may sound like heresy, but there is good evidence that far too much stress has been placed on this subject. Too many people drew rash conclusions from the scanty information available to them. We are now finding that we will need a great many more facts before we can speak with the confident tone many adopted some years ago. New vitamins are in the process of being tested daily, and there will be many others. Our knowledge will be incomplete and inconclusive for some time yet. Table VI gives a brief review of the vitamins about which we do know something.

The definition: a vitamin is one of a class of substances, existing in minute quantities in natural foods, and necessary to normal nutrition and growth, whose absence produces dietary diseases. Some are made synthetically.

Some vitamins are soluble in fat, as we have seen, and are found only in foods containing appreciable amounts of fat. Some are water-soluble. Some are destroyed by heat, some by rancidity, some by age.

Vitamins are necessary only in minute quantities. With a few exceptions, all essential vitamins are present in the normal diet. When all our information is boiled down, it seems certain that pigeons can get all the vitamins they need from grains and sunshine, provided the proper grains are fed and plenty of time is allowed to birds to 'absorb' the sunshine, especially during winter months when the actinic rays are at a minimum.

Many vitamins have individual but very similar functions. In maintaining health some are useful only in conjunction with others. It is often difficult to break down the better sources into their individual components. For our purposes, it is quite unnecessary to discuss each of the vitamins individually in order to understand the effects of the groups in

What You Should Know about Foods and Feeding

which they occur and in which we handle them. The B complex is an excellent illustration. It embodies many essentials. All may be found together and are used together medicinally.

Table VI gives in outline form the major properties, function and sources of the principal vitamins and vitamin groups which are of interest to pigeon fanciers. There are many more sources of vitamins which are of interest in human diets other than the ones we have listed, but these refer to nutrition as it concerns pigeon health.

TABLE VI

VITAMINS: THEIR PROPERTIES, FUNCTIONS AND SOURCES FOR PIGEONS

Vitamins	*Concerned with*	*Sources*
A (and carotene)		
Fat soluble	General metabolism	Yellow grains
Stable at boiling temperatures	Growth	(Maize)
	Skin, feather health	Dark green vegetable leaves
Spoils with age if exposed to air	Muscle co-ordination	Alfalfa leaf meal
Body stores it	Fertility	Milk
	Calcium utilization	Fish, Synthetic liver oils
	Digestion	
	Hearing	Halibut liver oil or
	Vision	Percomorph oil
	Prevention of infection	
	Nerve health	
	Pituitary-gland function	
B Complex		
Biotin	Growth promotion	Cereal and other grains
Pantothenic acid	Nerve health	
Riboflavin, Thiamin	Heart health	Alfalfa leaf meal
Folic acid	Liver function	Yeast
Niacin	Appetite	Rapidly growing plants
Pyridoxin	Gastro-intestinal function	
B₁₂		Bacterial growth in digestive tract
Water soluble	Intestinal absorption	
Body storage—small	Fertility	
Some destroyed by high cooking temperatures but not riboflavin	Muscle function	
	Prevention of anaemia	
	Kidney and bladder function	
	Blood health	

What You Should Know about Foods and Feeding

Vitamins	Concerned with	Sources
C		
Ascorbic acid	Not necessary in pigeons	Synthetic ascorbic
Water soluble	except in disease treat-	acid
Unstable at Cooking	ment	Alfalfa leaf meal
temperatures		Fruit and vegetable juices
D		
Irradiated ergosterol	Regulation of calcium	Fish liver oils
Well stored by the body	and phosphorus in	Synthesized in
Stands considerable heat	blood	pigeon's skin in
Resists decomposition	Calcium and phosphorus	presence of sun-
Fat soluble	metabolism	light
	Prevention of rickets	Irradiated foods
	Normal skeletal develop-	
	ment	
	Muscular co-ordination	
E		
Tocopherol	Muscular co-ordination	Seed germs
Fat soluble	Fertility	Green leaves
Body stores it	Sound heart	So abundant none is
Perishes when exposed to	Survival of young	needed by healthy
air	Growth	pigeons
Stands ordinary cooking	Pituitary gland health	
temperatures		
K		
Fat soluble	Normal blood clotting	Green succulent
Body stores it		leaves
		Alfalfa leaf meal
		Vegetable oils
Unsaturated Fatty Acids		
(Sometimes called vitamin F)		
Linoleic acid	Skin and Feather Health	Seed oils such as
Linolenic acid		wheat germ, rape-
Arachidonic acid		seed oils
		Linseed oils
		There is so much in natural grains pigeons need no more

In studying the above table, you see that feeding extra vitamins to healthy pigeons is usually a waste. And there is a further reason why they are unnecessary. A goodly proportion of the digested mass in the

1. Two types of scraper

2. A wide-bladed hoe helps greatly in rapid cleaning. Its blade should be kept sharp and free from nicks

3. A wide shovel, its blade kept sharp and smooth, is an important adjunct. A ball-pointed hammer is issued to smooth the shovel and the peen, in order to drive nails evenly into the floor

4. For efficient loft cleaning, the trap-door opening on to a wheelbarrow is a great help. Note wire-mesh floor on the porch above the wheelbarrow

5. Feeding and watering on a shelf which is easily scraped, makes for hygienic conditions. The devices to right and left of the fountain can be used for either food or water

6. A food tray, which is easily scraped after the birds have been fed, can be tipped on end to keep it clean

7. A simple and useful 'hospital' for the isolation and treatment of sick pigeons. This one is suspended from a low ceiling

8. An aluminium or galvanized-iron roof over a porch keeps out wild birds, and pigeons cannot stay on it

9. An uncovered porch is a menace to health

10. A neat and useful fly where the birds can sun, bathe and mate. It is enclosed with half-inch mesh wire cloth

11. The floor in this fly is of one-inch mesh heavy welded wire strong enough to bear a man's weight. Rain drives in from all angles so the fly remains clean

12. Youngsters raised under a nestbox. Both he and his nestmate could not hold legs under them but kept them extended

13. One result of lice damage. The feathers are not worn or picked off, but are cut off by lice

14. A 'one-eye' cold, a condition easily and quickly cured

15. A pigeon with pigeon pox. Completely unnecessary because so easily prevented

lower bowel is bacteria which are decomposing the waste and also synthesizing amino acids and vitamins. The same thing goes on throughout the entire digestive tract; with the bacteria making vitamins. Small amounts? Yes, but vitamins are needed only in small amounts.

Moreover, in disease conditions, these bacteria cannot function. Diarrhoeas wash them out. So, in sickness, some vitamins are essential, as we shall see when we read what their uses are as an aid in treatment.

Since so little work has been done on vitamin requirements of pigeons, we must draw on the enormous literature of the requirements and diseases caused by a lack of vitamins in chickens. Yet there is a difference: the pigeon is grown in 27 days and the chicken in 150 or more. Pigeon growth is much faster and probably requirements are much greater. But the food consumed is also much greater in amount. So if we calculate the vitamin requirements per pound of food, we should arrive at a fair comparison.

Although it is, therefore, a theoretical question since pigeons obtain their vitamins from proper grain mixtures, it is practical to know what the safe minimums are in the case of sick or undernourished birds.

Whatever one says about the value of maize as a source of vitamin A or of carotene, one must always keep in mind one fact, namely, that both of these deteriorate with age. In whole grain the deterioration is less than in pellets but even in whole grain the loss may be 75 per cent in either improperly stored or aged maize.

The vitamin A used in pellets today is usually in a stabilized form, made so by addition of a chemical which prevents oxidation and therefore prolongs its active life. Untreated cod liver oil loses its vitamin A activity more rapidly than whole maize loses its ability to supply carotene.

The point to remember is to use fresh foods, either of grain or pellets wherever this is possible.

Vitamins   A—3,000 International Units (I.U.) per pound of food.

          D—30 minutes of exposure to sunlight per day during winter, 10 minutes during spring and autumn, 3 minutes during summer, or 600 I.U. of D_3 per pound of food.

          Thiamine—100 micrograms a day.

          Riboflavin—2,000 micrograms per pound of food.

          Nicotinic Acid—10 milligrams per pound of food.

          Niacin—2,000 micrograms per pound of food.

What You Should Know about Foods and Feeding

Pantothenic Acid—5,000 I.U. per pound of food, or 6 milligrammes.

Biotin—5075 microgrammes per pound of food.

B_{12}—$\frac{1}{2}$ gramme per 100 lb. of feed of Aureomycin, Terramycin, Bacitrocin waste, less of Penicillin.

Water. That water is essential to living is obvious. Everybody who observes at all has seen what its absence produces in the way of dehydration, knows the sensation of thirst, the dry mouth. Every pigeon owner has seen squeakers a few days after weaning sit about hunched up and blinking, and has also seen what a good drink will do to revive them. And since blood, the very vehicle of transportation of nutrition to the cells, consists mostly of water, the need for water is patent. Besides its internal uses, its evaporation regulates temperature.

Water carries out waste products; it bathes the cells and carries off their excreta as it carries useful substances to them, to mention only a few of its uses. But supplying water is so easy that it is not a problem. A pan from which the pigeon can drink at will is all he asks. Then, if there is enough water in his food so that he needs no more he is satisfied, and if his food is of such a type that he must have additional water, he drinks.

Seventy per cent of our pigeons' bodies is water. Here are the percentages for the separate parts:

Cartilages	55·0	Brain	79·0
Bones	60·0	Blood	88·0
Skin	72·0	Urine	93·0
Muscles	75·0	Lymph	96·0
Ligaments	77·0	Gastric Juices	97·0

Nearly all the water drunk is absorbed. Normally about 20 per cent passes out with the breath, and in hot weather more is thrown off in this manner. Almost all the rest is passed in the urine. Very little water is used in combination with other substances. It acts as a solvent or vehicle. As water it enters the body: as water it leaves.

In foods, water content varies greatly. The most succulent greens which pigeons like contain so much water that in nutritional studies they were difficult to evaluate because a pigeon could not eat enough in a day to nourish it. But grains contain little (6 to 14 per cent) unless soaked, as is the practice with some fanciers in the forced feeding of orphan squeakers. Grains, if dried below a normal water content, simply absorb water from the air.

What You Should Know about Foods and Feeding

Water can be a vehicle for the transmission of disease, as we shall see, and it is highly important that it be fed pure and in such a way that droppings cannot fall into it. But more about this under Sanitation.

Inadequate water supply will cause pigeons to fly away from their lofts in search of it. The drinking of salty water by thirsty race birds may cause nausea and the inability to continue flying. Growth slows perceptibly in squeakers when sufficient water is not available to the parents, who find regurgitation of food difficult.

Pigeons, like other poultry, prefer warmed water to icy cold water. Hens' egg production falls when their water is not warmed. Unlike hens, however, pigeons do not drink frequently, so a constant water supply need not be furnished. Breeding birds do need a constant supply, but non-breeders do not, provided water is brought to them three or four times a day. Electric heating devices for water containers are useful and worth while.

The amount of protein and salt in the diet affect water consumption. Higher protein diets cause more water to be consumed and the amount of faeces is increased. Higher percentages of salt cause more watery faeces.

Food Deterioration. Rancidity destroys vitamins. This is especially true of the important vitamins A and E. It was once the practice to feed large quantities of cod liver oil to pigeons as well as to poultry in general. Don't do it. The oil in cod liver oil becomes rancid quickly if not refrigerated. This oil is poisonous. Moreover, the rancidity in it reduces the A and destroys the E vitamin. There is no reason whatever to feed cod liver oil, provided yellow maize is fed and, as we saw, the birds obtain all the D they need from sunlight. Synthetic A is much less expensive and is stabilized, and used liberally in pellets.

Mould in food can be harmless or deadly, depending on the kind of mould. Food should be stored in a dry area where mould fails to grow. If you find mould in food, don't feed it.

Insects and their larvae need no longer be a worry. They do little harm but the webs are annoying. A piece of Vapona bar put on top of the food in a container destroys them.

3

Pigeon Food Ingredients

Now, in 1968, most of the food fed to pigeons is in clean grains; seeds as many prefer to call them. What the future will open for us can be no more than a prophecy based on what has been proved in the feeding of poultry. But it would seem that, because of economy, pigeon pellets may and probably will, partly replace whole grains. For that reason, we shall have to include, among food ingredients, those which are or can be included in pellets.

Pellets are made by mixing the ingredients, and then forcing the mixture by revolving rollers through a circular plate with many holes in it, each hole the diameter of a pellet. A revolving blade below the plate cuts the pellets off at the desired length. Some are mixed with sticky substances such as molasses, steamed, then baked or dried after coming through the machine. Some mixtures of ingredients have enough oils to make firm pellets.

Pellets at present are fed by many fanciers as though they were supplements to grain. They are when the pellets are complete, but manufacturers do not market them to be supplements; pellets are sold as complete food. The only item to be fed with them is some form of calcium, oyster shells for example. No grit is needed.

Pellets, properly compounded, can include better sources of proteins than grains supply, they assure the owner that every bird receives the same diet. And this is important, as every fancier knows, because the stronger birds often eat all of the more tasty grains in a mixture, leaving the less desirable for the weaker birds. Pellets are easier to feed; no thought of proper grain mixture is necessary. Pellets are cheaper than top-quality grain and the manufacturers claim that they contain a higher percentage of digestible foods. The variety which can be included is amazing. Dried skim milk, dried milk whey, yeast, fats, fish, meat

68

Pigeon Food Ingredients

and bone, wheat germ and the best parts of the wheat, rice polishings, are all items which the pigeon man would seldom think of including in his birds' diet, yet they are all especially valuable for pigeon nutrition.

Here is a table showing the grain and by-products in some of the most successful pellets now on the market. You can see how varied the ingredients can be and yet completely nourish the birds.

TABLE VII

PELLET INGREDIENTS

Ingredient	Water	Protein	Carbo-hydrate	Fibre	Fat
Alfalfa Leaf Meal	7·8	20·0	41·1	18·0	2·5
Alfalfa Leaf Meal	8·6	17·0	37·8	25·0	2·0
Barley Meal	11·0	11·5	66·5	6·0	2·0
Blood Meal	9·7	80·0	3·8	1·0	1·0
Brewers' grains, dried	7·5	24·0	42·2	15·0	6·0
Brewers' Yeast, dried	6·3	46·0	35·7	2·8	1·2
Buckwheat	—	11·0	—	10·0	2·0
Buttermilk, dried	7·6	32·4	43·3	—	5·0
Maize Meal	15·0	8·9	68·9	2·0	3·9
Maize Germ Meal	7·8	13·7	56·1	11·0	6·0
Maize Gluten Meal	8·6	42·9	40·1	3·9	2·0
Cottonseed Oil Meal	7·8	41·0	26·3	9·0	7·0
Distillers' Grains, dried	6·9	28·8	41·7	9·0	8·9
Distillers' Solubles, dried	6·9	28·0	47·6	3·3	6·7
Fish Meal—					
Menhaden	6·4	62·2	4·2	0·7	8·5
Sardine	6·9	67·2	5·4	0·6	5·0
Whitefish	6·9	63·0	0·1	0·1	6·7
Fish Solubles, dried	7·0	32·0	—	—	3·0
Hominy Feed	10·1	10·8	63·9	4·7	5·7
Kafir Meal (Milo)	7·1	11·0	71·1	2·5	2·5
Linseed Oil Meal	8·8	35·0	36·9	8·1	5·6
Meat Scraps, dried	6·9	52·9	7·3	2·2	7·3
Meat Scraps, dried	6·2	60·0	1·1	2·4	8·8
Meat and Bone Meal	6·4	50·6	2·0	2·0	10·0
Molasses, Cane	26·0	2·9	62·1	—	—
Oatmeal, feeding	9·3	15·0	64·4	2·0	7·4
Oats, Rolled	7·9	15·5	66·1	2·5	4·5

Pigeon Food Ingredients

	Water	Protein	Carbo-hydrate	Fibre	Fat
Peanut Oil Meal	7·2	43·1	23·0	13·9	7·6
Rice Bran	9·0	12·8	41·7	12·7	13·1
Rice Polishings	9·7	12·7	56·6	3·5	11·4
Rye Meal	10·5	12·6	70·9	2·4	1·7
Shrimp Meal	7·1	40·0	6·0	11·0	2·0
Skimmed Milk, dried	5·8	34·7	50·3	0·2	1·2
Soy bean Oil Meal, expelled	9·2	44·2	29·9	5·6	5·3
Soy bean Oil Meal, solvent	9·4	46·1	31·8	5·9	1·0
Wheat Bran	10·3	16·4	53·0	9·9	4·3
Wheat Germ Meal	7·1	26·0	—	2·5	8·0
Wheat Middlings	10·3	18·1	58·5	4·9	4·6
Whey, dried	6·5	12·2	70·4	0·2	0·8

In the following descriptions no analyses are given because they are all listed in Table VIII, page 81.

LEGUMES

First, let us consider the grains from plants known as legumes. These plants can remove nitrogen from the air as well as from the soil and, as a consequence, are able to add more nitrogen to their seeds thus making them higher in protein.

Field Peas (*Pisum arvense*) are grown mostly in the north because they require a cool growing season. They are sometimes grown as a winter crop in southern states of the U.S.A. Many are sold under the name *Canada Peas* or *Canada Field Peas*, of which there are several varieties.

Field peas are grown in white and yellow colours and there is little differences in the analyses among the varieties. It is not necessary for them to come from Canada to be good pigeon food.

Maple Peas. Brownish and with a speckled coat as compared with Field peas. They are grown 'down under' in New Zealand and Australia, the transportation making them rather expensive. Nor have they any great advantage over Field or Cow-peas.

Cow-Peas (*Vigna sinensis*). Cow-peas are widely grown all over the world but mostly for fodder, the seeds being too expensive for stock

Pigeon Food Ingredients

food, and pigeon fanciers are among the principal users. Cow-peas analyse about the same as Field peas and have little to recommend them in preference. Many feel that the choice of which to use depends on price. Nutritionally, they are slightly higher in calories due to the fact that the Field pea is somewhat higher in fibre.

Cow-peas are grown in a variety of colours: black, white, red, grey speckled.

Tic Beans. These are pretty much a European pigeon food. Some few tons are sent to America annually. The seed is large, being brownish with the 'eye' at one end (see illustration). Pigeons are often fed Tic beans as a staple and other seed fed as a treat.

Soy Beans (*Glycine max*). Soy beans are one of the great sources of human nourishment in Asia, but not yet in the West. They are also a principal animal food. Many varieties are grown, some with tiny round seeds, some with larger ones. The seeds vary in colour according to the variety. In the West they have been fed so little to pigeons that much remains to be learned about their value. Among the varieties are some with protein as high as 40 per cent. Their amino-acid complement is almost as complete in essentials as milk or meat.

Considering the high protein analysis, Soy beans are probably the cheapest vegetable protein available to the pigeon owner. Whereas Field peas or Cow-peas carry slightly over 1 per cent of fat, Soy beans have almost 18 per cent and furnish a large amount of heat calories.

Soy bean meal in pea size can also be purchased. This is the residue after the Soy bean oil has been extracted and it is even higher in protein, easily digested and an excellent food. It should be tried for pigeons, but as yet I can find no research reporting a study of its trial.

You may have heard it said that Soy beans are not good for pigeons. I attended a pigeon club meeting once where a member was expostulating on food. He said Soy beans should never be fed. Then he told us how he used half pellets and half grain, naming the kind of pellets he fed. We had been using the same kind in the Speedome Lofts, so when I returned home I looked at the guarantee which accompanies the bag. The only grains included in it were maize and Soy beans. The rest of the ingredients were composed of by-products or vitamins, minerals, etc. The manufacturer, therefore, has demonstrated that Soy beans are good pigeon food because so many thousands of pigeons eat them in that mixture.

Tares, Vetches (*Vicia Spp.*). Tares produce round or oval seeds, according to the species and there are many species: Woolly Pod, Hairy,

Pigeon Food Ingredients

Common, Hungarian, Perennial, Purple, Bard, Bird Vetches and many others.

They analyse much like the other legumes except Soy beans. They furnish variety to pigeon feeds and the birds like them.

Horse-Beans (*Vicia faba*). Horse-beans are related to the vetches but are grown in southern countries which have little temperature variation and plenty of warmth because they cannot stand cold.

The Horse-beans are relished by pigeons and are much like the vetches in quality of nutrition.

Garden Peas (*Pisum sativum*). Now and again seed growers find themselves with large quantities of Garden pea seed which they have been unable to sell and which has become so old it no longer germinates sufficiently well for agricultural purposes. Instead of throwing it away, they sell it for poultry food at reasonable prices. Some are wrinkled peas and some are smooth, almost impossible to distinguish from Field peas. They vary little in analysis from Field peas and are worth about as much. In 1968 the price was about half that of Field peas. Pigeons must be educated to eat the wrinkled varieties.

Lentils (*Ervum lens, Lens esculenta*). Lentils are grown for human food and when these round flattish seeds are puchased for pigeon feeding, we must pay the same price as the wholesale prices of the human food.

Lentils have the least amount of fibre of any of the legumes and probably a little more nutritional value, although the rest of the analysis corresponds closely to that of Field peas.

Peanuts (*Arachis hypogaea*). Peanuts differ from the other legumes: they bear their fruit underground. They are available in several types: Virginia, Runner, Spanish and unclassified. The Virginia peanuts are long and are sold in shells or shelled for human consumption, as stock feed and as cake (residue left after peanut oil has been extracted). Spanish peanuts are small, almost round and not too large for pigeons to swallow easily. They can be had already shelled and with or without the red husk, and are available in the shell.

Peanuts are rich in protein and nearly half their substance is fat (48 per cent in some). They are rich in fat soluble vitamins, but are not to be recommended as the sole article of diet.

OTHER GRAINS AND SEEDS

It is difficult to classify the other grains we feed our birds. We could do it by the size of seed, the protein content, or the character of the

Pigeon Food Ingredients

plant on which they grow. Each classification has its faults, however. Suppose therefore, since most of the seeds come from grasses, that we look them over in alphabetical order:

Barley (*Hordeum*). Barley is from a grass-type plant. The grains are commonly used and not particularly relished when there are more attractive grains available. Barley is quite laxative, although not especially high in fibre. It is low in protein and fat, useful in maintenance rations and relatively inexpensive. Unhulled barley is often fed to livestock but pigeons usually have the hulled product. Some breeders use unhulled, believing that the additional roughage is good for their birds.

Buckwheat (*Fagopyrum*). Buckwheat is a grain, but it does not actually belong to the true cereals because the buckwheat plants are not grasses, as anyone who has seen any of them growing will remember. The seeds are triangular and pointed at the ends. There is considerable difference in size of seed among the species. *Tartary* is probably used more often than any other. Its seed is small and easily eaten by pigeons. The flinty seed coat which is indigestible adds materially to the fibre and detracts from the more concentrated nourishment of some other grains.

Corn or *Maize* (*Zea mays*). The word 'corn', when used in Europe, signifies all kinds of grain. The early American settlers who first encountered this huge grass-type plant, with its seeds growing on ears produced part way up the stalk instead of on the top, called it 'Indian Corn'. On the American continents the name is now used without the prefix 'Indian'. Americans who read European pigeon books and magazines are often at a loss to know what grains are being referred to when they read the word 'Maize'. It is simply what Americans call 'corn'. Europeans who read American books have some trouble thinking about the specific word 'corn', which to them is an inclusive, general term.

In the table of grain compositions, maize is presented as having 8·9 per cent protein, 68·9 per cent carbohydrate, 3·9 per cent fat in the form of oil, but the maize you use may be quite different from this analysis for the following reasons: the different varieties vary greatly, the percentage of water varies anywhere from 10 per cent to 16 per cent depending on the length of storage period and the process of drying. The carbohydrates in maize are starch and sugar, and some varieties have more sugar than others.

Back in 1912 to 1916, when I was flying pigeons as a boy, we fed 'Canada peas and Canadian corn'. A 50–50 mixture was considered to

73

Pigeon Food Ingredients

be all that could be desired. Our Canadian corn was Flint maize. Each kernel was roundish with a flinty hard outer surface and a softer germ end. Today very little Flint maize is grown, having been replaced by 'Dent maize', each kernel of which has a dent in its outer end. The kernels are long and narrow as compared with Flint and much softer as one may determine by crushing a kernel with one's teeth—which would be a difficult task with Flint maize.

White maize is almost devoid of carotene, so it is almost never grown any more. Before we learned the relationship of carotene and vitamin A, however, White maize was grown more than yellow. In Argentina, Flint is still grown and exported to England and the United States.

Maize is one of the finest grains to include in pigeon rations. Some birds gulp in swallowing the large kernels. Yellow maize is so rich in carotene (each unit of which splits into two units of vitamin A) that a pigeon receiving rations containing one-fifth of maize will be getting all the vitamin A it needs.

Maize, however, does have some disadvantages which make it unwise to use too large a proportion in a ration. While being rich in vitamin A, it is relatively weak in the B-complex vitamins as compared with some of the richer grain sources. A study of Table VI shows that difference.

Pigeons relish maize, the mature birds often eat it all from a ration before touching any of the other grains present, unless hemp seed is included.

In addition to the Flint and Dent types of maize, it is often possible to buy popcorn and sweet corn seed; also types of maize. Seed growers who find by test that the germination rate is too low, will, as in the case of garden peas, sell the seed for pigeon food.

When sweet corn is eaten it absorbs enough moisture in the crop to make it enlarge or swell considerably. Popcorn in its raw state is so hard as to make one wonder if it ever can soften sufficiently for the stones in the gizzard to grind it. But they do and these small grains are digested well.

Parts of the maize kernel are much richer in certain substances than are the other parts. For example, the gluten meal separated from the whole kernel contains 8 times as much carotene proportionally as the whole kernel, $2\frac{1}{2}$ times as much niacin, 5 times the protein of the whole grain, 10 times the calcium, 24 times as much iron. Pellet manufacturers can take advantage of such facts and make better pellets without using whole corn meal.

Pigeon Food Ingredients

When corn or maize becomes cracked and the oil, together with the sugar and starch, becomes exposed to the air, it is believed that it becomes easily rancid, that it develops moulds and deteriorates; and as a result has become taboo as a pigeon food. And yet, we all know of breeders who have broken all rules, fed 'scratch' food composed of cracked corn, whole oats, and other grains of a less desirable nature, who still raised good pigeons. Is it luck which will 'run out'?

Sorghum (*Sorghum*). This is a corn of which *Kafir* and *Milo* are two of the species. Sorghum, when it starts to grow in the row, appears much like maize but as the season progresses, the leaves and stalks are more slender and the seed grows on the terminal part of the plant in the manner of the tassel on the maize plant. Varieties grow from a few feet to 15 feet tall. The yield of seed is large and there is also fodder to be gained from the crop; hence the low cost of the grain.

Kafir kernels are roundish and may be white, pink, or reddish in colour. Milo seeds are somewhat flattened, white or yellowish in colour. Sometimes Kafir or Milo grain is actually from a hybridization product of the two. Seeds may be brownish or like the parents, depending on the particular cross.

Kafir or Milo seeds are quite low in fibre, rich in carbohydrate, and about average in protein and fat. They are fairly well liked by pigeons and make a good food for the inexpensive part of a maintenance ration.

Oats (*Avena*). Oats are a low yielding crop and the grain is expensive. The seed kernel is enclosed in a tight sheath which accounts for most of the 11 per cent of fibre they contain. Some are fed to pigeons, but since the oat kernel is one of the finest cereal grains in completeness of amino acids and B-Complex vitamins (although deficient in carotene), they could be used more.

As a pigeon food, hulled oats, clipped oats, or groats are generally used. Hulled oats are the kernels produced from undried grain in the process of hulling. Clipped oats are oats with the husks clipped off short, thus leaving less fibre and weighing considerably more per bushel.

Groats are kernels left during the process of making oatmeal. Since they are low in fibre they make an excellent addition to the ration.

Rice (*Oryza sativa*). Rice, along with Soy beans and wheat which make up a great part of the staple diet among human beings, is also one of the best pigeon foods. Rice for pigeons should be the whole brown product, not the devitalized polished product which human beings eat.

75

Pigeon Food Ingredients

However, because it is susceptible to weevils, brown rice is often difficult to obtain. White polished rice can best be thought of in terms of starch calories, for it contributes little else. Since it contains under 7 per cent protein and 80 per cent carbohydrate of which only 1·5 per cent is fibre, it is easily understood why it is one of the constipating foods.

Then think of the wonderful properties produced from the by-products of which polished rice has been robbed: rice polish, so rich in vitamins that it was once used as a chief source of them; and rice bran, one of the best cattle food supplements. These remarkable and inexpensive items can be pellet materials for pigeon food, while we consume the calories and not much more of the nutritious elements.

Broken rice is nothing more than broken grains of polished rice. It is also called 'brewer's rice'.

Canary Seed (*Phalaris canariensis*). Canary seed comes from a grass which is grown for the most part in Europe, especially in Spain, Turkey, and North Africa. The seeds are golden yellow, pointed at both ends, firm and slippery. They contain an average amount of protein—about 14 per cent—and 5 per cent fat. Canary seed is too expensive for pigeon food and adds little or nothing which cannot be furnished by other kinds of grains or seeds.

Millet (*Panicum miliaceum*). Millet is a small, oval, yellowish seed which grows on a coarse grass and is one of the principal grains fed to budgerigars. It is sometimes found in pigeon foods and sometimes can be bought cheaply enough to be tempting, yet it offers little, and has a low degree of palatability. It is usually the last of the food mixture to be eaten. Its analysis is much like that of canary seed, but is a little lower in protein content.

Millet can be obtained in yellow or white colours; budgerigar breeders usually prefer the white, which is more expensive.

Rapeseed (*Brassica napus*). Rapeseeds are round. tiny, black or red seeds which newly weaned squeakers sometimes enjoy picking up and are one of the richest seeds on the bill of fare in fat, of which they contain about 40 per cent. They are moderately well supplied with protein, but the lowest of all grains containing carbohydrate, which amounts to only 16 per cent, making them unique. Like millet, rapeseed is chiefly a canary food and is sometimes used to feed budgerigars. It is not used much as a feed for pigeons, but sometimes in trapping mixtures.

Linseed or *Flaxseed* (*Linum usitatissimum*). This is another of the oily seeds which contain a great amount of fat—36 per cent. Some

Pigeon Food Ingredients

fanciers feed it during the moult, believing that it adds lustre to the feathers. It is seldom used in commercial mixtures.

Poppyseeds (*Papaver somniferum*). Poppyseeds look like rapeseeds, as anyone who has eaten poppyseed rolls remembers. They are rich in fat with 40 per cent, fairly rich in protein 18 per cent, and are also used for squeakers to pick up. There is a general opinion that poppy-seeds have a medicinal property of producing a constipated condition in birds with loose bowel movements and that they are useful in counter-acting laxative foods included in the food mixture. Just how much truth there is in that belief is problematical; this also holds true for the amount of opium they are said to contain.

Hempseed (*Cannabis sativa*). Hempseed is the most relished of all of the foods fed to pigeons. Even when fed hempseed for the first time, our birds seem to know instinctively that these globular oily titbits are their first choice. How they know at first sight is a mystery. Hempseed is low in carbohydrate, moderately high in protein, and quite high in fat (30 per cent). Because of their high cost, only small amounts are found in mixtures. Bought in 10-lb. lots, the cost is about four times the cost of maize. It is strictly a titbit—excellent to use as a lure to coax pigeons in.

Sunflower Seeds (*Helianthus*). Sunflower seeds are large, striped, and pointed with a considerable amount of fibre (28 per cent). They are also quite oily (32 per cent fat), and are expensive. They are the chief food fed to parrots but are fed only occasionally to pigeons.

Wheat (*Triticum*). Wheat is, like Soy beans and rice, one of those grains which are mainstays of human diets. Wheat is also an excellent pigeon food. Pigeons are fortunate in having it fed to them in its whole form and not in the devitalized form in which we human beings eat it. As in the case of rice, the outside layers contain some of the most valuable elements and the germ is rich in oil and some vitamins. There are many species and varieties of which the Hard Red or White wheats make the best pigeon foods. Fortunately, some of the parts removed from the kernel can be incorporated in pellets.

Wheat is a rich source of food, low in fibre despite the fibrous bran and middlings, contains an average amount of protein and very little fat (1·8 per cent).

Acorns. Acorns, the fruit of many species of oak trees, have been fed with some success in the past. The difficulty is in finding the best sorts and in having the help to pick them up. In some parts of the world, acorns are used to feed many species of livestock. Wild pigeons often

77

Pigeon Food Ingredients

eat the smaller kinds whole. Passenger pigeons of the United States consumed enormous quantities; game birds, such as pheasant and grouse whose heads and beaks are not much larger than those of pigeons, can negotiate fairly large-size acorns.

For pigeon feeding these oak fruits should be gathered and those with worm holes rejected. They are spread in thin layers under cover until they are dry (not fed before that), and then stored in barrels or bins.

To feed, acorns are generally cracked first. They can be eaten day after day and the tannic acid in them seems to have no adverse effect on the pigeons.

If you see your pigeons picking at young grass, think of the value it contains before you shoo them away from it. About a month after planting, the grass leaves are at their best nutritionally. Compared with lettuce and cabbage, grass is outstandingly better: 19 per cent of it is solids, while lettuce contains 5·3 per cent solid.

In the B complex, grass contains (in micrograms per gramme) Thiamine 12·8, Riboflavin 26·2, Biotin 0·22, Panthothenic Acid 17·0, Niacin 77·7, Growth Factor 14·6. Carotene runs 0·58 milligrams in each gramme. Grass has 24 per cent protein, 8·3 per cent fat, 18·3 per cent fibre, and it is rich in chlorophyll. Grass may be one factor in pigeon health if they are permitted access to it.

SALT

Pigeons need salt and they know enough not to eat too much of it. Salt blocks can be supplied to them with good effect. If you feed all grain and some greens, moisten the greens with iodized salt. Or leave a little coarse salt where the birds can reach it. Best of all is a soft salt brick which can be made to contain all of the known minerals in it as well. There are salt bricks available, but I have seen none which gives the mineral composition. The salt blocks for cattle and sheep, although well supplemented with minerals, are too hard for pigeons to chip off; our birds need much softer blocks.

In the matter of diets, it is amazing what a wide variety of foods pigeons can live on. We are interested in knowing the best for each special condition, but knowing some of the diets they have eaten makes us realize that there is no one that is essential.

Colin Osman in his excellent book, *Racing Pigeons*, cites an old time

Pigeon Food Ingredients

fancier of Woking, England, who fed acorns throughout the war years, 1939–1945, during the racing season and who 'achieved more than his share of success'.

Pigeons in city parks often consume large amounts of popcorn which kind-hearted persons buy from vendors and feed the birds. Other pigeons fill up on roasted peanuts. Think of the bread-fed pigeons which are kept satiated by their benefactors who toss it out on to pavements and streets. During the war, races in Britain were won by birds on stale bread and butter diets!

Pellets are coming more and more into favour and they are a far cry from grains or seeds. Squab breeders have tried providing a variety of grains in separate hoppers so that the birds could choose the grains they wanted.

When it comes to grain mixtures, pigeons have shown their ability to live on the widest variety imaginable. Ordinary cheap poultry scratch foods with whole oats and cracked corn, diets of peas and beans, other mixtures of a dozen expensive seeds, beechnuts which pigeons pick up under trees.

Pigeons will eat boiled potatoes, will drink and thrive on milk, sweet or sour, and I know a farmer who permits his barn pigeons to eat the poultry mash from the same trough as the hens; indeed, he feeds the pigeons nothing else.

FOOD FOR RACING

When a pigeon is flying, in a long race that is, is he digesting food as he flies or is he living on food stored in his liver and muscles? Have you ever felt the crop of a bird just home from a 500-mile race? Then you know that he does digest food while flying. Since this is so, what should our birds be fed which will furnish the most food in the smallest amount of bulk? Foods rich in protein, carbohydrates, or fat? Since every gramme of fat burns into $2\frac{1}{4}$ times as much energy as 1 gramme of either protein or carbohydrate, it would seem sensible to provide high fat foods.

But we must remember that the pigeon has a great deal of fat stored in his body, and sugar too, in liver and muscles. For short races these are sufficient. Perhaps an investigation of the foods which have been fed to human athletes or to dogs which are called upon for long, gruelling periods of exertion, will help in determining the answer.

Lumberjacks use so much energy in their work that some eat six

Pigeon Food Ingredients

meals a day. Their food is greasy to such an extent, that persons on a sedentary diet would become nauseated from the high percentage of fat. They consume large amounts of sugar for quick available energy. Marathon runners use fat and sugar.

The experienced hunter, whose foxhounds often run for 24 or more hours at a stretch, learned long ago that a high-fat diet keeps hounds running and builds them up more quickly after the chase than any other kind of food. The sled-dog driver feeds his dogs pemmican, which usually contains about 70 per cent fat, and these dogs pull heavy loads for hours at a time.

Protein, of course, is necessary because it repairs muscles, but fat releases the most energy per ounce, and for that reason should be the kind of food chosen for the long races. Here, for example, are two grains: peanuts and maize. Suppose a pigeon eats 25 grammes (a little less than 1 oz.) of either one. Which would supply the most energy?

Peanuts with 30 per cent protein, 11·6 per cent carbohydrates, 47·5 per cent fat;

Maize with 9·3 per cent protein, 70·3 per cent carbohydrates, 4·3 per cent fat.

One hundred grammes of peanuts would have 41·6 grammes of protein and carbohydrate combined:

$$41·6 \times 4 = 166·4 \text{ calories}$$
$$\text{Fat} \quad 47·5 \times 9 = 427·5 \text{ calories}$$
$$\text{Total} \quad 539·9 \text{ calories}$$

One hundred grammes of maize would have 79·6 grammes of protein and carbohydrate combined:

$$79·6 \times 4 = 318·4 \text{ calories}$$
$$\text{Fat} \quad 4·3 \times 9 = 38·7 \text{ calories}$$
$$\text{Total} \quad 357·1 \text{ calories}$$

Thus, a cropful of peanuts would supply our 500-mile flier with 563·9 units of energy vs. 357·1 in a cropful of maize.

This is not to say that peanuts make the ideal racing food. There may be reasons why they are not, but the comparison indicates that we can, by thought and action, help our birds sustain themselves by what we feed them. Perhaps mixtures of high fat foods are the answer. For one day's racing we need not be concerned with vitamins, amino acids and other essentials. Racing takes energy and the essentials beyond that can be supplied before and after the race.

Table VIII—Composition of Grains

Grain	Water	Protein	Carbo-hydrates	Fibre	Fat	Digestible Calories Per Pound
Acorns (Dried)	15·0	5·7	61·6	11·6	4·1	1080
Barley	10·6	12·7	66·6	5·4	1·9	1405
Buckwheat	14·0	11·3	69·2	14·4	2·6	1296
Canary Seed	7·0	17·2	59·1	5·7	5·5	1492
Cow Peas	9·8	23·8	57·1	4·3	1·4	1430
Field Peas	9·2	25·2	57·8	5·6	1·1	1432
Flaxseed (Linseed)	7·2	24·2	28·4	5·5	36·5	2300
Hempseed	9·0	18·3	36·2	14·8	32·6	2018
Horse Beans	12·5	25·7	48·8	8·2	1·4	—
Kafir Corn	11·1	11·2	71·1	2·3	2·9	1555
Lentils	8·4	25·7	57·5	1·7	1·0	1461
Maize (Indian Corn)	15·0	8·9	68·9	2·0	3·9	1506
Milo Maize	10·6	11·3	71·3	2·2	2·9	1550
Millet Seed	9·1	11·8	64·7	7·8	3·3	1369
Maple Peas	14·0	22·5	59·1	5·4	0·9	1405
Oats	9·8	12·0	68·3	11·0	4·6	1432
Peanuts	5·5	30·2	11·6	2·8	47·6	2622
Rice, unhulled	12·0	7·4	64·3	9·3	2·6	1229
Rice, polished	12·6	6·7	79·5	1·5	0·4	1537
Rapeseed	14·0	19·4	16·4	7·8	38·5	2239
Soy Beans	10·0	33·2	34·6	4·1	17·5	1851
Sunflower Seeds	7·5	14·2	42·6	28·1	32·3	1822
Tic Beans	14·3	25·4	53·3	7·1	1·5	1350
Vetch	13·2	20·0	55·8	6·0	1·7	1420
Wheat	10·4	15·2	70·9	2·6	1·8	1572

Pigeon Food Ingredients

In long-distance races the food in the bird's crop is that fed them in the baskets. What is fed in the last meal in the loft before the pigeons are basketed will last no more than over night. Therefore, the food fed the pigeons in the basket must be food which all the birds have been trained to eat, and thus no one has an advantage from his study of nutrition, unless he can find a way of feeding which will load his birds with stored nutrients.

What is the quickest way to fill the storage capacity in the liver and muscles? Obviously, the way is to feed enough protein, which need not be more than 14 per cent, and see that the ration is high in fat and that it contains a reasonable amount of carbohydrates. Some maize and a fairly high percentage of oily seeds should suffice.

You may see a list of *digestible* calories in various foods and wonder at the discrepancy in your own calculations. But you need not wonder if you will remember that some of the food eaten is not digestible. At the present state of our knowledge, it is not possible to present a table showing the digestible calories for all species. Most of the tables available show the percentages which cattle can digest. Some tables have been worked out for dogs and human beings, but neither of these species can begin to extract the amount of nourishment from foods which cattle can, because cattle can digest much of the fibre.

To compute digestible calories for pigeons, the fibre must be subtracted from the total carbohydrates and, even then, not all of the remaining carbohydrate is digestible. It is a safe rule to figure the digestible protein and carbohydrate about 10 per cent less than the total.

In some tables one reads 'nitrogen-free extract'. This need not confuse one either if one remembers that protein contains nitrogen. The fat is removed and measured and the elements left are protein and carbohydrate. The element left after the protein is removed and measured is the extract, free of nitrogen: nitrogen-free extract or carbohydrate. Subtract the fibre from this and one has the total of starches and sugars, most of which is digestible.

One study on pigeon digestion in which a variety of ingredients were investigated, showed that pigeons could digest almost all of the starch in the foods, but the ability to digest non-starch carbohydrates ranged in percentage from 7 to 49. Protein digestion measured from 78 to 95 per cent, and fat from 62 to 100 per cent, depending on the food.

We must not draw conclusions about pigeon digestion from the results obtained from studying the same processes in chickens. Pigeons

Pigeon Food Ingredients

digest fat and protein better than chickens do, but chickens can utilize fibre and nitrogen-free extract better than pigeons.

HOME-MADE MIXTURES

Almost all local corn merchants will mix any formulas desired, or you can mix them yourself by putting, say, 25 lb. of each into a barrel and stirring. The charge made by a manufacturer for all pigeon food has to include the labour of mixing and the cost of a new bag. These are items which run to shillings in England, dollars in the U.S., and can be saved by home-mixing. But it is admittedly a nuisance.

When we buy small quantities of ingredients we generally pay much more than the corn merchant who buys in car-load lots. But suppose we find several ingredients available at a satisfactory price: how do we know whether we are giving our birds a complete meal? An example will suffice to show how we should proceed. We find we can obtain maize, wrinkled garden peas, wheat and Milo all for about 37s. per 100 lb. This will save us money. So we calculate this way, using 100 lb. of each:

		Amount	Protein	Carbo-hydrate	Fat	Fibre
Maize (Corn)		100 lb.	8·9	68·9	3·9	2·0
Milo		100 lb.	11·3	71·3	2·9	2·2
Peas		100 lb.	25·2	57·8	1·1	5·6
Wheat		100 lb.	15·2	70·9	1·8	2·6
		400 lb.	60·6	268·9	9·7	12·4
	In	100 lb.	15·2	67·2	2·4	3·1

We refer to our table of amino acids and find that there is ample of all of the essential nine of these protein building blocks. So as a maintenance ration we decide to buy the separate ingredients. If we ask a corn merchant to mix them we must expect to pay for his services, because his profit on the several ingredients is not sufficient to warrant opening bags, mixing and sewing bags again.

A local farmer has a good supply of the beans at 50s. a cwt. Maize costs 40s., wheat 35s., and barley 35s. a cwt. What would a mixture of 2 parts beans, 1 of maize, 1 wheat and ½ barley cost us?

Pigeon Food Ingredients

	Amount	Protein	Carbo-hydrate	Fat	Fibre	Cost £ s. d.
Tic Beans	224 lb.	50·8	106·6	3·0	14·2	5 0 0
Maize	112 lb.	8·9	68·9	3·9	2·0	2 0 0
Wheat	112 lb.	15·2	70·9	1·8	2·6	1 15 0
Barley	56 lb.	6·3	33·3	1·0	2·7	17 6
	504 lb.	81·2	279·7	9·7	21·5	£9 12 6
	112 lb.	18·0	62·1	2·1	4·7	£2 2 9

FEEDING FOR A QUICK START IN LIFE

Every year fanciers lament that chicks in the first pairs of eggs die in the shell, or that eggs failed to hatch from one cause or another. Usually these are eggs laid before spring has made the grass grow green. Pigeons have been on winter diets. The eggs laid later in the spring are more likely to hatch.

Few realize the importance of proper feeding during the month preceding egg-laying. A much higher percentage of hatching would doubtlessly occur if proper attention were given to the diet at this time. You have read the tables on vitamins and amino acids and now know what to furnish your pigeons, to ensure hatching and provide the nutrients in the yolk to carry the chicks through the first days of life.

Every year thousands of pigeon eggs fail to hatch. We have seen that some vitamins are concerned with fertility. Of these vitamins A and E deficiency is extremely important. But both are almost always present in grain; A in the yellow pigment of maize and E in the germs of all grains. The one outstandingly important vitamin lack, from a practical point of view, is Riboflavin.

Riboflavin is the one vitamin which must be kept in mind by every pigeon fancier as a first consideration when eggs fail to hatch. They incubate apparently normally but the youngsters fail to pip out. When the eggs are moving down the oviduct of the pigeon, there is an area where Riboflavin is added. If only grains are fed, there is insufficient Riboflavin available to add. Hence, the eggs can't hatch. Feeding pellets rich in Riboflavin is the simplest solution. But the feeding should start at least two weeks before mating.

Pigeon Food Ingredients

THE PROPER COMPONENTS OF "GRIT"

Pigeons use stones in their gizzards to grind the food which the fluids in the crop have softened. They pick up angular pieces which eventually become so smooth and round or oval that they pass out of the gizzard and are replaced by other angular stones.

Until recently no published study has been available as to just what and in what amounts of grit pigeons do pick up. Watching them pick at mortar between bricks one realizes they are probably trying to satisfy their need for calcium. Watching them picking up pieces of charcoal where fire has charred wood, one realizes that pigeons seem to need it.

The simplest method of supplying stones, calcium and charcoal is in granite or lime stones, ground oyster shells and charcoal. If ground limestone is fed, it wears smooth quickly but granite stones last longer.

The author conducted a long study from which the following information was derived:

Granite and oyster shells come in three sizes; the so-called pullet size was found to be the best by far. Number 6 charcoal was the preferred size of that ingredient.

At all times of the year, except during the reproductive period, the proportions of grit, shells and charcoal eaten were 8 : 8 : 1 respectively. During breeding, the proportions change to 8 : 16 : 1.

Colouring the mixture red made no difference in the amount consumed nor did scenting with anise change it.

During the non-breeding parts of the year the birds consumed 2 ounces each per month; during breeding season, double that.

This should provide a guide for those mixing their own grit or for suppliers of pigeon foods.

4

Drugs and Their Uses

Not so long ago a pigeon losing weight was practically doomed. Respiratory diseases progressed unhindered; intestinal infections often proved fatal. Today we are able to treat all of these diseases and many others with confidence. We have developed new uses and better methods of administering many of the older drugs. The discovery of the sulphonamides, and such antibiotics as penicillin, streptomycin, and chlortetracycline (Aureomycin) has made it possible to cope with many of the most devastating diseases. We have developed new insect destroyers of great potency and seem to be on the verge of perfecting others in the near future. Equipped with a vastly improved arsenal of drugs and aided by an enormously expanded knowledge of the actions of those drugs, veterinary medicine has made astonishing progress in the last decade.

The value of these life-saving drugs is too often taken for granted by the pigeon-owner. All of them are actually of the greatest importance to him, for in a very real sense it is they that have made it possible for him to keep his birds healthy and vigorous. If the fancier is to be able to take full advantage of this new science of health, he must know some of the fundamental facts about drugs and their actions, so that he can use them more intelligently and more effectively. Obviously there is no need for him to understand the pharmaceutical intricacies of the various medicinal preparations, but he should certainly know the characteristics of the several general types of drugs and be familiar with their common usage.

In order to understand the uses of drugs, you must first understand that drugs work in several different ways. Some drugs do not kill germs outside the body as well as they do in the blood stream; working in combination with the bacteria-destroying white cells in the blood, they

Drugs and Their Uses

are highly efficient. Without the white cells the drugs are of little value, and the cells without the drugs are helpless. This might be called a synergistic action. Phenols (such as cresol, thymol, tars), and mercurial salts, such as mercuric chloride, kill by causing the protoplasm of the cells to precipitate. Other drugs, such as arsenic, prevent the multiplication of bacteria. Still others combine chemically with some constituent of the protoplasm of the organism. Some have oxidizing properties and some interfere with the functioning within the bacteria themselves.

The success of all drugs depends on their being used in proper concentration. They must be strong enough to kill bacteria, yet weak enough to cause no harm to the tissues of the bird. The required strengths for the various drugs have been worked out by long study and testing. When a veterinarian gives you pills or tablets, with instructions to give them at certain intervals, he is usually calculating how fast the drug is eliminated, in order to be sure that your pigeon always has enough in his system to accomplish results.

Which brings us to the question of body repair. Always remember that the body of a bird is composed of many delicate organs. Its potential length of life is more or less determined at conception. With good care and no exposure to some diseases against which it may not be resistant, it should live its normal life-span. But when it becomes sick there is no certainty that, with the jab of a needle and a dose of medicine, it will recover. Life isn't like that. Recovery takes care—and time. Think how long it takes for a cut on one's hand to heal. Cells slowly grow together, scar tissue forms and shrinks, and several weeks may pass before the area looks normal. Yet, too often, we expect birds to recover in a day or two from disease more telling and debilitating than influenza is to human beings.

Drugs can and do have marvellous properties, but they cannot abolish the element of time.

Great care must be taken not to overdose, a common tendency on the part of laymen. If a teaspoonful cures, then three teaspoonfuls should cure in a third of the time, he often reasons. Sometimes it kills. Doses have been worked out by pharmacologists with great care. The bird's size and the effect desired determine the dose. Overdoses are wasteful and dangerous. Where measurements are given in gallons, either British Imperial gallon, or the slightly smaller American gallon, may be used, for the dosage is not sufficiently critical to necessitate distinguishing between the two measures.

Drugs and Their Uses

ANAESTHETICS AND DEPRESSANTS

There are many drugs used in general surgery for desensitizing animals, but pigeon fanciers are not likely to try to use any, except local anaesthetics which may be obtained from a veterinarian if they want to do some simple surgery.

Local anaesthetics can be injected to cause loss of pain in a given area and are a great boon to animals, doctors, and pigeon-owners. They may be injected over a main nerve trunk, around the area to be anaesthetized, for example, around a bad gash which needs to be sutured, or around a tumour which requires removal.

Procaine or *Novocain* is most commonly used as local anaesthetic and must be injected. This is a job for the veterinarian, unless he decides to supply you with some for minor operations.

Cocaine is not made from opium, as so many think, but from leaves of trees which grow in Peru and Bolivia. It is dangerous to human beings because of addiction, but pigeons cannot develop addictions without human help. Used locally, it blocks off nervous conduction. Much higher concentrations are needed for main nerve trunks than for terminal branches.

Ethyl Alcohol. Clients are for ever telephoning their veterinarians to say that they have just given their pets a dose of alcohol, such as brandy or whisky, as a stimulant. Somewhere the layman has picked up the idea that alcohol is a great animal saver. Actually it has so few warranted uses in veterinary medicine that it need be mentioned only to emphasize the fact that it is actually a depressant, rather than the excellent stimulant which most people believe it to be. It stimulates neither the respiration, the heart and blood system, nor the muscles.

Alcohol irritates the skin, injures the cells, has an astringent action, and shrinks tissues; it causes irritation and inflammation to mucous membranes. Alcohol has very little germ-killing power, and only at 70 per cent by weight—a percentage difficult to approximate—is it worth using for this purpose.

Never give alcohol to 'warm' a pigeon. All it does is lower his temperature by bringing the blood to the stomach and producing a false sensation of warmth. Nor should it be given as an aphrodisiac. I have known fanciers to use it in an effort to get shy breeding cocks to attempt copulation. They have found it often makes them worse.

88

Drugs and Their Uses

DRUGS ACTING ON THE ORGANS OF REPRODUCTION

Nearly every pigeon-owner has wondered whether there is not some drug he could use to affect some phase of the bird's reproductive cycle, the desire to nest, maternal instinct, desire to hurry home to the mate or to youngsters. There are such drugs, but they must be obtained from a veterinarian or physician and used under his directions.

The Hen. Perhaps it may sound like a sacrilege, but it is a fact that 'mother love' is chemical. Injected into a cat it will make her want to mother kittens. This chemical hormone is *prolactin*, discovered in experiments with pigeons. It causes pigeons to produce crop milk. It can be purchased but is relatively expensive. Crop milk can be digested by the pigeon itself and there is evidence that a bird uses what is in the crop in a long fly but does not make more while it is flying. All of the hormones mentioned in Chapter II are needed, but as far as I know, none is useful to the fancier for treating pigeons.

Of the vitamins, the one most often found inadequate in diets is vitamin A, which affects egg hatchability and fertility. Carotene, or a fish-liver oil, or yellow Indian corn in good quantity generally suffices. Vitamin E is so abundant in grain that giving any more is a waste. In some grain mixtures riboflavin is much too low.

The Cock. You may have heard of feeding vitamin E as wheat-germ oil to make pigeons eager to mate or become fertile, or of injecting testosterone for the same purpose. They are both a waste. Testosterone is substitutive therapy and seems to do nothing to help fertility, but it does increase the male desire to mate. I have injected baby chicks and had them crowing when they were three days old, but they were not fertile. The hormone which acts on the testicles and thus on fertility is the Anterior Pituitary, and doses for a pigeon are extremely small.

DRUGS TO KILL INTERNAL PARASITES

The drugs which are used to eradicate the worms which infest pigeons (the helminths) are called anthelmintics. Some are flat worms (platyhelminths) and some are round (nemahelminths). This class of drugs is of vital importance to us all, since the most prevalent group of diseases to which birds fall heir is caused by worms and external parasite infestations, with the consequent symptoms. The life histories of all of the

Drugs and Their Uses

common parasites will be considered in a later chapter. Here we will discuss only the drugs used in their elimination.

Male Fern. One of the oldest worm expellers is the dried root of a common fern (*Aspidium*) or extractions from it. It has been used since ancient times and is still in use.

Several pharmaceutical concerns sell it for pigeons and claim excellent results. Other drugs used for the removal of tapeworms in pet animals are Arecolene Hydrobromide, Dichlorophene, Santonin. They were described in an earlier edition but it was found by fanciers that the drugs were not available in small enough doses for pigeons. Arecolene Hydrobromide dose is $\frac{1}{84}$ of a grain and no pills containing so little were marketed, whereas Male Fern is, in small enough dosage for a one-pound pigeon.

In an earlier edition of this book, Carbon Tetrachloride, Tetrachlorethylene, and Butyl Chloride were discussed as being useful for the elimination of Roundworms from pigeons. These, when used with caution, were safe and effective but already we have so much better remedies that we can forget those once commonly used drugs. We think now of Piperazine and Mintic.

Piperazine. This is the newest in the field of deworming drugs. It is an English discovery, used first for ridding children of pinworms. It has been found effective against many of the roundworms and has low toxicity so that the dose need not be exact. It was first reported effective in pigeons by the author. I dewormed hundreds of pigeons before publishing the paper in *Veterinary Medicine Magazine*. One of the unusual features of the drug was the rapidity with which it was effective, roundworms being found under perches as early as 4 hours after the birds drank the solution.

Piperazine will not rid a bird of capillaria worms nor tapeworms, but almost 100 per cent of ascarids are killed by it. Piperazine is usually employed in the form of its adipate, citrate, hydrate or phosphate.

The effective safe dose is 8 grammes of piperazine in each gallon of drinking water. Make a solution in a jar first and when the piperazine is completely dissolved, put it in the fountain. In the Speedome Lofts we keep papers of 12 grammes made up in advance because all of our fountains hold $1\frac{1}{2}$ gallons of water. Any chemist will be glad to weigh it out for you.

Research with chickens and pigeons indicates that 60 hours ($2\frac{1}{2}$ days) of medication is quite enough to clean up a flock. The slight salty taste of the solution is not objectionable to pigeons.

Drugs and Their Uses

Mintic. The chemical name for this remarkably effective drug is methyridine. In Europe it has been used for many years to deworm poultry but had not been researched for safety on pigeons. With the assistance of two other fanciers, I experimented with this drug for safety and efficacy and learned that it was the first drug which could be successfully used to eliminate Capillaria worms. After a careful study with many individual pigeons and then, by treating flocks, we learned that a dose of 40 c.c. (1⅓ ounces) per gallon of drinking water was remarkably efficient.

The objection to it was that the pigeons wouldn't drink the solution unless they were thirsty. This was managed by withholding their water from evening of one day until noon the next. The birds were then thirsty enough to drink a crop full of water before they realized it was treated. A few vomited but all were rid of their Capillarias. The solution was left all afternoon, removed at night. That was sufficient.

DRUGS TO KILL EXTERNAL PARASITES

Dozens of drugs can be used to kill insects, but most of them will kill mammals and human beings too. There are several modern drugs which are quite safe if used with reasonable care, and new ones are appearing and being tested annually.

Rotenone (Derris; Cubé). Rotenone and a number of closely related substances are the active insecticidal constituents of the roots of certain tropical plants, notably various species of derris and of the lonchocarpus or cubé plant. Powdered derris or cubé root, as commercially available, is usually blended to contain about 5 per cent of rotenone. For dusting purposes a powder adjusted to contain about 1 per cent of rotenone is generally used. When less than a year-old dust is used it is one of the most potent, safe insect killers known. It kills insects by paralysing their respiratory tracts. Birds can eat it in small amounts, usually with no ill effects. It is more poisonous if inhaled, and is especially so if it gets into fresh open cuts.

Derris also kills fish. If you use it, don't allow derris dust to blow on to the water in a fishpond, nor permit freshly dusted birds to bathe in such waters.

Probably derris in dusts, diluted to contain 1 per cent of rotenone, is as safe for flea and louse powders as anything one could ask for, but no pigeon should be put in a closed box and dusted, since it is then

91

forced to breathe the dust. It is hard to believe that birds could be so mistreated, but they often are—by people who want to keep the powder off their clothes.

Incidentally, with some people—but not all—derris causes numbness of the lips and tongue tip. The sensation soon passes. If you are sensitive, dust the pigeons in the open where the breeze blows the dust away from you.

It pays to keep some 5 per cent derris or cubé powder on hand. One per cent powder is effective, but the 5 per cent has done no harm in our lofts and we have used many pounds. It is light and fluffy. We put $\frac{1}{2}$ teaspoonful on each perch once a month and no red mites exist in any loft. The birds fan it about, much eventually sifts into cracks and crannies in the loft and we are free from insects. Some of course settles among the feathers of all the birds.

Before we used perch paint, we relied on derris powder, sifting a few pinches among the feathers of new birds to delouse them.

Derris powder can now be purchased in a wettable form which, when mixed with bath water, muddies it somewhat but does not repel the pigeons and kills all insects on them.

Pyrethrum. Chrysanthemums contribute pyrethrum to our store of drugs. In pure form, the chemical agents made from it are called pyrethrins. They are mentioned here because they are so often ingredients of flea powder, but the fact that they are included here is not an endorsement, since they merely stun the insects. The early powders were sold with the advice that you dust the animal, brush the fleas and lice on to a newspaper, and burn the paper. You burned it because the insects usually refused to 'stay dead', and manufacturers knew it.

Pyrethrum has a wonderful psychological effect on the fancier. When it is used as an ingredient of a powder or rinse, the insects appear to die instantly. They drop off, and that is what fanciers love to see. Mix in some derris and the bugs not only drop off but they stay dead. The combination of the two drugs makes a fine treatment for the owner as well as for the pigeon.

DDT (Dicophane). This is also called by the simple (to a chemist) name of diphenyldichlorotrichloroethane. It really kills insects and lasts for weeks without decomposing and losing its potency. It finds uses in fly sprays, mists, dusts, rinses, and all vehicles for spreading bug death.

DDT is one of the best ingredients to use in residual sprays, those sprayed on to screens and walls to kill bugs which touch them. It is

Drugs and Their Uses

generally used as a 10 per cent powder or spray, but since it is slightly poisonous, the dust or spray must be kept away from all water and food trays. Particular care must be taken with unfledged youngsters.

Sodium Fluoride. This poisonous drug was for many years the substance used to kill several external parasites of pigeons. It was never used in water in which pigeons bathed because they might drink a little and die; rather the solution was made up and the birds were dipped one at a time. Sodium fluoride is available to anyone and the recommended dilution is 1 oz. to a gallon of water.

In comparisons of sodium fluoride dip with DDT powder, Signal Corps pigeons in the U.S. were tested with the results that while sodium fluoride produced a satisfactory kill of insects, it took much longer than when 10 per cent DDT powder was used. In recent years it has been largely replaced by potassium sulphite used in a similar manner.

Benzene Hexachloride (BHC). This is also called *Sixide* and *cyclochlorohexane.* It is one of the newest of lethal products and kills ticks as well as other insects. It is probably one of the safest for pigeons, since it may be used in powders at a dilution of 1 per cent. This is relatively non-toxic in the amounts that would be used to kill fleas or ticks. The form called *gamma isomer* (Gamma Benzene Hexachloride, Gamma BHC, Lindane, or Lorexane) is by far the most toxic to insects. Like DDT, this drug has a long-lasting effect. It is used in a very wide variety of ways, even for killing mange mites.

Vapona. Probably the greatest boon to the pigeon fancier who is interested in destroying parasites on his pigeons is the Vapona Bar, made and sold by the Shell Oil Company. It was marketed as a fly and mosquito killer. In 1966 I studied the effects of the chemical which these bars give off to see if it might not destroy pigeon feather lice and pigeon flies. The results were published in The American Racing Pigeon News.

Since that time much has been learned about this non-odorous, remarkable chemical. When hung in a loft with 1,000 cubic feet of space, all pigeon lice will be dead in 36 hours. Pigeon flies take a little longer or even a shorter time to die if the space which the bar has to fumigate is reduced. The same is true of poultry lice which cut off feathers covering a pigeon's throat and crop. One bar lasts three to four months.

Malathion is, in 1961, principally used on farm crops as an insecticide against both chewing and sucking insects. It comes as a liquid which makes an emulsion with water, 1 tablespoonful to the gallon. With more

93

extensive research, it will be found useful in pigeon lofts. I have used it as a spray on walls, floor, and screens, with excellent results. If it is used, naturally, food trays and water containers must be removed. Malathion is already used in flea powders for mammals and in perch paint for poultry.

PERCH PAINT

The several methods and drugs mentioned above as reliances to destroy insects are good but another idea makes all except Vapona obsolete. This is a mixture of drugs which can be brushed or sprayed on to perches, into nest bowls, and in nest boxes as well as into cracks and corners where bugs may breed. These mixtures are offered for sale in quart and gallon bottles and even in aerosol sprays, the latter being more expensive.

Agricultural chemists have found that drugs which turn into vapour can actually carry with them vapours of other insecticide drugs with the volatile substance. One of these is Xylol or Xylene as it is also called. White oil, petroleum oil, or refined kerosene may be a part of this mixture.

Here are the contents of one such mixture of known effectiveness:

Malathion	2·80
Lindane	1·45
Pine Oil	2·50
Xylene	15·00
Petroleum Oil	75·00
Emulsifiers	4·25

There are others of varying percentages all of which impart a not objectionable 'chemical odour' to the loft, which also repels mosquitoes.

These mixtures can be sprayed or just daubed on the sides of perches by using a one-inch-wide paint brush. If the perches have been painted, less need be daubed than is needed on unpainted perches which absorb some of the perch paint.

The volatile substances turn into gas, permeate the birds' feathers and kill every form of insect life. It is quite amazing to treat the perches of birds liberally infested with feather lice and on the next day be unable to find a single louse on a bird. Even pigeon flies leave or are killed. The treatment works best in warm weather but also does its work in winter.

94

Drugs and Their Uses

Many loft owners use it methodically once a month.

As we use one of the commercial products in Speedome Lofts, one quart treats 400 perches and can be applied in 30 minutes. We pour perch paint into a coffee can and use a small paint brush to apply it.

DRUGS FOR CUTS AND SCRATCHES

Because skin-tears are one of the commonest injuries to pigeons, every fancier's medicine chest should contain one or more disinfectants to clean the wound and prevent the growth of bacteria. In this list we could include a large number, but only a few are necessary.

Disinfectants, germicides, antiseptics, bacteriostatics, fungicides, bactericides—what are these things? *Disinfectants* free areas of infection by destroying bacteria, fungus organisms, viruses—all kinds of infective organisms. *Antiseptics* inhibit the growth of bacteria or other infecting agents, but do not necessarily kill them. *Germicides* and *bactericides* are agents that kill germs. Contrary to what you may have thought, there are not very many which will kill germs and not injure tissues too. *Bacteriostatics* arrest the growth of bacteria. A *viricide* is an agent which kills viruses. *Fungicides* are agents which destroy fungi.

Phenol (Carbolic Acid). This is a coal-tar derivative. Phenol is the standard by which other germicides are compared. We speak of Phenol Coefficient of 5, meaning that a comparison of germ-killing power of a certain dilution has been made with a given dilution of phenol.

Only weak solutions should be used, as phenol is a poison. It precipitates proteins. When applied to the skin, it first produces a whitened area which later turns brown and sloughs. It is a topical anaesthetic, for which reason it is often incorporated in skin preparations by those who do not object to its odour. But it is always used in extremely small amounts. If half a teaspoonful will kill a dog, one can easily see how foolish it is to bathe a pigeon in a solution made by pouring phenol or one of its relatives indiscriminately into a bucket of water.

True, it will kill fleas and lice and mites outside the skin. But it is too harsh to be recommended for use on birds.

Tincture of Iodine. One of the mainstays of veterinarians of a few years ago, as it was in the average household, tincture of iodine still has its uses. It is germicidal against all bacteria and many fungi and viruses, regardless of their race, creed, or colour. It is twice as potent as phenol as a germ killer. Since a number of applications to the same area may

Drugs and Their Uses

result in burning, when several treatments are indicated, it is better to use the tincture diluted by an equal amount of water. Iodine discolours, and feathers once discoloured with it may retain the stain for months. This, plus the fact that the treated area burns and smarts when it is applied, makes its use of limited value for pigeons.

Hydrogen Peroxide. When you apply this product to raw tissue there is a strong fizzing, and a white foam appears. This means that the, peroxide is decomposing into water and oxygen. And only while this decomposition is progressing is the treated area being disinfected. But this fizzing helps wonderfully at times to loosen debris in wounds. As a germ killer, it is less efficient than many others. I have found a 3 per cent solution the best for all such tasks. This is the standard strength supplied by American drug stores and is sometimes called 10-volume hydrogen peroxide. The standard strength supplied by English chemists is 6 per cent, often called 20-volume hydrogen peroxide.

Potassium Permanganate. There are many veterinarians who use this chemical for wound treatments, though it is now used less than formerly, because we have so many better antiseptics. It is a purple crystalline substance, generally used in concentrations of about 1 to 5,000 parts of water. Some fanciers use it in pigeon bath water and occasionally a few crystals may be put in the drinking water. A concentrate is sometimes prepared known as Vin Rouge (Red Wine) but this must be tightly corked, otherwise it will turn brown, when it is useless.

Mercurial Compounds. Our first thought is mercuric chloride (mercury bichloride) when we think of mercury. The large blue or coffin-shaped blue tablets are synonymous with poison in the minds of many and are dangerous to have around for humans or pets. Best forget mercuric chloride, but don't confuse it with mercurous chloride which is much less dangerous.

But there are many other useful mercurial compounds, such as thiomersal (thimerosal in U.S.A.) or Merthiolate. Recently much publicity has been given to the failure of these mercurial compounds to kill germs. The inference is that they are worthless. Actually, as supplied by the chemist, they are bacteriostatic, and to some extent bactericidal. To my knowledge, that is all the manufacturers ever claimed for them. If bacteria or their spores cannot grow in the presence of these drugs, then they serve a useful purpose. As an application to sutured incisions, they prevent infection, but used under bandages, they may cause irritation.

Drugs and Their Uses

THE SULPHA DRUGS

The person who did not own pigeons B.S.D. (Before Sulphonamide Drugs) can hardly appreciate what their discovery has meant to all of us. True, some are already outdated, and some are being replaced for some purposes by the antibiotics, but veterinary medicine is now a far happier profession because of them.

The first to be discovered was sulphanilamide. Shortly thereafter, unfounded claims were made for it as a cure-all; it was said to be a specific for coccidiosis, viruses, all kinds of bacteria. But genuine study showed that its field was very narrow—that it killed only a limited number of bacteria and was ineffectual against viruses, coccidiosis, warts, bad disposition and ingrowing toenails!

Laymen cannot normally obtain the sulpha drugs without prescriptions. Let your veterinarian tell you why he prescribes the sulpha drug he prefers for your birds. Here, in general, are a few things you should know about them, which will save his time in instructions and explain why he tells you to use them as he does.

Some of the sulphas do not kill certain bacteria. Some are more toxic than others. Some are much more soluble. Sulphathiazole and sulphadiazine accomplish approximately the same germ-killing effects, but the sulphadiazine, being slightly more soluble, is a better bladder and kidney disinfectant. Some sulphas are but slightly absorbed from the digestive tract. Phthalylsulphathiazole (sulphathalidine) disinfects the colon principally; sulphaguanidine, the whole tract. Some leave such acid residues that it is wise to prescribe bicarbonate of soda with them. Some do their best work when injected, some when taken orally.

In spite of all their wonderful effects, no sulpha drug and no combination of them has yet been found which will kill all the bacteria, and none affects viruses.

One of the most important facts to remember when you use the sulphas, which are absorbed, is that many of them are excreted via the kidneys quite soon after they are administered. Others, sulphadimidine (sulphamethazine) for example, need be injected only once a day. If your veterinarian says 'give every six hours', don't stretch the interval to eight hours. For some, his instructions may be every four hours. The reason for giving them frequently is that sulpha drugs will not kill germs when their concentration in the blood drops to below 1 to 50,000.

Given in drinking water, the soluble sulphas, such as sulphamethazine

97

Drugs and Their Uses

or sulphaquinoxaline in their sodium salt form are taken into the system several times a day by the birds and the necessary blood concentration is thus maintained.

Powdered sulpha drugs are often sifted into surgical incisions and wounds, where they are of great help. They are being used in solutions, such as propylene glycol, and poured into inaccessible wounds where they often prove to be true miracle drugs and life-savers.

THE ANTIBIOTICS

When researchers learned that some bacteria and moulds give off substances toxic to others, a new branch of bacteriology was born. When further research demonstrated that these substances would kill bacteria and not poison animals, a life-saving blessing of inestimable value was bestowed upon both us and our pigeons. We are told that wonderful as penicillin, streptomycin, and chlortetracycline are, they are but heralds of far more wonderful drugs to come. Several have a specificity for certain types of bacteria. As yet, none has been found specific for viruses, except the tetracyclines in the case of ornithosis.

The antibiotics, like sulphas, are prescription drugs. At first they were given in quickly absorbed doses, mostly intramuscularly and at very frequent intervals. Later, a way was found of combining them in a wax-and-oil solution from which they were slowly absorbed, so that now, injections once in 24 hours suffice to furnish a high enough concentration in the blood to destroy effectively the germs against which they are being used.

Soluble antibiotics can be given to pigeons in drinking water with excellent effect, but injections of them are somewhat more certain. The injectible types are prescription items and while in the U.S. the water soluble kind for poultry are available to all, unfortunately, in Great Britain, no antibiotics are obtainable without a prescription.

Penicillin. This was the first of the safe antibiotics developed for injection purposes. It is useful in several pigeon diseases but probably not as useful as the tetracyclines.

Tetracyclines. For several years, Aureomycin and Terramycin were thought to be distinct entities. Chemical analysis revealed that they and others were basically the same, but with differences due to the addition of oxygen or chlorine. Thus *aureomycin* is chlortetracycline, *terramycin* is oxytetracycline and *achromycin* is tetracycline.

All of the above are prescription drugs. Each differs from the other

98

Drugs and Their Uses

somewhat on the basis of what diseases they are most effective against. Probably all are useful against our pigeon diseases. The authorities in some countries, but not Great Britain, have become lenient in permitting some forms to be sold to poultrymen and pigeon fanciers. Soluble Aureomycin for dissolving in drinking water, soluble Terramycin and others can be had even from corn merchants.

Chlortetracycline (Aureomycin) used in the drinking water is given as a treatment to cure birds of a disease, or as a preventive measure. The material is marketed in a concentration of 25 grammes in each pound. One level teaspoonful contains 200 milligrams of chlortetracycline, which is the recommended amount to be added to a gallon of water, or to 2 gallons as a preventive or for continuous treatment. It is necessary to make fresh solutions daily.

Cattle farmers in the U.S.A. can purchase these drugs in 2 oz. tubes with pointed applicators. These tubes contain the antibiotics in sufficient concentration to kill germs in cows' udders. The base in which the antibiotics is dissolved is harmless when spread over eyes or put in cuts and when the proportion of antibiotic is not too strong. Pigeon fanciers, therefore, can take advantage of the low cost of these medicines and buy them instead of capsules, salves, eye ointments, etc.

Streptomycin. This is an injectible antibiotic often used either by itself or in combination with penicillin. It is a valuable aid in the treatment of several diseases and in salves for treating cuts and abrasions.

Chloramphenicol (Chloromycetin). This drug is now being produced chemically instead of from moulds. Some poultry scientists prefer it as a general antibiotic for certain purposes above any of the other drugs. It is especially useful for eyes; high claims have been made for it in treating blood poisoning and diarrhoea; and as a 1 per cent mixture in cream bases, chloramphenicol makes an excellent wound dressing. It may be obtained in the U.S.A. in tubes for cattle udder treatment, and in this form is inexpensive. In Great Britain it is, of course, like all antibiotics, only obtainable on prescription.

Doses of Antibiotics. All of these drugs are measured in milligrams, and for a pigeon 25 mg. is more than enough. The smallest sized capsules on the market are 50 mg., and while this amount is more than enough, many fanciers give one capsule a day to a pigeon. If ointment is used, the amount to carry 25 mg. squeezed down the throat is enough and the salve base is harmless.

In drinking water, enough of the soluble drug is dissolved so that

Drugs and Their Uses

each bird obtains about 25 mg. a day. In a level teaspoonful of Aureomycin soluble, there are 200 mg. of Aureomycin. How much should be given to birds in their drinking water? If a pigeon consumes 2 oz. of water daily, a level teaspoonful is enough for 16 oz.; 2 tablespoonfuls for a gallon. For some ailments, like Sour Crop, one day's dosing may effect a cure but systemic diseases usually need four days' treatment.

In addition to the antibiotics we have discussed useful products which have been developed from the waste derived from the manufacture of these drugs, which are used as food supplements. Bacitracin, gramicidin, neomycin, tyrothricin and several others may induce increased growth, but as yet, we have little evidence of their effect on pigeons.

Malucidin. A drug which may prove to be one of the most versatile of the antibiotics, yet is in a different class from the rest, is Malucidin which is made from residues from the brewing of beer. It has proved to be an effective fungicide and prevents growth of many kinds of bacteria as well. Its first use in pigeons was applied by the author and an associate, where we found it had a repressive effect against Coccidiosis when injected. Recent studies prove its effectiveness against Paratyphoid organisms.

In mammals it must be injected because the stomach juices digest the drug, but in poultry enough apparently is absorbed when taken in drinking water to be effective. Studies are currently being made in the several fields of its probable usefulness. As yet Malucidin has not been given clearance by the official government agencies for its use as an injectable agent but large quantities are sold for external applications for skin disease treatments.

So far as present research has determined, malucidin does its most effective work when injected. A small gauge needle and a 1 c.c. syringe are sufficient, as only 1 c.c. of the solution is needed.

Aminonitrothiazole. This is a drug for curing canker. It is sold under a variety of names but originally was sold only as Enheptin. The drug is seldom packaged as the pure product. It was suggested first for blackhead—a turkey disease—and can be bought without a prescription.

Aminonitrothiazole is sometimes marketed in capsules and in pills, which must be given to a pigeon once a day. This is tedious but one is certain that each pigeon gets the proper dose.

In the United States, the drug is sold under a variety of names, but Enheptin is the most widely known. Two strengths of solution are recommended, 0·03 and 0·015 per cent. Aminonitrothiazole is commercially available in a form suitable for adding to the drinking water

Drugs and Their Uses

to ensure correct concentrations. British trade names include Harkanka and Entramin.

Follow the directions on the package.

Copper Sulphate. Blue vitriol, the old canker remedy, is now supplanted by aminonitrothiazole, which is safer and surer. It is thought that the copper sulphate kills the trichomonas in the crop and intestines only, while the newer chemical also acts in the blood.

Nutritional Deficiency Remedies. These are principally vitamins, minerals, and amino acids discussed in a later chapter. Here we must state that in every case of a pigeon being in a run-down condition with a loss of appetite, aneurine (thiamin or vitamin B_1) is practically a medicinal must if the bird is to live. Every pigeon fancier's medicine chest should have a bottle of 50 mg. size aneurine pills and a bottle of brewer's yeast tablets for the vitamins they contain.

Glucose. This is also called grape sugar. It can be purchased as a liquid or as powder. The liquid is so thick that it must be diluted with water or milk to make it thin enough to give with a syringe. The powder must be dissolved in water. Glucose is used as one of the best supporting treatments in poison cases or as a detoxifying substance. It is also used in supplying quick energy for sick birds.

An Important Note on Administering Drugs

I have observed some cases when I have furnished drugs to pigeon fanciers and they reported that the drugs produced a toxic effect on their birds. Investigation showed that the solutions had been mixed in the drinking fountain. *This is a mistake. Always* make the solution in a transparent bottle or jar and be sure every bit of chemical has gone into the solution before you pour it into the fountain. If this is not done, you will have a heavy concentrated solution at the bottom of the fountain and a weak one above. The birds may refuse to drink, or if they do, may take such an overdose due to the concentration that they will be poisoned and vomit the drug, thus obtaining little benefit from it.

5

Diseases and How a Pigeon Catches Them

If one of your pigeons 'goes light' you will know that it is sick. But unless you know more than that, there is little that you can do for the bird. On the other hand, when you know something about the types of diseases and their causes and your bird becomes ill, you can handle the situation much more intelligently. You may be able to recognize the symptoms well enough to diagnose the condition and treat it yourself.

A knowledge of the cause of the diseases to which your birds are subject and of the way they may contract them is even more important from the standpoint of prevention. Many diseases can be avoided by observing a few simple precautions. Some of these maladies, once contracted, are difficult or impossible to cure. To the pigeon-owner and to veterinary medicine, the prevention of disease in birds is as important as it is in the case of human beings.

A simple understanding of the basic facts about disease is sufficient for the pigeon-owner. He doesn't need to learn and remember a series of names or technical terms. He should know the broad general classifications into which all diseases are divided; he should be familiar with the common characteristics of each, and he should have a general knowledge of the way each affects birds. This is hardly too much to expect of any person who is really concerned with his pigeons' welfare.

To most pigeon owners all diseases are more or less alike—the result, they think, of some vague thing called 'germs'. Actually, of course, there are a number of distinct types of diseases, and they are classified according to their causes. Some are caused by bacteria, some by viruses, and others by fungi, or parasites, growths, or deficiencies. To under-

Diseases and How a Pigeon Catches Them

stand the diseases themselves it is necessary to know something about these causative agents.

BACTERIA. Bacteria are single-celled organisms: those which cause disease are called *pathogenic*. There are many forms causing disease, and all are, in some way, transmissible from one pigeon to another.

Since bacteria are too small to be seen without magnification, they must be studied through the microscope. There they appear as different from each other as the various farm animals. Some are spirals, some are little balls, some have whip-like attachments, and some look like baseball bats.

Coccal bacteria are round. *Streptococci* (pronounced strep-toe-cox-eye) are round bacteria which grow in strings. They produce such diseases as Pneumonia and pus infections. *Staphylococci* are round forms which grow in groups like bunches of grapes. They are notorious pus producers and abscess formers.

Bacilli are rod-shaped bacteria, many of which are mischief-makers, sometimes complicating other diseases. Rod-shaped forms, of which there are many, cause Bubonic Plague, Tularemia, and some pigeon diseases. *Salmonella* organisms cause food poisoning and other diseases in pigeons. *Shigella* cause dysentery in birds and Bird Typhoid; *Clostridia* cause Lockjaw, food poisoning (Botulism), Gas gangrene; *Mycobacteria* cause Tuberculosis. *Spirochetes* are corkscrew-shaped organisms which cause diseases such as Leptospirosis.

Since they are all comparatively large forms, too large to enter the cells of the body, bacteria float or propel themselves about in body fluids or remain stationary. Some invade the blood; some are specific for certain tissue, such as *pneumococcus* types for lungs; others are found confined to the stomach and intestines.

SAPROPHYTES. There is another general class of bacteria which are important to pigeon breeders which do not cause disease with specific symptoms; in other words, are not pathogenic. They are classified as *saprophytic* bacteria. One finds them complicating other diseases. A good example of these germs are what the author and his associate found in studying Coccidiosis in pigeons. It had been thought that Coccidiosis infection was a disease in itself. We found that when a simple Coccidiosis infection occurs there is little sickness. But, very seldom is it a simple infection, because the tiny parasites weaken the intestinal wall and permit the entrance of these saprophytic bacteria. In

103

Diseases and How a Pigeon Catches Them

one very sick pigeon studied, we found five kinds of germs in the blood and it was because of these that the pigeon was sick. When we killed them by injection of an antibiotic (Malucidin) the pigeons took a new lease on life.

RICKETTSIAE. *Rickettsiae* are different from bacteria. They are smaller —so small that they have been found inside cells. They are responsible for such diseases important in America as Rocky Mountain Spotted Fever, which is spread by the parasites of rodents, dogs, human beings and pigeons.

FUNGI. A third class of infecting organisms most interesting to the veterinarian and to the pigeon owner is *fungus* (plural *fungi* or *funguses*). Fungi are plants of a low order; they produce spores which are like seeds. Spores resist drought, heat, cold, and other environmental factors. When conditions of moisture and temperature are right, they grow into mature forms.

Some diseases in pigeons are of fungus origin. Moulds are fungi. There are a great many kinds of fungi—good, bad and neutral types. Several antibiotics, some of the most extraordinarily effective drugs ever discovered, are made from moulds.

VIRUSES. *Viruses* live in the cells. They are so small that they are invisible through an ordinary microscope. Photographs of them made through the electron miscroscope indicate that, like bacteria, they grow in various forms. Their exact nature is not understood, nor have cures for most of the diseases they cause been discovered.

Viruses, even more than bacteria, have affinities for certain tissues in the body. Rabies, for instance, is *neurotropic*, which means that it attacks nerve tissue. Some have an affinity for the *epithelial* tissue (skin and mucous membranes). Some viruses attack the lining of the nose and throat, and others attack lung tissue.

One of the tragic facts about viruses is that they so weaken tissue that bacterial diseases can get a start and develop. Certain bacteria are such constant companions of viruses; we once believed that bacteria caused a number of virus diseases because bacteria were constantly present.

DISEASE TRANSMISSION

Before birds can contract a disease, they must in some manner be

104

exposed to the infecting organism. Exposure can come about in many ways.

Bacterial diseases may be contracted by the bird's eating infected food, by getting the bacteria into cuts or puncture wounds, by insect stings or bites, or by inhaling them. If a pigeon is pecked by another, the wounds may fester by the multiplication of bacteria inserted by the beak. Bacteria may be drawn into the system, or they may be present in air passages, waiting for a virus or general loss of resistance to weaken tissue and set up conditions favourable to their growth.

Some virus diseases can be passed from one bird to another, by inhaling one brief sniff of a sick bird's breath, or even by inhaling air in a room in which a sick bird has sneezed and left minute droplets floating about carrying the virus. Other virus diseases can be transmitted by drinking water previously infected.

Fungus diseases are spread in several ways; by contact, by wind and by water.

IMMUNITY

Some knowledge of the body's defence against diseases and of immunity is necessary, in understanding methods of prevention and cure.

When a bird develops an abscess, his body builds a dam around the area and walls it off from the rest. The next time he is bitten, other infections may develop from the same bacteria. But if, instead of developing a localized abscess, the bacteria invade the blood stream, a different condition develops. If the bird survives by its own bodily mechanism or chemistry, it will be immune to that species of bacteria for a long time afterward. But if it is treated with medicine such as *sulphathiazole*, which destroys all bacteria of that type in the body within a few days, then solid immunity may not be developed. Why?

Because the body builds up defences to overcome bacteria or viruses in several ways; white cells may engulf them, or the body may develop antitoxins which counteract the toxins produced by the bacteria. All birds' bodies have the power to develop specific counter-chemicals which will act to destroy invading bacteria. We call these defence chemicals *antibodies*. It is amazing how specific they can be. The antibodies against one disease organism are seldom of value against another. If a pigeon recovers from Pox, for instance, he can still contract other virus diseases. If he recovers from one species of Coccidiosis, he can still contract another form. But if the bird is to develop immunity,

Diseases and How a Pigeon Catches Them

he has to recover without medication. If the recovery from a bacterial disease is due to chemicals added to his blood, he does not always develop antibodies which will solidly protect him against that form of disease in the future.

There are different kinds of immunity. *Passive immunity* is conferred by additions of biologics to the blood which insure temporary protection. *Inherent* or *Inherited immunity* is transmitted from parent to offspring. *Acquired immunity* is acquired after birth. *Active immunity* is produced by a pigeon's own tissues or fluids. It may be produced:

By having a disease and recovering;
by constant mild exposure to the disease-producing organism;
by injection of dead bacteria, or products of dead bacteria;
by injection of attenuated (weakened) or dead viruses;
  (a) Attenuated by the addition of chemicals to live virus;
  (b) Attenuated by passing the disease through other species, or
      growing it on eggs of another species;
by injection of toxins.

PARASITIC DISEASES

Parasitic diseases from which our pigeons suffer are real diseases, often tragic in their consequences. Have you ever thought of lice infestation as a disease, or capillaria worms? Fortunately these are the easiest diseases to manage, so long as we remember that the cure is only half of the job; the important part is to prevent re-infestation. For this reason every pigeon owner should know, in a general way, the life history of all the common parasites. Lice, ticks, fleas, mites, flies and bedbugs belong in this class.

Internal parasites which damage the inside of the body, in contrast to those which attack from the outside, consist of worms (round and flat), flukes and protozoan organisms of which *coccidia*, *toxoplasma*, and *trichomonads*, are important.

DEFICIENCY DISEASES

Negative as well as positive factors cause disease. Many pigeons have died from lack of oxygen. There are the obvious cases of suffocation; the carrying cage or shipping crate may be insufficiently ventilated, and when it is opened the bird or birds are found dead. Lack of oxygen,

Diseases and How a Pigeon Catches Them

obvious as it is, constitutes a deficiency disease. There are many more subtle deficiencies.

Some deficiencies produce what should be called conditions, not diseases. A disease is a morbid process with characteristic symptoms. Thirst is neither a disease nor the result of a disease. The symptoms of dehydration are cured by water consumption. Anaemia is a disease in one sense, a condition in another. Millions of human beings go about in an anaemic condition. In general, deficiency diseases are quite easily cured, simply by furnishing the body with the missing elements.

ANAEMIA is caused by a shortage of oxygen. We have considered the obvious form but not the symptoms. *When a pigeon suffocates, the pink colour of the tissue turns blue.* A lack of oxygen in the tissues can be produced by many causes other than lack of air. The blood may simply be unable to carry it about the body. This, in turn, may result from a diminished supply of red cells in the blood. There may be too few, or the chemical composition of their components may be inadequate. Capillaria worms and strongyles are a common cause of an inadequate supply of red cells in birds. Their blood consumption strains the blood building equipment, which cannot keep up with the loss. A worm-infested bird lacks animation and gets out of breath easily. He shows all the symptoms of anaemia, as though blood had been drawn from his arteries or veins.

Heavy infestations of sucking lice may also cause anaemia. The bird can't stand cold and loses its appetite. The basic condition is probably aggravated by toxins from the lice. Pigeons are often seriously weakened by these parasites and have actually been known to die from lice infestation.

A lack of iron or copper or both causes anaemia. Insufficient iron is responsible for a shortage of haemoglobin and although there may be a full quota of red cells, they cannot pick up and transport oxygen properly. Copper deficiency also causes anaemia. Copper is not part of haemoglobin, but it is concerned with its formation.

RICKETS. After anaemia, Rickets is probably the most common deficiency disease. It is a result of a lack of one or more of these factors: vitamin D, calcium, or phosphorus.

MINERAL DEFICIENCIES. The only two minerals of great consequence to birds are calcium and iron, but in passing we must recognize that the

107

Diseases and How a Pigeon Catches Them

absence of others causes dire consequences. Iodine is essential. Common salt is also essential. Since 99 per cent of the calcium in the body is found in the skeleton, obviously a calcium deficiency results in poor skeletal development, as we saw in the case of Rickets. But calcium does more than develop bone. It is necessary to proper nerve function and acts almost like some vitamins as a catalyst or 'marrying agent' between other chemicals. Cobalt and boron, although needed in minute quantities, produce sickness through their absence. Potassium deficiency causes paralysis, and so forth.

VECTORS

Many diseases depend for their spread upon some means in the form of a live creature to transmit them. An example of a vector is the house fly which feeds on pigeon droppings and then carries the germs of Paratyphoid, which have stuck to its feet, to food about to be eaten by a healthy pigeon.

The mosquito which stings a pigeon infected with Pox and later stings another healthy bird, leaving the Pox virus at the site of the sting is a vector. You can be a vector if you walk into a loft where a highly virulent form of Trichomoniasis is present and then walk into your own loft, for you will be transmitting the disease to your own birds.

INTERMEDIATE HOSTS

Vectors and intermediate hosts are not the same. A Sow or Pill Bug which eats the eggs of a stomach worm would not infect a pigeon if it were eaten at once, because the egg must undergo changes within the bug before it becomes infestive. Snails are in the same category. The vector transmits the infective agent directly.

POST-MORTEM EXAMINATION

If no pathologist is near and you wish to know what killed a certain bird, or what disease or parasite is ailing your flock, you may want to do two things: (1) make a faecal examination and hunt for eggs; (2) examine a dead pigeon for some hint, some marks at least, which certain diseases leave on the internal organs. Since there are a few fairly certain marks left by various diseases; you may learn enough to assist you greatly in saving the rest of the flock.

Diseases and How a Pigeon Catches Them

I have no intention of suggesting that you try to pit your knowledge against that of a poultry pathologist. These men are marvels at diagnosis. Although I am a member of the Pathology Department of a medical school and have studied poultry pathology in veterinary college, I know I am a rank amateur in pigeon pathology compared with these experts. All I am suggesting here is that it may pay you to try to find certain lesions, if there is no poultry pathologist whom you can consult.

How to Make a Faecal Examination

Equipment needed:
1 microscope of 100 power or more;
6 test-tubes;
6 miscroscope slides;
small test-tube rack;
$\frac{1}{2}$ lb. sodium nitrate;
gauze for straining.

A faecal examination is made to discover whether there are worm eggs present in the faeces. By simply mixing a small amount of droppings in water on a microscope slide and studying this, it is often possible to find eggs or coccidia oocytes. But this is an inefficient method and it is quite possible for you to miss seeing the things for which you are looking. It is better to use a method by which you concentrate any worm eggs present into a few drops. Examinations may be done in several ways, but the following method may be put to use by anyone owning a microscope with results on a par achieved by any scientist.

1. Make a saturated solution of the nitrate of soda by putting it in a container and covering it with hot water. Shake it well until you make certain all the nitrate possible is dissolved. The resulting solution will be $1\frac{1}{2}$ times as heavy as water and will float worm eggs.

2. Mix about $\frac{1}{4}$ level teaspoonful of droppings with a tablespoonful of the sodium nitrate solution.

3. Strain it through gauze and pour the liquid into a test-tube. Fill the tube until the fluid is level with the rim, using additional sodium nitrate solution if necessary.

4. Place the test-tube where it will be steady and place a microscope slide on the top of it. The slide must touch the solution.

5. Let the tube and slide remain in this position for 6 or 8 hours, or more, to allow the eggs to rise. Then pick the slide up straight so the surface of the solution comes with it. Turn it over quickly.

Diseases and How a Pigeon Catches Them

6. Study the surface of the fluid with the miscroscope. Compare what you see with the photographs of the eggs or oocytes. You may not, without considerable experience, be able to determine the severity of the infestation, but you will be able to know whether your birds are infested or not and, if so, with what kind of parasites.

Some students use corn syrup instead of sodium nitrate, but this makes a sticky mess compared with the nitrate. If you cannot get nitrate, use a heavy solution of glucose.

6

Diseases Caused by Bacteria

PARATYPHOID

Typhoid Fever in man is a dreaded disease, principally attacking the digestive tract and spleen. It produces fever, diarrhoea, nose-bleed, pain, and rapid loss of strength. Everyone has heard of it, but few persons have it any more. If we know that *para* means *closely resembling*, and that *typhoid* means *delirious*, and realize that Typhoid Fever starts as an intestinal ailment, we might logically expect that Paratyphoid in pigeons is a mild intestinal disease which causes delirium. But this is not the case.

The history of discovery of diseases caused by bacteria of the *Salmonella* group is long and interesting. To avoid confusion it was generally agreed among microbiologists that nearly all of the diseases which were caused by the *Salmonella* group, whether they produced intestinal upsets or not, should be called paratyphoid diseases. *Salmonella* bacteria are a chief cause in many cases of food poisoning, abortion, swollen joints. They are often complicating organisms in virus diseases.

In pigeons Paratyphoid may well be the most important disease. It often kills half the squeakers hatched, it cripples birds by infecting and stiffening leg and wing joints, it may have produced internal changes unrecognized, but so serious as to make racing an impossibility. In the case of some forms of Paratyphoid it may be a disease of insanitary conditions. But in the case of pigeons, it often creates havoc in the most meticulously clean lofts. Experience indicates it is worst in warm damp weather.

Insanitary conditions definitely seem to induce it. Damp, poorly ventilated lofts, shipping long distances in crowded race baskets, overcrowding lofts, permitting birds to drink dirty water, permitting food to contact faeces, these are all contributing factors. But we must remember

111

Diseases Caused by Bacteria

that *Salmonella* germs are to be found in almost every loft, *latent*. We must try to prevent conditions which can 'start a fire'.

A great deal of research has gone into the present understanding of pigeon Paratyphoid. It was at first held that the disease, as in poultry, could be caused by any of several varieties of *Salmonella*. Today, one thorough study after another discovers for us that among 60 or more different types found in poultry, the *only* one found in pigeons was *S. typhi-murium* and some 97·5 per cent of these were the Copenhagen variety. Of the more rare types, one scientist found three pigeons carrying but not sick with *S. abortus equi*, the germ which causes abortion in mares.

Records as to the occurrence of Paratyphoid in pigeon lofts indicate that it is much more likely to be a warm or hot weather disease. Not a few mature birds show wing and leg boils during cold weather, but when many youngsters die and the disease takes on epidemic form it is usually in the summer months. But so is canker much more prevalent in hot weather and losses of nestlings from that disease have been attributed to Paratyphoid.

CONTROL. With the above information in mind, how is one to deal with an outbreak or, better still, prevent one? Suppose a bird shows a drooping wing or a flexed leg? You feel a lump and are sure the disease has appeared. Kill or isolate the bird? What good will it do when you realize that the incubation period is many days and that the bird has already spread Paratyphoid via drinking or bath water. If it happens during racing season, surely you want to keep the rest of the birds flying.

If and when the disease breaks out what can be done? Recalling that the carriers have the organisms in their lungs, the best precaution would seem to be to disinfect the drinking water. Soluble Terramycin can be given, or chloromycetin for two weeks. The parents will not spread the disease and will fill the crops of their youngsters with the solution of the drug and thus kill the organisms in their crops and digestive systems.

Furazolidone has been tried in a grain mixture with no appreciable effect in stopping an epidemic but good results are claimed for it when administered in pill form where each pigeon received a stronger dose.

One method of control, if the owner does not want to use medication, is to rest all the birds of a loft for a season and to breed the following year without introducing new stock. This will give the birds a chance

Diseases Caused by Bacteria

to recover and build anti-bodies against the disease, so that they will not transmit it to their young. (*See footnote on page 126*).

At present one drug concern is offering vaccine. It should be widely used by pigeon owners.

Symptoms. These differ in young and old birds. Old bird symptoms first: It is most important to understand that the disease is often mistakenly diagnosed. The average fancier thinks that Paratyphoid is characterized by wing or leg "boils". He finds a swelling in a wing or leg joint and at once calls it Paratyphoid. Indeed they can be a symptom of that disease but not always. When Dr. R. Arch at Yale and I began to study the disease, what we needed was a pure culture of *S. typhimurium var Copenhagen*. Thinking that all we needed was some fluid from the swollen joints, we withdrew samples from 12 pigeons and cultured the fluid. To our surprise 10 of the 12 showed only a species of Staphylococcus, the organism so commonly found in human boils; only two samples yielded the true pigeon Paratyphoid, *Salmonella*. From the two we had a pure culture for study. And these two birds had different symptoms from the ones whose swellings did not yield the true organism. The 10 with Staphylococcus were affected almost entirely in their joints but without losing weight or otherwise showing sickness.

The two with the true pigeon Paratyphoid lost weight, showed a decrease in appetite, acted droopy and had green, loose droppings. And these are the chief symptoms of all of the birds we have studied since. None of the adults died, but all had a long illness, some as long as eight weeks before they were back to normal, except in many cases for stiff wing or leg joints. Sometimes the first indication that a mature pigeon is affected will be a slight lopsidedness in flight.

In nestlings and squabs the symptoms are especially severe. Baby birds may show a complete lack of resistance and rapid loss of condition. Diarrhoea is copious, the feathers stand out, the vent is usually coated with an accumulation of faeces. Often the sudden loss of numbers of squabs is the first inkling that the disease has struck in the loft.

In the case of young squeakers, the coating of the vent and failure to grow should not be confused with a symptom of canker, namely, infection of the navel. Should you find a squeaker in a nasty condition, feel for a lump in the navel. It may be as large as a walnut. Treat it with drugs to reduce the lump and the squeaker will usually grow again. This will allay your fears.

Another symptom which should make an owner suspicious is

113

dizziness or some other evidence of brain inflammation. If the organisms invade the brain the pigeon may twist its head always to one side, it may put its head between its legs or do the opposite, pull its head backward until it falls. Occasionally a bird has a convulsion, fluttering about crazily. Such an action usually panics the other birds in a loft and more than one fly-away by young birds has been reported as a result.

Epidemics of Paratyphoid vary in severity. In one, 10 per cent of 200 birds died quite suddenly and finally 80 per cent were lost or killed because the owner thought, when they showed "wing boils" that they would be lifelong carriers.

If a post mortem study is made, one finds enlargement of the liver, spleen and kidneys. Sometimes the lungs show small dead areas, as does the liver, where bacteria have been particularly destructive. If squeakers die soon after the symptoms show, no lesions will be found.

Human Typhoid Fever, as nearly every one knows, can be transmitted by carriers. The same is true of pigeon Paratyphoid and it has been found that about 37 per cent of all healthy pigeons are carriers, the organisms living in the lungs but not causing the disease. Just what does cause these latent organisms to start an epidemic no one knows. It would almost seem that some, as yet not isolated, virus was responsible. In the case of dog distemper, it was long believed that a bacterium was responsible. And finally the true organism—the virus of Carre—was found to be the real infecting agent.

Fanciers have usually killed the pigeons left with deformities because they feared such birds were carriers and thus dangerous to use as breeders. In order to test this opinion, I assembled 12 pairs of pigeons. Both parents of five pairs were cripples, either because of their stiff wings or stiff legs. In the other seven pairs, one parent was a cripple. The 12 pairs were kept in a separate loft and allowed to breed. In all, they raised 60 youngsters, not one of which was in any way crippled; all were sound, healthy birds. So we must ask: Does the fact that a pigeon has had an active case of Paratyphoid confer permanent immunity and, because of the anti-bodies built up, render them no longer carriers?

Since this original study was made in 1963, all the parents not too old, have been producing youngsters and no Paratyphoid has been produced.

Treatment. Before we knew as much as has since been learned about treatment of pigeon Paratyphoid, it was assumed that the drugs which had proved so successful in controlling the disease in poultry would do so in pigeons. But such is not the case; the pigeon form of Salmonella is particularly resistant. Our pure culture was sent to several pharmaceutical companies and each reported one or two drugs which would kill the organism in vitro (in test tubes). When we tried these drugs (in vivo) (in drinking water) they apparently had no effect. They were Sulfamethazine, Terramycin, Chloromycetin and two others still in the experimental stage. What effects cures in poultry cannot be relied upon to do so in pigeons.

What can we do to treat birds with "boils"? First we should know that the joint fluid is infected. This brings serum, together with the clotting and healing power of the serum. When the inflammation subsides the healing effect is shrinkage of the fluid, or pulling together just as a blood clot does. This is what produces the stiffness in the joint. So if we can incise the skin and joint capsule and squeeze out as much of the fluid as possible, there will be less to shrink. Pressure must be placed under the wing as well as on top. The cavity may be flushed with peroxide or some antibiotic to kill germs which can enter through the incision. As fast as the lump of fluid reappears it should be opened and drained. It will eventually heal over and, if it has been treated before shrinkage and stiffening has set in, the wing may heal so that no lopsided flying will be noted. Should the boil be due to staphylococcus, treatment is the same. Many a fine pigeon is flying well today as the result of this management.

SPIROCHETOSIS

As we saw in Chapter 5, there are diseases produced by spiral-shaped bacteria called *Spirochetes*. At least one of these produces a disease in pigeons. Birds seldom die of the disease, but are ailing during its course. If the blood is studied, the Spirochetes can be shown to increase up to a crisis point and then disappear rather rapidly. Spirochetosis is one of those minor diseases which can at times account for a short illness in a pigeon, but one from which it recovers spontaneously. Should the owner be able to recognize it, tetracyclines would doubtless be the most effective treatment as they are in the case of spirochete-caused diseases including human and rabbit syphilis.

Diseases Caused by Bacteria

CHOLERA

Cholera is a disease prevalent in warm climates but less frequently found in northern countries. Cholera attacks all kinds of birds and may infect certain mammals which help to spread it. Fowl Cholera was more prevalent a generation ago that it is today.

While it has been demonstrated that pigeons are quite resistant to it, cholera can nevertheless infect a pigeon by mouth, through the eye or the nose; it is not necessary that there be an injury to the intestinal tract as was once thought. In natural infection, the nose and throat are probably the portals of entry. It is strange that a pigeon, after surviving an epidemic in the loft, can succumb to another, later infection. In the cases of many diseases when a pigeon comes through an epidemic safely, it can usually be assumed that the bird has either natural immunity or has previously had a light case unobserved by the owner. This is not so in the case of cholera.

SYMPTOMS. In some cases the disease is so devastating that you may find your birds dead before you had realized they were sick. Death strikes so suddenly that owners often suspect poisoning. If an epidemic starts this way—if you find dead birds when you didn't know there was disease among them, and from then on birds continue to sicken and die —it is a fairly safe assumption that the disease is none other than cholera.

Sick birds are usually stupid in their actions and refuse all food and water. Rapid emaciation occurs; some become lame and seldom make any attempt to fly; their breathing is difficult. If a bird lasts long enough diarrhoea can be expected. The death rate is very high.

DIAGNOSIS. A positive diagnosis depends on actually recovering the causative organism. In very acute cases post mortem reveals nothing abnormal. But in birds which have lingered, a characteristic finding is generally little pin-point haemorrhages on almost any of the mucous membranes, such as the intestines, lungs and liver, as well as on the abdominal fat. A cheesy substance resembling the yolk of hard-boiled egg may be found in the abdominal cavity. The spleen is nearly always greatly enlarged.

The causative organism is *Pasteurella avicida*, sometimes called *P. aviseptica* and *P. cholerae gallinarum*. It is a resistant bacterium, living as long as a month in bird manure and for three months in the decaying body of a bird which it has killed.

116

Diseases Caused by Bacteria

SPREAD. The disease is spread in many ways. Wild birds may become infected and spread the germs in their droppings. Mice drop the germs where birds can become infected. Drinking water can be a hazard. It is thought that flies which have had access to infected birds can also spread the disease. The incubation period is anywhere from 2 to 9 days.

Great care must be exercised not to bring birds suspected of having the disease among healthy birds, and if cholera should break out, a careful disinfection is in order.

TREATMENT. As soon as the disease is suspected, dose the flock with one of the effective sulpha drugs or inject the birds with Malucidin which you can procure from your veterinarian. If a soluble sulpha drug such as sulphamethazine is used, medicate the drinking water for 48 to 60 hours. Repeat 4 days after the end of the first treatment.

ERYSIPELAS

This disease does considerable damage to pigeons. The lesions are so characteristic that the birds are often used to test the presence of the disease in swine.

A pigeon infected with the disease will usually pass it to its squabs. Squeakers as young as 4 days have been found infected.

The same erysipelas which affects swine is also often transmitted to pigeons and by several different insects, by several species of mosquitoes, by the stinging fly, *Stomaxys calcitrus*, and by other stinging insects. Several species of insects studied were found to harbour the virus for from 1 to 4 days in their bodies. A single bite by one can transmit the disease.

The infection also enters the body through skin abrasions and scratches.

SYMPTOMS. Loss of appetite, green diarrhoea, lassitude, hanging head, ruffled feathers, and an apparent shortness of breath are the symptoms. If the bird dies and is 'posted', an enlarged spleen, inflamed intestinal tract, and enlarged liver covered with small spots of infection and a great many pin-point haemorrhages will be found.

CAUSE. The disease is caused by the bacterium *Erysipelothrix rhusiopathiae*.

117

Diseases Caused by Bacteria

DIAGNOSIS. It is sometimes so difficult to differentiate the lesions of erysipelas from other diseases in pigeons, that only a bacteriological examination of the blood will establish the diagnosis. The fact that penicillin cures it when it is valueless against organisms of the Pasteurella and Salmonella groups is also helpful in identifying the disease.

Erysipelas occurs mostly during the autumn and winter. Since inadequate diets help predispose the birds, proper feeding is important in prevention.

TREATMENT. Antibiotics such as tetracyclines, penicillin, and Malucidin injected by a vet are most effective and fairly large doses are administered. Penicillin, 5,000 units per pigeon twice a day for 4 days are recommended; Tetracyclines 50 mg. daily for 4 days; Malucidin 1 c.c., and again 2 days later.

Soluble tetracyclines in the drinking water are favoured by some, but the disease is such a quick killer that it is probably better to inject and use tetracyclines for several days in the water besides.

SOUR CROP

This is primarily a disease of pigeons. The affected birds drink a great deal more than the normal amount of water. The grain they eat becomes sour and they vomit it. The regurgitated kernels are usually eaten by other pigeons, which in turn become infected.

Some authors believe Sour Crop to be caused by improper feeding, but it is more likely the result of an infection. No causative organism has as yet been described. Probably the disease may be caused by several organisms.

TREATMENT. The old method of treatment consisted of holding the bird upside down and squeezing the crop until the surplus fluid ran out of the mouth. Then a pinch of baking soda or several pinches of charcoal were placed in the bird's mouth. The bird was allowed only a small amount of water. The sweetening agent was administered every day until the condition was cured—usually within a week.

The more modern way of curing, and one much easier to administer, is simply to add solible tetracyclines to the drinking water and thereby treat the flock because there is no way of knowing which birds have eaten the infected grain vomited by the sick pigeon. Usually no more than two days are required to effect a cure.

Diseases Caused by Bacteria

INFECTIOUS CORYZA

When pigeons sneeze frequently or seem to clear their throats, and show nasal discharge, when the normally white cere becomes brown or grey and when the face, including the eyes, swells somewhat, the birds probably have Infectious Coryza (which most persons call a 'cold' and many pigeon fanciers call 'the Gawks'). In poultry an early scientific name for the disease was *Contagious Catarrh*. It was also called *Roup*. In poultry there has been a tendency for Infectious Coryza to accompany Fowl Pox, and this is sometimes found to be the case with pigeons.

SYMPTOMS. The usual effects of the disease are sneezing, a rattly cough, accompanied by mucous discharge. This precedes the discoloration of the ceres. The tissues surrounding the eyes, the cheeks appear slightly inflamed and swollen. There is a diminishing appetite and thirst. Since breathing is difficult, no afflicted bird wants to fly and will drop gasping, with mouth opened wide, if forced to fly. Sometimes the windpipe and bronchial tubes are involved in which case one can hear a rasping sound with each breath. Recovered birds are carriers.

CAUSE. The organism causing the disease is *Hemophilus gallinarum*. The incubation period after exposure is about 24 hours, more or less, and symptoms show from soon after infection up to three days. If the disease runs its natural course, it drags on for many weeks and may last throughout the cold months. But if it is contracted in spring, the time is shorter as hot dry weather helps the bird recover.

Unfortunately, other bacteria gain a foothold from the weakening effects of Infectious Coryza, a fact which makes it imperative that the disease be treated as early as possible.

Then, too, there are many different strains of *H. gallinarum*, some of which are more virulent than others.

PREVENTION. Since we know that recovered birds are carriers, once the disease has infected a loft, we must be everlastingly on the watch for a fresh outbreak among the new crop of youngsters. Watch for evidences of the disease in birds coming home from races. The disease is frequently contracted in baskets.

TREATMENT. Sulpha drugs in drinking water, or antibiotics are quite effective. Sulphathiazole, sulphamethazine can be given for two or three days or at least for one day after the majority of birds are over the symptoms.

Diseases Caused by Bacteria

Helpful and effective as these treatments are, they do not compare in efficacy with daily injections into the chest muscles of 1/10 c.c. of a mixture of penicillin and dihydrostreptomycin. Many pharmacological firms manufacture and distribute the mixture. Several trade names are used for the product such as Bicillin, Duocillin, etc. So effective is it that the author has cured racing birds for his clients so quickly that they were able to continue racing. I have supplied my clients with a 10 c.c. vial and a 1 c.c. syringe and 22 ga. needle and instructed them to part the feathers over the keel, expose the breast muscle and insert the needle directly into the muscle. Injected under the skin, a lump is formed and has little medicinal value. Larger doses than 1/10 c.c. are wasteful and sometimes harmful.

WHEEZING

Birds seem to have asthma, if one judges their breathing by similar human behaviour. Wheezing is not, however, a disease but a symptom of other diseases or accidents.

The bird wheezes during its inhalations and exhalations. This may follow diphtheria, or any disease which causes scar-tissue formation to constrict the throat or harm the delicate tissue involved in the breathing operation, or may result from throat inflammation.

A sudden attack of wheezing should alert the bird's owner. The infected bird should be segregated from the others, and the owner be on the lookout for more serious symptoms. It may be an early symptom of a disease which with proper treatment could be aborted.

Keep the nostrils and throat as clear as possible. Feed laxative diets with green vegetables and a drop of percomorph oil each day for its vitamin A content, and treat as above.

URINARY SYSTEM DISEASES

Pigeons are not immune to infection of the kidneys and other parts of their urinary tracts. Birds' urine may well contain crystals, carbonates and quantities of various bacteria. Since a bird possesses no urinary bladder, however, infection is a matter of the kidneys and ureters only.

SYMPTOMS. When a pigeon consumes an excessive amount of water, you are justified in suspecting a kidney ailment. If it discharges so much urine along with its faeces that the droppings are unduly liquid, and still does not become dehydrated as it does when suffering from diarrhoea, this is another sign of a kidney disorder. Though the bird neglects seed and dry foods, it often seems unduly fond of green foods, so that its appetite may even appear to increase. There may be no evidence of pain, and not until the latter stages of the disease will the bird appear droopy. Experienced breeders have noticed that droopy birds which have been voiding copiously and showing great thirst will often die when exposed to a sudden drop in temperature, whereas healthy birds are unaffected.

DIAGNOSIS. How can a kidney ailment in a given pigeon be diagnosed? Since the bird secretes no liquid urine, and since it cannot be catheterized and its urine tested, how can the disease be properly identified? The specific symptoms above are an indication. If a post mortem is performed, the kidney of the bird may be obtained to give us some idea of the cause, for we then see the kidneys enlarged by the inflammation. A chemist or biologist can dissolve a bird's droppings in water, strain it through a fine gauze strainer, and examine the filtrate. This may even be tested for albumin and studied microscopically for various abnormal constituents of urine. But such diagnosis is highly specialized and ordinarily would not come within the experience of the pigeon owner.

Poisons can and do produce nephritis, or inflammation of the kidney, but such poisons generally kill the bird and the damage is discovered only on post-mortem examination.

CAUSE. Bacterial invasion is doubtless the most frequent cause of kidney ills in pigeons. Some fanciers believe the draughts are certain to 'bring on kidney trouble', and to produce 'cold in the kidneys'. Today this is questioned by scientists. 'Colds' are confined to the upper respiratory tract. However, draughts may lower the bird's resistance and perhaps indirectly cause kidney damage by preparing the way for infection.

Diseases which affect the kidneys exclusively appear not to be contagious. However, the inflammation is often the result of generalized diseases which may, of course, sweep through a flock of birds in a few days. In such cases it is of utmost importance that the kidney condition as a danger signal and treat the causative disease as quickly as possible.

TREATMENT. When you are reasonably certain that the diagnosis is an exclusive disease of the kidneys, try sulpha drugs or antibiotics in the drinking water.

Diseases Caused by Bacteria

TUBERCULOSIS

This disease is universal in its spread and exempts no species of bird from its ravages. In the United States it is particularly severe in the north-central group of states. Some mammals also can be infected by this specific form of the disease. Rabbits and swine have low resistance to it; dogs, cats, goats, and most other animals very seldom have been reported infected with the bird form. Few cases of this type of tuberculosis have been reported in human beings.

SYMPTOMS. If a pigeon has a good appetite and a normal temperature but appears depressed, less lively and animated, tires easily and shows a slow, steady loss of weight, T.B. should be suspected. The breast muscles shrink, making the breastbone more prominent. The feathers lose their lustre and are ruffled. Instead of walking, the bird will hop with a jerky one-two-jump, one-two-jump gait. Flying is a great effort and tubercular pigeons may take off from a height, glide, and crash into a wall, unable to navigate. Birds with tuberculosis may die in a month, or may live for more than a year.

Now and again a pigeon shows a shrinking of the eyeball, a condition known medically as *Phthisis bulbi*. This may be caused by avian tuberculosis germs; they have been recovered from such eyes more than once.

DIAGNOSIS: The best way of ascertaining positively if an ailing bird has tuberculosis is to make a T.B. test. This is done by injecting a drop of avian tuberculin within the skin; if the disease is present, a bleb (swelling) will be found at the site of the injection 48 hours later.

In dead birds tuberculous lesions may be found almost anywhere in the body from the bone marrow to the liver. These are greyish-white or white nodules of any size. The spleen and liver usually are well marked by them and greatly enlarged. If you cut through a nodule, it may be found to have a yellow cheesy centre. The bird form of T.B. is caused by *Mycobacterium tuberculosis avium*.

It is found in pigeon lofts—usually in new lofts—when birds are brought together from many old lofts, and in very old lofts without proper sanitation. T.B. is transmitted from bird to bird.

Before long we may have cures by the use of antibiotics, but so far there is no better way of controlling the disease than by elimination of every infected bird, isolation of all suspicious ones, careful attention to cleanliness, and prompt removal of droppings.

Diseases Caused by Bacteria

PSEUDOTUBERCULOSIS

Unlike Tuberculosis, Pseudo- (meaning *deceptive resemblance*) Tuberculosis is of short duration. It starts as a blood poisoning (septicaemia) which is followed by the formation of lesions much like those of T.B. It has been found in many species of birds (farm and sporting), and song sparrows may spread it. Even canaries and finches die from it. It is also found in rabbits, rodents and other animals.

Pseudotuberculosis seldom attacks birds in tip-top condition, but seems to strike those weakened by worms, by having been lost in races, chilled, or underfed. Youngsters are more susceptible than older birds. The disease seldom sickens more than one or two birds at one time in any loft.

SYMPTOMS. The incubation period is three to six days. In acute cases, pigeons may die without showing symptoms, or may live two or three days. Diarrhoea is a first symptom. But more often the bird has the chronic form in which case he presents all the symptoms of 'going light'. The bird steadily loses weight although some appetite remains, sits hunched up, has diarrhoea which is sometimes bloody, becomes weak, stiff, has difficulty walking, acts sleepy and a day or two before it dies the pigeon quits eating altogether. These are symptoms of other diseases, as you have already observed.

CAUSE. *Pasteurella pseudotuberculosis* which gains entrance through the intestinal tract or through cuts and scratches in the skin.

DIAGNOSIS. Since the symptoms are similar to those of other diseases, the only sure method is to have the diagnostic laboratory make a bacteriological study. Post-mortem lesions are suggestive: spleen and liver enlargement, kidney and lungs inflamed, little yellowish-white 'millet seed' lumps in the spleen, liver, kidney and even through the breast muscles. You will find the intestines inflamed with contents often bloody. In the chest and abdominal cavities there may be considerable clear serum.

TREATMENT. Pasteurella organisms are susceptible to the tetracyclines. Isolate the sick bird and give Aureomycin, Terramycin in drinking water.

Diseases Caused by Bacteria

PREVENTION. Sanitary hygienic conditions do much to prevent the occurrence of Pseudotuberculosis.

ONE-EYE COLDS

In no other species of poultry has there been described, so far as I have been able to ascertain, this disease which affects the pigeon. It is occasionally found affecting both eyes, but when the disease becomes established in a loft, the vast majority of birds which have it at all, will have it in one eye only. It is not a vitamin A deficiency.

Actually, the eyeball itself is not diseased, but rather the surrounding tissue (conjunctiva) and the cere, all of which become inflamed. Often the inflammation becomes so great that the eye is almost closed. The increase in size of the tissues makes the affected eye appear much larger than the other. One bird among all the flock, when it is thus affected, seems to stand out, unless of course the bird's colour obscures the trouble (grizzle, for instance). So there is little excuse for failing to detect the disease and to treat the bird.

SYMPTOMS. We are considering the simple one-eye cold. As you have seen, the eye inflammation can be a symptom of other diseases. In one-eye cold there are no other symptoms, except those naturally accompanying inflammation, which are itching or pain. The pigeon may scratch at his eye or he may simply reach for it with a toe and appear to want to scratch, but be deterred by pain. Some birds sneeze.

TREATMENT. The cause may not always be the same. Several bacteria have been isolated from eyes of affected birds. But it is quite certain that the infection is of bacterial and not virus origin, because it responds so readily to antibiotics and sulpha drugs.

Untreated, the disease may last for weeks, whereas, with proper medication, the eye may become normal in a few days. It reminds a doctor of Pink-Eye, usually caused by streptococcal organisms, in the way it responds to treatment so quickly.

Eye salves (ophthalmic ointments) are good; effective but not in the same class for a quick cure as penicillin-streptomycin injected *into* the breast muscles. Give 1/10th of 1 c.c. daily. Sometimes one injection effects a cure. Two or three are almost always sufficient.

Diseases Caused by Bacteria

PULLORUM DISEASE

This once devastating disease of chickens has been reported as a natural outbreak in pigeon flocks from time to time. Compared with chickens, pigeons are quite resistant. English sparrows are very susceptible. When pigeons, which have had no contact with chickens, show symptoms, there is the probability that sparrows spread it. Birds which have recovered from the disease become permanent carriers. Actually, Pullorum disease is one of the minor pigeon diseases, only rarely causing trouble.

SYMPTOMS. *S. pullorum.* The disease, not too distantly related to the cause of Paratyphoid, may easily be mistaken for others. There is diarrhoea, emaciation, 'going light', increased thirst, loss of appetite, droopy appearance.

In a dead bird, the pathologist will often find the reproductive organs badly infected, the heart with the pericardium thickened and adhered to it, liver enlarged and yellowish green, spleen soft, kidneys enlarged and many other characteristic lesions.

The Pullorum organism, *Salmonella pullorum*, persists in a virulent form at ordinary temperatures, in feathers for a month.

DIAGNOSIS. Only methods of the expert suffice. Take suspected birds to him, the poultry pathologist. He will attempt to isolate the organism from the blood or he may use agglutination tests.

TREATMENT. No satisfactory medication has, in 1968, been reported. A Pullorum-infected bird is not safe to have in a loft; isolate it. Clean up the loft. Change the floor covering (sand, etc.), use immaculately clean feeding devices, arrange water containers so that no droppings can reach the water and so that no feathers can be blown into it.

SALMONELLA AERTRYCHE

This is another of this group of diseases which may, but rarely, produce a fatal disease, especially in undernourished birds. It produces anaemia and serious effects throughout the body, even in the bone marrow.

Diseases Caused by Bacteria

Occasionally pigeons have been reported to have been naturally infected with less important diseases. For instance:

Fowl Plague is now and again reported, but it is uncommon and pigeons seldom die from it, unless they are injected with organisms directly into the brain.

One form of streptococci, *S. gallinarium*, cause a blood poisoning, but it is rare indeed. The disease is *Avian Streptococcosis*.

Note to page 115.

The drugs do not eliminate the carrier state. Birds may never become non-effective. But if we eliminated all carriers from our lofts, there would be precious few birds left for breeding. Or, plan to have breeding over with before warm weather sets in. So, from a practical point of view, it is wise to use our recovered birds as breeders and to watch for outbreaks and treat accordingly.

7

Diseases Caused by Viruses

These highly contagious diseases take on many forms, all the way from respiratory diseases to malignant growths. Several of the most important of all pigeon diseases come within this group.

NEWCASTLE DISEASE

Poultrymen speak of it as ND, but most pigeon fanciers have never heard of it. Yet it may be of decided importance, not only for what certain strains can do to our birds, but because it may infect the eyes of human beings. Few diseases spread more easily and few viruses live as long outside the host nor as long in dead birds; and few viruses, except rabies, infect such a wide range of birds and mammals. All farm poultry, many flying birds and game birds, many farm animals, including cats and dogs, rodents and other animals kept as pets have been found susceptible, although the effects in some species are not as severe as they are in chickens.

Only in 1926 was ND recognized as a poultry disease, although there is evidence that it has been known under different names in the Orient for many generations. In 1927 some types were found infective to pigeons.

ND is now understood to be a disease of many strains (some say 35), each differing in its effects. Some strains kill in a few days and destroy many birds of a flock; others kill only a few. All birds are carriers for long periods. Even dressed poultry carcasses stored for a year and a half contained infective ND virus.

Pigeons may have the disease in a mild form, unsuspected by the fancier. In one study, ND virus was given pigeons both by mouth and by inhalation. A few died but most of them showed no symptoms.

However, ND virus was recovered from their faeces which infected baby chicks. Thus these pigeons were spreaders to healthy birds. Some research results may indicate that ND does not infect pigeons, but other students insist the first were working with one of the harmless strains.

SYMPTOMS. Typical of upper respiratory infections, infected birds have trouble breathing, show drooping wings, paralysis of the legs, partial closing of the eyelids. They act depressed and eat much less than normal birds. Profuse diarrhoea is an early sign. In some cases, when the virus invades and damages the brain, nervous symptoms are apparent; the head may be pulled backward, sideways, or be held twisted and under the legs. Birds may fall off their perches and act like parlour tumblers which can't stop tumbling, creating panic in the rest of the birds.

Because of the variability of ND virus, there is no constant picture of the internal effects. One strain may produce many haemorrhages. The spleen may be mottled, or it may be shrunken. The strains which have an affinity for the respiratory tract may cause a grey or yellowish film to coat the air sacs and to thicken their walls.

DIAGNOSIS. Pathologists use any one of several methods, all highly technical, to determine whether a suspicious case is definitely ND. Even though the symptoms are sufficient to warrant a diagnosis, there is so much chance for confusion with other diseases that a blood study is generally needed.

PREVENTION. Since we have no cure as yet, prevention should be our watchword. This ND virus changes so often that we never know if a more or less specific pigeon form might decimate our lofts, as it has so many flocks of chickens.

IMMUNIZATION. Should such a catastrophe occur there will still be time to immunize. Poultrymen are resorting to vaccines with excellent results. One of these immunization techniques is called atomizing or fogging, which makes it possible for birds to breathe in the vaccine which is carried on the minute droplets of fog discharged into the coop or loft.

Hygiene is of the greatest importance and isolation of all sick pigeons at the first sign of the disease is essential.

Diseases Caused by Viruses

RABIES

Rabies could infect our pigeons as it can other birds and mammals, although studies indicate that it is difficult to infect old pigeons. Nestlings may be bitten by rabid bats, but it is difficult to think of any other mode of infection.

PUFFINOSIS

This is one of the rare diseases of pigeons, one which affects the feet and legs so far as outward appearances are concerned. If you see a bird with blisters on the webs between the toes, and with spasms of the legs, you can suspect Puffinosis.

MENINGO-ENCEPHALITIS

The *encephalon* is the brain, the *meninges* are the membranes covering the brain, *itis* means *inflammation of.* Thus the disease means an inflammation of the brain and its covering. This virus disease can be a serious problem in lofts and pigeon breeding establishments. In one flock of 14,000 squab breeders, 140 died with it and Meningo-encephalitis is more important and more likely in lofts than most fanciers realize.

SYMPTOMS. Once the disease is established, the pigeon may lie quietly prostrate, simply turning its head to one side in a corkscrew fashion. Pick it up and it may try to turn sideways or struggle violently. It may spin in wild gyrations about the floor. I went into my loft one morning and found the birds so panic-stricken they refused to eat even though they were hungry. I let them out and they flew for nearly three hours, seemingly afraid to enter the loft. As soon as they had flown out, and upon hearing a noise, I looked under the feeding tray which stands on legs and there was the cause: a battered ball of feathers. This was a bird I had only recently acquired. Examination showed the brain and meninges highly inflamed.

There are several other causes of such behaviour. Some bacterial diseases can cause it, Paratyphoid for example, and so can other viruses. Thus this kind of behaviour in a bird is not a certain sign of Meningo-encephalitis.

129

Diseases Caused by Viruses

There is no cure. The mode of spread is not well known as yet. Mosquitoes may be the vectors carrying the virus from bird to bird.

PSITTACOSIS and ORNITHOSIS

This is the disease which created a world-wide pandemic, which has caused the destruction of millions of dollars' worth of parrakeets and pigeons and which may be a danger to human beings. But it is much less of a danger than it was, as we shall see. *Psittacosis* as a name was derived from the *Psittacine* bird family which refers to parrots, macaws, parrakeets, etc. *Ornithosis* is often used for the name of the disease when it is found in birds of other kinds and in mammals.

Psittacosis affects many species of birds, including ducks, which are now known to be one of the most frequently infected species. In one state of the United States, the only human cases reported during one year were all contracted from ducks. Mice, too, are often carriers as are cats, especially cats which have eaten birds.

Few would deny that the disease spreads from parrakeets and canaries to our species; the evidence is too overwhelming. Remember that reported cases are woefully incomplete; there are many times the number reported because of the difficulty of diagnosis.

Here is the result of a study of cases in Great Britain and the United States from 1931 to 1950 which shows which is the greater danger, parrot family birds or pigeons. The figures show the reported cases contracted from parrots and parrakeets, and from pigeons. It is very important to note that these figures, although obtained from reputable sources, unfortunately do not state the type of pigeon. In most cases they are known to be common street pigeons, a few are squab or fancy pigeons and a few are not identified. It is possible that there may be a few racing pigeons therefore among the cases reported.

TABLE IX

PSITTACOSIS IN GREAT BRITAIN AND THE U.S.A. 1931–50 AND THE
NUMBER CONTRACTED FROM PSITTACINE BIRDS AND PIGEONS

	Psittacine Birds		Pigeons (All Types)	
	Cases	Deaths	Cases	Deaths
Great Britain	8	0	0	0
United States	384	43	136	7

Diseases Caused by Viruses

This table shows no pigeon infection in Great Britain because no serological tests demonstrated the disease. Nevertheless, when 1900 patients recovered from acute respiratory disease and were blood-tested, 27 showed they had recently had Psittacosis. There is far more of it than has been suspected.

The discrepancy in the percentages of wild pigeons in various cities of the world found to have, or to have had Ornithosis, is amazing. Whether this is true Psittacosis has not always been determined. The test often consists of making vaccines of the suspected virus, using this to immunize mice and then injecting the mice with known Psittacosis virus. If the vaccine renders the mice immune, it is concluded that the suspected virus is probably Psittacosis.

In every city where studies of wild pigeons have been made, some birds are found infected with the disease or show evidence that they have recovered from it.

In Birmingham, Alabama, U.S.A., 55 out of 91 were found infected. In Washington, D.C., 35 per cent of those trapped and tested, reacted positively. In Ontario, Canada, birds from three cities showed that of 146 examined 16·4 per cent reacted positively; 15 per cent of the pigeons studied in Baltimore, Maryland, had or had had the disease (33 per cent of those in one location); 60 per cent of another group of 91 birds. In California, the infection rate in some private lofts ran from 30 to 40 per cent. When human infection was traced to private lofts in California, 204 out of 524 pigeons proved to be dangerous to non-infected pigeons and to their squabs. The author of the study does not state categorically that the birds infected their owners. In another study, 50 out of 60 birds were positive. In Paris 70 per cent of the birds examined may have been latent carriers.

SYMPTOMS. In pigeons, the symptoms are vague. Some birds die without showing symptoms. Many lose weight, appetite, have diarrhoea, and in time the symptoms of thiamin deficiency. In squabs, there is slow growth, diarrhoea, matting of the vent with sticky matter which may cover it over. In squeakers and adults alike, however, the weakening effects of Psittacosis provide a fine environment for other latent diseases—Canker and/or Paratyphoid—to thrive. Then there are combinations of diseases from which the birds seldom recover.

Internally, the liver of squeakers is swollen, mottled, and haemorrhagic. The spleen is somewhat enlarged but soft and spongy, easily

131

Diseases Caused by Viruses

ruptured. The heart covering (pericardium) is highly inflamed and one finds a coating of secretion around it.

Adult pigeons show one striking feature which helps greatly in diagnosis; an enlarged liver with its rounded edges and pinhead speckles all over its surface. Also, the spleen is enlarged, so much so in some adult pigeons that it ruptures and the bird bleeds to death. One should be very careful in handling pigeons which may have the disease or who have died from it. Making a post-mortem examination should be done with gloves, unless you have been blood-tested and know you are no longer susceptible.

The manner in which squabs react to tests for Psittacosis is something of a mystery. In one study 5 out of 27 showed evidence in serum tests that they had already built up immunity. It is possible that they can, while living on pigeon milk, have such mild cases that they do not show it and become immune.

DIAGNOSIS. The gross lesions one can see in a dead bird have been described. The positive techniques of blood testing had better be left to your poultry pathologist. Neither you nor your family would be quarantined if he should find the disease in your loft.

TREATMENT. Attempts to produce a satisfactory vaccine seem to have failed, but we now have the tetracyclines and other antibiotics. The virus of Psittacosis is among the largest of the viruses and aureomycin or terramycin seem to stop the increase of the virus in the pigeon's body. When a bird is sick with the disease, tetracyclines seem to shorten the course of the disease, but do not eliminate the virus altogether.

If a fancier desires to clean up his loft after all sickness is over, he can inject his birds twice a day for 5 or 6 days with aureomycin and in this way eliminate the carriers.

Thereafter, he must be most careful about introducing new pigeons into his loft, injecting them first for the prescribed course of treatment.

Since antibiotics help so greatly to cure the disease, and since virus pneumonia does not yield to them, any pigeon owner who develops what the doctor calls atypical pneumonia should let it be known that he does keep pigeons. For in virus pneumonia the doctor can do nothing but depend on the patient's constitution to cure itself; in Ornithosis the doctor can give antibiotics with the expectation of hastening recovery. One interesting point: blood tests may not reveal anti-bodies until the disease has progressed for more than a week.

Diseases Caused by Viruses

Very few children have been made ill by Ornithosis; it is a disease contracted by persons of middle age or older.

PIGEON POX

This virus disease is one of the most important of all pigeon diseases.* It eliminates a bird from racing, it often disfigures, and may kill. But happily, it can be prevented. There is no known cure.

There are many kinds of pox, each more or less specific for birds of one particular kind. Canary pox produces the disease in canaries; pigeon pox in pigeons; but each may affect other species of birds. Pigeon pox will infect chickens, for example. Pigeon pox is most prevalent in warm weather and seems to disappear in cold. If the pigeon recovers, it is immune for life.

SYMPTOMS. Pigeon pox seems to produce most of its lesions (wart-like growths) on the unfeathered parts, with occasional lesions on the body. The legs below the hocks and toes are favoured areas, as are the base of the beak and membranes of the mouth, and borders of the eyelids. These are the areas which mosquitoes settle on and sting.

In pigeons, there are two forms of pox: the throat and the skin. Birds often recover from the latter. The throat form, sometimes called diphtheria, produces a higher mortality. In that form, no skin lesions are found. In the skin form there will be some lesions in the mouth and around the eyes, where the swellings often become so large as to preclude vision. The head may be so swollen, one might suspect roup if there were no other lesions.

It has been demonstrated that pigeons can have the disease in such a mild form that they show no symptoms or lesions whatever. Recovery results in lifelong immunity, and the majority of pigeons recover, some quickly, others more slowly.

SPREAD. Several forms of mosquito can carry pox virus from one bird to another, and they may be the principal means of infection, which is probably why it spreads so fast in warm weather and disappears in cold. Since the virus cannot enter sound skin, it frequently gains entrance through wounds, scratches, pecked spots, and sores in the mouth. When the virus was fed in capsules, the birds failed to become infected,

* Although relatively common in some countries, reported cases in Great Britain are rare.

133

Diseases Caused by Viruses

which would seem to indicate that some break in the skin is necessary for infection.

IMMUNIZATION. Vaccination against Fowl Pox can be done successfully in pigeons but not in canaries. The method is simple. For example, with a squeaker, vaccine is rubbed with a brush into follicles where a few feathers have been pulled on the breast or leg.

Pigeon-pox vaccine is grown in hens' eggs, packaged and dried by a special method and packed in a vacuum ampoule in which it lives for many months unless it is permitted to become hot. If you have a failure in the vaccine's use, the vaccine is most likely dead and worthless. Failures seldom occur when it is kept cool during transportation and used as directed.

When vaccinating a flock, do them all, since the virus may be spread to unvaccinated birds and bring them all down with the disease. Be sure to permit no contact with the brush you use or the empty ampoule.

In the case of pigeon pox we have another example of why birds fail to come home from training or racing. The early symptoms of mopiness and loss of appetite may be missed, the birds basketed, and the poor sick things are unable to fly far. Imagine yourself starting a five-mile run with a good case of influenza! One can't say 'chicken pox' because it is often a mild disease in human beings. Pigeon pox probably makes the pigeon at least as sick as a person with influenza.

Following vaccination, it is probably safe to train birds for 4 or 5 days, but when the fever stage occurs, keep them home. You can often tell by the way the birds appear when the worst is over and they are eager to fly. In 1957, 221 young birds were vaccinated in the three Speedome Lofts on July 19th. On July 27th, when they were let out to fly, not more than half of their number flew out. The ones that did, instead of routing, came down in ten minutes.

Food was in the pan in one of the lofts, so it was not hunger that kept them back. On July 30th the birds were still showing ill effects. The vaccinated birds landed after ten minutes of flying, most of them with their mouths open, panting hard. Another lot of younger birds, not yet vaccinated, flew an hour and landed fresh and not panting. Yet both were flown at the same time and the day was hot.

Examination of the birds that night revealed swelling in the feather follicles of every one handled. A week later further examination revealed well-developed pox on the denuded areas in many of the pigeons.

Diseases Caused by Viruses

TREATMENT. In pigeons, throat and mouth lesions can be swabbed with tincture of iodine or potassium-permanganate solution, 2 teaspoonfuls to a pint of water, or with a solution of 1 oz. borax and $1\frac{1}{2}$ oz. boric acid to a quart of water. The external lesions can be treated with carbolated ointment or some softening agent such as sweet oil or glycerine. Wash this off in an hour and touch the lesions with tincture of iodine.

ENCEPHALO-MYELITIS

The word means inflammation of the brain and spinal cord. This is a rare disease of pigeons, so far as we may know, although it may be more common than is realized. There are several strains. Pigeons are the only other known bird naturally susceptible to the North American strain, which has killed so many horses. Therefore, pigeons are considered spreaders of the disease to horses. It is a virus-caused disease affecting the nervous system.

Mosquitoes are thought to be a vector. In horses the disease occurs principally in the summer and naturally, since mosquitoes fly only during the warm months, observers wonder whether pigeons may not be the reservoir, mosquitoes going from bird to horse. More work remains to be done before pigeons can be blamed for the epizootics.

Pigeons have been shown to be less susceptible to one of the strains, the Venezuelan. When this virus was passed from pigeon to pigeon, the virus died out at the third passage.

SYMPTOMS. In the pigeons used in studies, the symptoms have been entirely nervous: loss of balance, sleepiness, lack of interest in food and inability to drink because of unsteadiness.

I.N.I.

A newly described disease of pigeons, which in the past may have been mistakenly diagnosed, is tentatively known as I.N.I.

SYMPTOMS. The symptoms are somewhat similar to those of other diseases; diarrhoea, ruffled appearance, a somewhat prolonged sickness and death.

Damage by the disease consists chiefly of lesions of the digestive tract. The tissue becomes congested and areas of dead tissue can be seen. A pathologist viewing stained cells can find inclusions of virus in them.

135

Diseases Caused by Viruses

The virus is smaller than that of Ornithosis and is not infectious to rabbits, guinea-pigs, or mice. In the course of the study, pigeons were found to be infected with both Psittacosis (Ornithosis) and with I.N.I. simultaneously.

8

Diseases Caused by Fungi

The diseases caused by fungi, constitute a different class from the bacterial and virus diseases and until recently were a type of disease for which no cure was known. In the U.S.A. they are important because some fanciers use antibiotics in their birds' drinking water. Fungus diseases are actually assisted by penicillin, aureomycin, terramycin and others which is probably why we see more of them than formerly. The principal fungus diseases are *Aspergillosis* and *Thrush*.

ASPERGILLOSIS

This is a disease not only of pigeons and poultry in general, but also of man. It is called in some countries *Gaveurs des Pigeons* disease; which, translated, means *pigeon feeders* disease. It is primarily a disease of the lungs but occasionally infects cuts and skin scratches.

CAUSE. *Aspergillus fumigatus* is the most often seen of the several aspergilli spores. The seed-like forms of the organism are prevalent in nature, travel as dust, settle on feed, or are inhaled. The fungus produces toxins which poison the victim's blood, nerves and body cells generally, but, curiously enough, pigeons are much more resistant to the toxins than many other species.

Because aspergillosis spores are so widely distributed, it is held that some other influence which lowers resistance is necessary for the disease to develop. Respiratory diseases frequently afford such influence and if it gets a start and certain antibiotics are given far too long, the respiratory disease may be cured, but the aspergillosis increases.

SYMPTOMS. Whereas several respiratory diseases cause gurgling or
137

rasping (gawks), in aspergillosis the bird makes no sound but shows shortness of breath, rapid breathing and gasping for breath if it exerts itself.

The 'going light' symptom is present, loss of appetite, a sleepy attitude, thirst and fever are more or less constant symptoms. In the later part of the disease the faeces may become liquid and greenish.

DIAGNOSIS. In addition to the conditions described above, examination of a dead bird may show accumulations of fungus in the windpipe and lungs. They may show, too, in air sacs and even in the abdominal cavity. A pathologist can demonstrate the fungus by culture to be doubly sure.

TREATMENT. In poultry in general, when the disease is found, the first thought is to remove the source. Mouldy food, mouldy floor covering and dampness must be corrected as preventive treatment.

Medication with Malucidin may prove the answer. This fungicide has proved excellent in many fungus diseases where other antibiotics have been proved worse than useless. In treatment of skin lesions, it may be applied in the soap-base form and rinsed off a day or two later.

THRUSH

This is not a common disease of pigeons, but has been reported sufficiently often to be worthy of consideration. It has devastated poultry flocks, especially chicks under 60 days of age, and there is always the possibility that pigeons can contract it from fowl, also from game birds, turkeys and geese. Thrush is principally a disease of the digestive tract. It is more serious in youngsters than in old birds.

SYMPTOMS. *Moniliasis* is its scientific name. As a disease, Thrush is a slow killer and difficult to diagnose externally. Affected birds have the 'going light' appearance plus considerable vomiting. The 'sour crop' symptom in itself can be misleading. One way of diagnosing Thrush is to feel the empty crop of a normal pigeon and note the thickness. Having ascertained this, now feel the crop of a pigeon suspected of having Thrush; the walls of the crop will feel considerably thicker. In some cases, ulcerous patches may be seen in the mouth.

Post-mortem examination reveals white circular ulcers in the thickened crop wall which are easily scaled off. A mass of dead surface of

Diseases Caused by Fungi

the crop and intestinal lining is generally found. The proventriculus walls are swollen as is the small intestine, the latter sometimes having ulcers along its course. Under the ulcers one may find abscesses.

Strangely enough there is little inflammation accompanying the ulcers, even though they thicken the digestive tract walls.

CAUSE. *Candida albicans* is the fungal organism isolated from pigeons sick with Thrush, and this same organism, or varieties of it, produces diseases in mammalian species, including man.

TREATMENT. Until Malucidin was discovered there was no practical treatment. The value of this antibiotic was actually discovered when testing it against *Candida albicans* in mice, which it was learned could be completely protected by that drug.

At present Malucidin must be injected to be effective. In a short time it may be made practical to give by mouth, but in its present form it kills fungi better when injected. Inserted into the crop, Malucidin may kill all the fungi down as far as the stomach where it will probably be digested.

Other antibiotics are being tested for fungicidal activity. To my knowledge, there has been none so safe it had no toxic effects on the bird's system.

9

Diseases Caused by Protozoa

In addition to those already mentioned in preceding chapters, there is another kind of organism far larger than bacteria or fungi (but still microscopic in size) which produces a variety of diseases. I refer to protozoa, the lowest form of animal life. There are several kinds of protozoa which concern us. Some of the most important of pigeon diseases come within this class: *Coccidiosis, Canker (Trichomoniasis), Malaria,* and *Toxoplasmosis.*

The sporozoite *coccidium* (pl. *coccidia*) is the most important of these forms. These one-celled minute organisms live among the cells of the intestinal lining. Their life history is exceedingly complicated and the damage they do is accounted for by the enormous number that develop before the body eventually overcomes them, and by the fact that they permit bacteria to enter the blood stream through the mechanical damage they have caused. Coccidiosis is a self-limiting disease. Once a bird has recovered from it, the bird is immune for life to the specific form but it will always be a carrier.

Two other types, *Piroplasma* and *Anaplasma*, cause considerable damage as parasites of pigeons. The protozoan which causes Malaria is *plasmodium,* and two others of considerable importance are *toxoplasma* and *hexamata.*

COCCIDIOSIS

There is a species, and sometimes several species, of coccidia (pro-nounced cock-sid-ea) for every major species of mammal or bird. Fowls have eight, of which five are especially troublesome. We call this condi-tion by the term *species specific.* Although there are several forms which have been reported in pigeons, there is just one, *Eimeria columbae,* of which pigeons are the natural hosts.

Diseases Caused by Protozoa

In size these single-celled organisms are microscopic. With a 140×
magnification, the egg form can be seen clearly and when a properly
conducted faecal examination is made the degree of infection can be
determined. In the many hundreds of careful faecal examinations which

COCCIDIA

I have made of Belgian, Scottish, German and American pigeons, I
found no group free of coccidiosis. Some birds showed only an occasional egg form, and some showed thousands of egg forms in the stools.
Externally it would be difficult to see that anything was wrong, but the
inferior racing ability of the more heavily infected birds belies their
appearance.

Life History of Coccidia

The shape one sees through a microscope in a faecal sample is not
the organism which does the damage but the egg form (oocyte). It is not
important to remember all of the following details, but you will see
from reading about them why it is so important to keep the infection as
light as possible.

In the egg form, four sporoblasts develop outside the pigeon in from
2 to 6 days, provided the temperature and humidity are favourable.
Inside these, sporozoites develop and then the oocyte is capable of
infection.

When the infective oocyte is swallowed in food, on grit, or in water,
the coating is digested and the sporozoites penetrate the intestinal wall
where they increase rapidly in size, becoming roundish. They are actually within the cells, between the nuclei and the surface. These are called
schizonts. These divide and become *merozoites*, much like sporozoites.
These destroy the intestinal cells; and this act frees them into the intestinal contents from where they attack the intestinal lining; and again go
through the growth process to form more merozoites. After one or
more such processes, sexual forms arise called *microgametocytes* and
macrogametocytes. The intestinal lining cells are again ruptured in the

141

Diseases Caused by Protozoa

process. The microgametocytes fertilize the macrogametocytes which form *zygotes*, which in turn become cysts and form oocytes. They are expelled from the body cells and are passed out in the faeces. As we saw, from 2 to 6 days are required for the oocytes, now outside the bird, to become infective. The process is even more complicated than these 'highlights' indicate.

If you remember that every egg form swallowed by a pigeon develops into dozens of organisms and that the constant boring into the intestinal cells and the constant breaking out from the cells simply must weaken the infected bird, you will realize how imperative it is to keep chances of infection to a minimum.

SYMPTOMS. So far as I can learn no one has done any scientific work on the pigeon comparable to that done on the chicken. Symptoms vary according to the degree of infection. Many pigeons are killed by heavy infections which are frequently repeated. On the other hand, many have such light infections that it is not possible to observe symptoms.

A heavily infected bird subject to constant reinfection is droopy, has diarrhoea which may be bloody, lacks energy, loses weight and appears anaemic. The appetite is diminished but not the thirst.

Studies of the physiological effects in chickens, which are probably applicable to pigeons, show that on the 5th, 6th and 7th days after initial infection, the blood sugar per cent in the blood rises sharply. This is the same effect which artificial bleeding produces, but not starvation. And this is important: the glycogen content of the muscles is less than half of what it is in a bird starved for 19 hours.

As you may recall, glycogen is the food of the muscles. Now, if it is one-half that of a 19-hour starved bird, how can the bird be expected to fly any distance?

Dr. R. Arch and I, in making a study of coccidiosis in pigeons, learned another highly important fact which apparently has been overlooked. We studied the blood of pigeons sick with the disease. The thing we discovered, was that the element making the birds really sick was an abundance of bacteria in the blood—bacteria which doubtlessly entered the blood stream through the mechanically damaged areas of the intestinal lining, damaged of course by the coccidia. Our injections of Malucidin sterilized the blood and the pigeons soon lost their 'coccidia symptoms'. Our untreated controls showed no such effect.

DIAGNOSIS. Coccidiosis is easily diagnosed by a brine-float faecal

142

Diseases Caused by Protozoa

examination (see page 139). The oocytes are plainly visible in various numbers, from a few in each field up to so many as to preclude vision through them.

Watery and sometimes pink or bloody faeces, lack of tone, a droopy appearance, and a loss of ambition should alert one to the possibility that the bird is infected. Leg weakness is also a symptom, the infected bird preferring to rest on his heels rather than to stand. If it is a recently weaned youngster and no symptoms of Canker of Paratyphoid are present, it is likely the bird has coccidiosis. The appearance of symptoms a week or so after a damp spell is also suggestive.

One student wanted to determine whether there was any one period during the day when a pigeon discharged more oocytes than at any other time. He found that since 20 to 30 per cent of the faeces were discharged between 9 a.m. and 3 p.m., that this was the best time to collect faeces for faecal examinations, because they contained 80 per cent of the total number of oocytes passed during the 24 hours.

PREVENTION. Drying kills oocytes or prevents their development. Since the oocyte requires a minimum of two days to develop, even in the most favourable conditions, everything possible should be done to prevent droppings from getting into the birds' mouths. This applies especially to youngsters. Chances are the old birds have already had the disease and are immune.

The use of wire-bottom aviaries is one of the best means of keeping down coccidia and of lessening the severity of its ravages. Covered water fountains and feed troughs are essential.

TREATMENT. A number of drugs, notably sulphamethazine, have been recommended for pigeon coccidiosis. We found Malucidin to be remarkably effective when injected intraperitoneally with 1 c.c. on the first day, and 1 c.c. again on the third day, especially because it sterilizes the blood. Our question is, therefore: are not the beneficial effects of drugs reported as helpful due to their destruction of blood bacteria? We think indications are that this is the answer.

There are many new drugs being tested and used for farm poultry, some of which may become as useful for pigeons; glycimide is one. Watch for these developments.

Furazolidone is highly recommended by many poultry specialists as are other remedies, but no one should expect that any drug yet made available will do any more than lighten the symptoms by repressing development of the organisms.

Diseases Caused by Protozoa

From a practical viewpoint, it may be expected that squeakers in filthy lofts, even two-week-old youngsters, will show symptoms; slow growth, even death. Older youngsters may go through a six-weeks' or two-months' sickness seeming out of condition, and if they are homers, and are trained, will usually be lost.

In a clean loft, however, it is probably just as well that the birds should have the disease. The principal aim is to keep the disease from spreading and from becoming severe.

By following these simple rules you will aid greatly in preventing coccidiosis from ravaging your flock: keep the loft floor as clean as possible with no droppings more than two days old during warm or hot, damp days. Arrange feed troughs so there is no possible chance for droppings to touch food or grit, nor for the birds to step on droppings and track them on to food or grit. Change the drinking water at least once a day and be sure there is no chance for droppings to reach it. Bath water should be removed within twelve hours after it is presented to the birds; and there should be no opportunity for the birds to drink from puddles. Lofts should be kept screened from flies or sprayed with substances which repel them. As long as there is not one infection on top of another, the disease will be moderate and in time the birds will have built up immunity, never again to be troubled by coccidiosis.

If the bird's stools are not watery but normally firm, it is safe to conclude that it is either having a mild case or has recovered and it is safe to train or race the bird. A pigeon with watery stools may return from a short training fly, but it is cruel to send such a bird on a long one.

CANKER (TRICHOMONIASIS)

This is one of the greatest killers and cripplers among pigeon diseases. It kills in several ways and cripples the internal organs. making racing out of the question until complete recovery has occurred. Other species of birds have the disease. Duck hawks are found with the organism in their bodies. It affects doves and kills a large proportion of the birds it infects.

Strains of trichomonas vary considerably in the severity of the disease they produce. In one study, one strain, called the Jones Barn strain, killed 93 per cent of the pigeons infected; another killed none of the birds but all showed signs of infection.

For the information of those who think of canker only as a yellow cheesy growth in the mouth of the pigeon, here are the results of a study,

Diseases Caused by Protozoa

including both live and dead birds. In this study 2,168 birds were examined. These included mourning doves, ring doves and all sorts of pigeons. Every bird, whether sick or not, was found to have trichomonads in the crop. Seven per cent died with the disease. In the majority of cases the lesions were in the intestine between the crop and the stomach (pre-gastric). Occasionally the lesion was in the intestine beyond the stomach. Sometimes lesions were in the muscles, in which case the muscle liquefied and the cheesy growth developed. This was walled off by the body and after twelve days regressed.

TRICHOMONAS

In another study, five strains of this protozoan parasite were investigated, five birds being used to test each strain.

Strain I killed 4 out of 5 birds;

Strain II killed none, nor did any of the infected birds show any evidence of the disease;

Strains III, IV and V, caused some cheesy growths but only a few birds died.

CAUSE. This disease is caused by the protozoans *Trichomonas gallinae* or *T. columbae*, which are egg-shaped organisms having flagella or whips which propel them. Each parasite is 0·25 of an inch long; a microscope is needed for a clear view of one. They move forward spirally propelled by the beating of the flagella at the front end of the body. Along the side is a movable flange-like membrane which undulates. It is thought by students that there are two forms, one inhabiting the upper respiratory tract, the other the lower portion. It is possible that another strain has an affinity for the navel.

Diseases Caused by Protozoa

In general these are harmless organisms found in the crops of most, if not all, pigeons. They apparently lie in wait for some constitutional weakening in the pigeon's body to produce the disease we call *canker*. Of the *T. gallinae* there are several strains, some much deadlier than others. Some strains produce a serious disease in turkeys, infect chickens, quail, ducks, canaries and English sparrows. Students feel that the pigeon is the primary host, however.

SYMPTOMS. Failure of the bird to swallow larger grains, swelling of the throat and cheesy growths in the mouth area are certain evidences of the disease, but usually not of the type which kills. Loss of flesh and ambition, loss of appetite and weakness are chief symptoms of the bird with liver and intestinal damage. 'Going light' best describes it.

Some strains are especially virulent in squabs. One student described such an infection in this manner: the whole digestive tract was inflamed and parts of the walls were sloughing off; there was an accumulation of a pus inflammation in all of the accessory cavities of the head, in the lungs, around the heart and in the navel.

The navel in youngsters often becomes infected and fills with a cheesy growth which frequently leads to invasion of the inner organs (liver, pancreas, lungs) and death to the youngster.

DIAGNOSIS. Except for the obvious form of canker, cheesy growths in the mouth, the gullet or on the nose, the disease is difficult to diagnose in a live bird because of the similarity of the symptoms to those of other diseases. The disease may be the principal one which caused old-timers to diagnose it as 'going light'.

In a dead or sacrificed bird, diagnosis is easy with the aid of a microscope and scissors. If no cheesy growths are found in the upper part of the digestive tract, small nodules may be found in the gullet. Each of these, if opened, may have a cheesy centre. Areas of the intestine may be necrotic (dead), or yellowish dead areas may be found in the liver.

Microscopic examination will reveal the trichomonads.

CARRIERS. Study after study reveals birds with trichomonas in their crops but without a history of sickness. Whether these birds have had a mild form and are immune, or whether the organism is simply waiting for a loss of condition to produce a disease, we do not know. But all such birds are carriers.

Some lofts are infected with more than one strain at the same time.

Diseases Caused by Protozoa

A bird recovered from a mild strain is believed to be immune to the more virulent types. It has not been determined how long a bird which has recovered from the disease may continue to be a carrier. Once a loft is infected, eradication of this parasite is a difficult task.

Since all pigeons are carriers, flock treatment is not of much value. Drug treatment may seem to destroy the organisms in the crops of all the birds, but within a few weeks they are back again, probably in the entire flock. Individual treatment is required.

One of the important facts about canker is that it is chiefly a warm weather disease. Records over many years show very few cases appearing before June, in cooler climates. The disease, when it ravages lofts, usually does so in July, August and September. Sometimes fanciers tell us they have no trouble with the disease but upon inquiry we learn that they breed early and have had little experience with hot summer breeding.

TREATMENT. Before the discovery of the value of the drug aminonitro-thiazole, copper sulphate was the drug of choice, and it is not to be considered useless, especially for those who find it difficult to obtain the drug. When a flock has a sub-clinical infection of trichomoniasis, copper sulphate used at the rate of 35 milligrams to each 100 c.c. of water (1/3 gramme per quart) provides a treatment which was found to be effective without producing toxic effects in breeding pigeons. When used at the rate of 100 mg. per 100 c.c. (1 gramme per quart) of water, the drug was most effective for non-breeders. The breeders were drinking more water because they were feeding squeakers and hence 35 mg. was the most they could take since some of the copper would be absorbed before being fed to the young.

Amino nitro thiazol, as we have mentioned, is preferable. It is available in the U.S.A. as Enheptin and in Great Britain as Entramin. Your chemist can weigh out any size dose you want of the drug. A quart of water (1 litre) is about 1,000 c.c. If your fountain holds a gallon (4,000 c.c.) of water, get the chemist to make up 1,400 milligram (1·4 grammes) papers of the drug and dissolve one in each gallon of water.

It is better to make the solution in a separate vessel and after it is thoroughly dissolved, add it to the fountain. Otherwise, the drug may settle and the solution be too strong at first and too weak later on. There is a lot to be said for the capsule form marketed under the name Harkanka.

147

Diseases Caused by Protozoa

Entramin (Enheptin) alone does a fair job of curing but if an antibiotic is administered simultaneously, the results are far superior. Furazolidone and amino-nitro-thiazole together make a remarkably good combination. These can be purchased in pill form or in liquid form. In the liquid, the drugs settle out and the mixture must be agitated before administration with a syringe and tube into the crop.

This combination reduces even navel canker in nestlings in a few days. With it, there is little excuse for ever losing a pigeon with canker.

The cheesy growths around the mouth or in the throat of the pigeon which hinder eating should be gently removed, but caution should be taken not to dig too deeply and cause haemorrhage. A pair of broad-nosed tweezers is excellent for this job, but as much as possible should be left until the drug begins to work for then the growths comes away much easier.

Every careful breeder observes the navels of his youngsters at intervals as the birds grow. At the first sight of canker in a navel, it should be opened gently and curetted with a blunt instrument and then treated with a strong entramin solution in their drinking water.

Some fanciers isolate all obvious canker cases, but in view of recent findings this seems hardly necessary. Although I would not advise against such isolation, I have had birds who returned home in a run-down condition after being lost, and developed canker; and I left them in the loft until they recovered spontaneously. The disease did not spread to other birds.

PROTECTION. It has been demonstrated that pigeons can be immunized against the devastations of the more virulent strains of trichomonias. But the question arises as to whether natural infection, plus a calculated risk, may not prove the more practical method for the average fancier.

Immunity against the severe strains can be established by inoculating youngsters with one of the mild strains. Having survived this infection, the bird is henceforth immune to the more severe strains. Some scepticism, however, has been expressed at this method, because we do not know as yet what happens when trichomonias occurs simultaneously with another disease, coccidiosis or pox, for example. Should the two infect a pigeon at one time, will either increase the virulence of the other due to having weakened the bird? Further research is needed to determine the answer.

Diseases Caused by Protozoa

MALARIA

When we think of malaria we usually think of mosquitoes which have become so closely associated in our minds with the disease. True, as we have observed, mosquitoes can be most annoying to our pigeons, but they are no more a part of malaria than they are of other diseases, such as pox for example, which they may help to spread.

CAUSE. One of the protozoan species of *Plasmodium*, transmitted by one of the species of mosquito, seems to be the most prevalent type. *Plasmodium reticulum* seems to be the natural species for pigeons and doves. *P. gallinacium* found in some species of poultry is seldom, if ever, found in pigeons.

SYMPTOMS. Not only have mosquitoes which transmit the malarial organism often made the pigeons anaemic, but the periodic attacks of the organism in the blood cause break-down of the red blood cells and they produce even more profound anaemia. Naturally the infected pigeon has no endurance. Even a short flight around the loft may cause the bird to open his mouth and breathe rapidly and with difficulty, such as a pigeon flying on a hot day may do.

DIAGNOSIS. Obvious anaemia and their study by a pathologist are the only certain means of diagnosis. Knowledge that one's birds have been subjected to mosquito attacks would also make one suspicious.

TREATMENT. Atabrine or any of the anti-malarial drugs used in man are also effective in use for pigeons.

Malarial symptoms are greatly enhanced by inadequate diets. Once the peak of the disease has been passed and the bird has only a latent infection, an inadequate diet will cause the parasites to appear in the blood again and the symptoms to show again. In any well-kept loft, however, it is unlikely that the birds will show a relapse.

HAEMOPROTEUS

A malaria-like infection of far greater importance to pigeon fanciers than true malaria is *Haemoproteus*. No one knows how widely disseminated the disease is. But apparently it is worse in those areas where the pigeon fly lives throughout the year and less prevalent where winter prevents the development of pigeon flies.

149

Diseases Caused by Protozoa

In Brazil more than one-half (57·7 per cent) of all the pigeons examined were found to carry the infecting organism. Pigeons (159 of them) from the loft of the Institute of Biology and from military barracks were among those examined. In Hawaii 82·2 per cent of a large number of pigeons studied had the organism in blood smears. The story was the same in Mexican pigeons.

Although this disease is not true malaria, it is so nearly like it in its effects that some investigators think first of Haemoproteus when they discuss pigeon malaria.

CAUSE. *Haemoproteus columbae* is spread principally by the pigeon fly *Pseudolynchia maura*. *Columbicola columbae* and *Pseudolynchia canari ensis* were found to transmit the disease in Hawaii. It seems to be a specific pigeon disease. Even doves appear immune, nor can it be transmitted to fowl. Mosquitoes do not transmit it: indeed, mosquito blood was found to destroy the organism.

Probably the reason for the disease being confined to pigeons is that the pigeon fly troubles no other species of bird. In addition, the period between generations of the fly is well over a month and winter cold checks the breeding of succeeding generations. As you will observe, as soon as a fly emerges from its pupa case it must have pigeon's blood or it will die. And homing-pigeon men separate their birds after two or three nestings and clean up the nests.

SYMPTOMS. Same as those described under the section on malaria.

DIAGNOSIS. Symptoms of anaemia should suggest the possibility of haemoproteus infection when you know that pigeon flies are present. Examine any strange small lump under the feathers on your bird, because the fly moves about under the protection afforded by the feathers. If you find one, examine nest bowls for pupa cases and watch squabs for flies.

TREATMENT. See treatment prescribed for malaria above.

PREVENTION. Prevent the breeding of the pigeon fly. This disease is the best argument for thorough cleaning of nest-boxes and bowls between every nesting and adding insecticide to the nest material. Control the pigeon fly and you prevent the disease.

Haemoproteus columbae causes the production of an antigen in pigeon blood. The serum can thus be used by a pathologist to test the blood of

Diseases Caused by Protozoa

suspicious pigeons, even when the organism cannot be found micro-scopically in the blood.

TOXOPLASMOSIS

This protozoan disease is probably more important to pigeon owners than it is to fanciers or owners of any other species of poultry. It is a disease of man, dogs, pigs, rabbits, guinea-pigs, wild birds, canaries, as a natural infection. It was first described in the gondi, an African rodent. In one study of 80 wild pigeons trapped on the roof of the U.S. Capitol building in Washington, D.C., 10 were found to have had toxoplasmosis.

CAUSE. A protozoan, *Toxoplasma gondi*, is the cause of the disease. There may be strains one or more of which are specific for mammals and others for birds. The appearance of the organism is no criterion as to its type; only behaviour tells the story. The mode of transmission is not known for certain. Biting or sucking insects may be the chief means.

SYMPTOMS. Shortness of breath, diarrhoea, loss of weight should make one suspicious, but these are also symptoms of many other diseases. If the mucous membranes appear faded and pale, the bird is anaemic,

TOXOPLASMA

which is a definite characteristic of toxoplasmosis. Post-mortem examinations usually reveal pneumonia and the pleura (lining of the chest cavity and covering of the lungs and heart) inflamed.

TREATMENT. When the disease is recognized by microscopic examina-tion, the remaining birds, if not too badly infected, may generally be cured by treating with any of the sulphas or antibiotics, sulphametha-zine, sulphathiazole, aureomycin or terramycin, for example.

151

Diseases Caused by Protozoa

HEXAMITA

Hexamita species attack and sicken several species of poultry, but that which interests us is *Hexamita columbae*, also known as *Octomitus columbae*.

The parasite is microscopic. It has 8 flagella, whip-like appendages, around its body. It has 2 nucleii.

SYMPTOMS. Pigeons affected have profuse diarrhoea, lose their appetite, sit hunched up and lose weight. And no wonder: the parasites accumulate in masses throughout the entire length of the intestine. Diagnosis is by microscopic study of the fresh droppings.

Another *Hexamita*, *H. maleagridis*, infection occurs in turkeys, causing considerable damage. Study shows that the pigeon cannot be implicated in spreading the turkey disease, because pigeons are not susceptible to that form.

10

Deficiency Diseases

As we have seen, certain vitamins are essential to the health of pigeons. Now we will consider the effects of vitamin shortage or deficiencies in the diet.

VITAMIN A DEFICIENCY

The needs of a pigeon for vitamin A have been quite well determined. As little as 40–50 International Units will keep one in good health. In studies, 40 to 100 I.U. are usually suggested as providing an optimum amount. Growing squabs may need 200.

Vitamin A, when inadequate in the diet, slows growth, produces an unsteady gait, sleepiness, ruffled feathers and loss of weight. It also causes infertility, lowering of resistance to disease, inability of the squab to pick out of the egg; and it affects the pigeon's flight.

SYMPTOMS. The principal symptom is an eye condition called *Xerophthalmia* which results in the eyes becoming crusty and sore. This must not be mistaken for the so-called one-eye cold because the deficiency affects both eyes equally. Xerophthalmia is an enlargement of the tissues around the eyes, but this is only part of the condition; the sinuses and mucous membranes of the head are all affected. Seldom is this condition limited to one bird. Instead, the entire flock is usually affected.

One finds nasal plugs, inflammation of the membranes of the throat, crop, gullet, windpipe and lungs. The kidneys usually show lesions. It is difficult to distinguish the lesions caused by vitamin A deficiency in the upper respiratory tract from those of other diseases, which cause a shedding of the mucous membranes. Pustules will be found in the windpipe and gullet after the bird has been affected for some time.

It is extremely rare, however, for pigeons to show vitamin A defi-

153

Deficiency Diseases

ciency because so many are fed yellow maize. This contains about 280 I.U. per ounce. A healthy pigeon eats about an ounce of grain a day, and if one-fifth of the ration consists of yellow maize, there is more than enough vitamin A for the daily requirement. Other grains, too, contain considerable vitamin A.

TREATMENT. This consists of assuring an ample supply of vitamin A in the ration and giving a drop of halibut liver oil to the affected bird once a day. Emphasis should be placed on *prevention*.

If the bird's diet consists of grain with inadequate amounts of the vitamin, add some by sprinkling tiny amounts of carotene on the slightly dampened ration, feed green vegetable leaves or add yellow maize so that 20 per cent of the ration consists of it. Commercial pellets are all provided with surpluses of the vitamin. If only 3 lb. of fresh alfalfa leaf meal is included in each 100 lb. of the mix before pelleting, the birds which eat the pellets will be amply supplied. In the case of pellets, remember that pelleting preserves the vitamin by keeping air away from most of it. Studies show that this protection lasts for as long as two years.

An excess of vitamin A is almost as harmful as too little. When given 25,000 I.U. per day, by the end of 60 days pigeons show the same symptoms as when fed inadequate amounts. It has not been determined what damage is done to the body, but the eyes are definitely affected.

It is a great mistake to give cod liver oil and halibut liver oil in large amounts. Animal feeders have learned that cod liver oil is poisonous when given in large amounts. For instance, a tablespoonful a day given to a 100-lb. calf will cause paralysis after 30 days. Halibut liver oil is rich in vitamins A and D, but does not contain a lot of toxic oil. It must contain more than 30,000 units of vitamin A and usually 3,000 units of vitamin D in a gramme ($\frac{1}{4}$ teaspoon). Cod liver oil, to be standard, must contain at least 600 units of A and 85 of D per gramme.

If one were feeding $\frac{1}{2}$ teaspoonful of cod liver oil to 20 pigeons each day, it could scarcely harm them. If the grain being fed is deficient in vitamin A, and no greens are given, it would pay to add a drop of halibut liver oil to each pound of feed and mix it thoroughly so that every grain has a little. If you feed more than that, you are wasting money. One drop a day on a pound of food will provide 16 pigeons with 2,000 I.U.

Fast-growing squabs need more vitamin A. If growing chicks are any
154

Deficiency Diseases

guide, then they require about three times as much, and even this amount is usually provided by the grains eaten.

VITAMIN D DEFICIENCY

Vitamin D deficiency produces rickets. A growing pigeon kept in the dark needs vitamin D. Since almost all squeakers are raised out of the sun's rays, they all need it. Mature birds in the sunlight need none, so far as anyone can discover. But during those times of year when the days are short, the sun rides at a slant to the earth and the actinic rays are weak, even adult birds, and especially those feeding squabs, need vitamin D.

There are many sterol derivatives which can prevent rickets. One that is useful for mammals is D_2, irradiated ergosterol. The protective which pigeons have formed in their feathers and skin is cholesterol, activated by the ultraviolet rays from the sun. This is found in fish liver oils also, and thus we need look no further for the prevention and cure of rickets.

When one speaks of the amounts of vitamin D required, one must take into consideration the amount of calcium and phosphorus also. A deficiency of any one of this triumvirate will produce rickets or abnormal bone formation.

Rickets is seldom found in pigeons because grains usually have sufficient calcium and phosphorus, and the sun creates the vitamin D. Calcium and phosphorus are easily supplied in ground bone. Pigeons when fielding are known to pick up snail shells and what intelligent fancier fails, today, to furnish grit and these contain oyster shells?

That pigeons need plenty of sunlight, or vitamin D, is attested to by the result of several studies. When raised without one or the other, rickets develops and usually the parathyroid glands enlarge markedly. In adult pigeons kept away from sunlight and fed inadequate amounts of vitamin D, studies showed their feathers turned dark. When vitamin D was fed and the feathers plucked, the regenerating feathers came in coloured normally.

Grains contain considerable amounts of calcium (Ca) and phosphorus (P). Whole rice has 90 mg. of Ca and 300 mg. of P per pound of food. Wheat contains 53 mg. of Ca and 375 mg. of P. Since approximately equal amounts of Ca and P are needed daily, we can disregard the P as there is always enough.

A grown human being needs only 700 mg. of calcium a day. A pigeon needs only about 5 mg. Parents of a growing squab need about 20 mg. If a pigeon eats 36 grammes of food a day, he will need no more Ca than is contained in his daily grain ration.

As to the amounts of vitamin D in grains, it is low compared with other vitamins.

Not more than one-tenth of 1 per cent of the sun's radiant energy has anti-rachitic effect, and yet if even this small amount shines on pigeons for no more than 10 minutes a day, if there is enough Ca and P present, the bird needs no other vitamin D.

SYMPTOMS. Egg shells too thin, embryo loses its hatching power. When youngsters show an inability to support their weight by the time they should be walking, if their bones lack stiffness, if the joints are tender and painful, if the skeleton is distorted, if the breastbone has a dent and/or is crooked, suspect rickets. (Crooked breastbones sometimes are not a sure sign; they may result from cramped nests.)

In chickens, one characteristic sign is an over-long upper half of the beak and a soft beak. This may be a sign in pigeons, too.

ANEURINE OR THIAMINE DEFICIENCY

Aneurine and Thiamine are both names given to vitamin B_1. Great amounts of investigation have gone into the requirements of different species of animals and much of it is highly controversial. The pigeon was among the first species to be used and for some time was employed as a test species in determining how much of vitamin B_1 various foods contained. If you read that a cow needs so many units of B_1 per pound of weight, that need does not necessarily correspond to the requirements necessary for pigeons or dogs. The amount of food in the digestive tract and the time it remains there is of great importance because bacteria manufacture B_1 and other vitamins. Then, too, some species can starve for long periods without dying from B_1 deficiency. Dogs can live 100 days on only water, but not pigeons. A chicken on a polished rice diet shows symptoms in 30 days, a pigeon in under 10 days.

The pigeon with its short digestive tract needs a large amount of Aneurine as compared with some other species. If we supply one milligram a day, we are sure we have given enough. A milligram is 1/1,000th of a gramme. But a pigeon eats about 40 grammes of food a day and most of the grains contain 20 mg. of B_1 in each gramme; so each pigeon gets many times as much as it needs.

Deficiency Diseases

Aneurine deficiency symptoms vary according to the rate at which the deficiency is produced. When pigeons are permitted to feed *ad lib.* on deficient diets, they become acutely or chronically deficient or die from loss of appetite. When tube fed, acute deficiency and nervous symptoms invariably develop.

In vitamin B deficiency, the weight of the pigeon's liver increases due to its becoming congested with water. Other changes, too, occur. The blood diastase doubles in some cases. The bird is greatly upset.

Pigeons fed polished rice show marked decrease in body fat as the B_1 deficiency develops. Aneurine in the diet prevents loss of weight, and when added to the diet of a pigeon previously fed a deficient diet results in rapid gain in weight. It functions to synthesize fat from carbohydrate.

Vitamin B_1 deficiency can be induced more easily by feeding certain raw fish flesh exclusively than by feeding polished rice. The student who uncovered this fact fed the birds crude entrails of carp which contained no B_1. The pigeons ate the entrails readily at first (another demonstration that they enjoy animal tissue), but the lack of aneurine killed the appetite. Raw fish flesh contains an enzyme which destroys vitamin B_1.

SYMPTOMS. It would seem that only in the case of sick pigeons is the vitamin of concern to us. Remember that in from 7 to 10 days of starvation, a pigeon's body can become so depleted of B_1 that it may start to show the symptoms of Polyneuritis, which is the involvement of nerves, so that there is leg and wing weakness, jerking of the head, unsteady gait, and finally, as the disease progresses, the head may jerk backward much like a fantail pigeon's and the bird falls backward and flutters to gain its equilibrium. Diarrhoea is another symptom, but so is it in many diseases. Before these symptoms appear the bird loses its appetite. But in most sicknesses the appetite is often lost with the consequence that Polyneuritis is naturally an accompaniment and the disease blamed for these symptoms which are not actually part of it.

TREATMENT. In all diseases which cause a loss of appetite, it is wise to administer thiamine as part of the treatment. One of the foremost students tells us that once a pigeon's body is depleted, ordinary daily doses will not cause a response. He found it necessary to administer 50-milligram doses daily to cure his Polyneuritic birds. Fifty-milligram pills of thiamine chloride can be had in any chemist's. Give one a day, or you can give four or five dried brewer's yeast pills a day.

Deficiency Diseases

RIBOFLAVIN DEFICIENCY

Of all the vitamins, a shortage of this one, B_2, is more likely to be found in pigeons because our birds are too often fed borderline or inadequate diets. Grain is not particularly rich in riboflavin, and although green vegetable leaves are, fanciers too often neglect to furnish them. Only 1·6 milligrams per pound of food need be eaten. Some grains do not furnish this much, others do. Here, for instance, is a feeding formula so low in riboflavin that it was used as a basis for studying the deficiency:

Sweet corn (maize)	40 per cent
Kafir corn	30 per cent
Wrinkled peas	20 per cent
Wheat	10 per cent

One of the finest sources of riboflavin is alfalfa leaf meal which may be included in pellets. Newly sprouted grains, of which pigeons are fond, are not often furnished and can be fed to good advantage.

Riboflavin has been found to increase hatchability of eggs. In a study in which a common commercial ration was supplemented with the vitamin, a significantly higher percentage of eggs hatched than was the case in the controls. It did not affect the number of eggs laid; controls laying as many as those provided with the vitamin.

SYMPTOMS. Leg weakness with a tendency to curl the toes is seen in chickens with riboflavin deficiencies and probably in pigeon nestlings, too. The appetite is good, but the birds are weak when they should be standing and coming forward to compete for the food from the parents. There is a tendency for the pigeons to rest on the hocks with a loss of tone in wing muscles so that the wings droop.

Old birds on diets deficient in riboflavin lay eggs of doubtful hatchability. It may be a chief cause of squabs found dead in the shell.

TREATMENT. Prevention should be our principal aim. We must provide synthetic riboflavin or feed plenty of green vegetable leaves or use pellets with riboflavin guaranteed adequate for daily requirements. Once we find we have neglected to feed enough, cure is dramatic when adequate amounts of riboflavin are supplied. Four or five days will be sufficient to show an improvement.

Deficiency Diseases

ASCORBIC ACID DEFICIENCY (VITAMIN C)

Research has not demonstrated that pigeons need this vitamin, chiefly because they manufacture their own. The subject is mentioned here because so many pigeon fanciers try unnecessarily to provide it. There are several vitamin C preparations on the market for which extravagant claims are made, claims without foundation in fact. Chickens have been found with scurvy-like symptoms which were prevented by feeding vegetables, especially cabbage.

VITAMIN E—TOCOPHEROL DEFICIENCY

Birds need this vitamin for normal reproduction. To feed any, such as wheat germ oil in addition to grain, is a complete waste of money. Whole grains almost all contain much of the vitamin. Many green plants also contain appreciable amounts. This is a vitamin pigeon fanciers can ignore. It is mentioned here only to assure you that seed germ oil is an exceedingly rich source. Only in the case where a fancier feeds a lot of cod liver oil may he observe the classical symptoms in his birds. Cod liver oil contains a factor which prevents the bird from utilizing vitamin E. In such cases embryos die early in the shell but egg production is not impaired.

PANTOTHENIC ACID DEFICIENCY

Nowhere can I find an account of anyone having studied pigeons in relation to the lack of pantothenic acid in their diets. If we draw on the effect such a lack has on chickens, we find the following:

SYMPTOMS. In adult birds, loss of hatchability in eggs, skin lesions, broken feathers, tendon weakness.

In chicks, the growth is retarded, emaciation occurs, scabs show at the corners of the mouth, the eyelids become stuck together with a mucus but of quite a different appearance from that of vitamin A deficiency. The skin peels on the feet in some cases.

TREATMENT. Give yeast tablets, feed milk instead of water for a few days (skim milk will do), feed pellets with alfalfa leaf meal.

Deficiency Diseases

Pyrodoxine Deficiency

This deficiency is almost never encountered in grain-fed pigeons. Almost all grains furnish much more than the minimum requirements.

Gizzard Erosion Factor Deficiency

This is in the same category as that above. Without it, the horny layer of the gizzard degenerates. But since many grains are well able to provide adequate amounts, it is unlikely that a fancier will ever encounter the ailment in his pigeons.

Choline, a deficiency of which causes slipped tendons, and *Biotin* deficiency, are both practically outside our concern since they are seldom found in pigeons.

Vitamin K is likewise so abundant in pigeon feeds that we do not encounter deficiencies. It is called *the anti-haemorrhagic* vitamin because when absent haemorrhages appear in the muscles, on the legs, wings and in other places. Pigeons synthesize vitamin K to some extent and when they eat pellets, or green leaves of plants (the greener the better), there is no danger of a deficiency developing.

Nicotinic Acid Deficiency

The best sources of this vitamin, such as yeast, milk, liver, are seldom available to pigeons except in pellets. There is probably more of this inadequacy in diets than is commonly thought. The flesh of pigeons is rich in nicotinic acid, but there is considerable difference as to age and sex. In their breast muscles, male squabs contained 71 micrograms per gramme of fresh flesh; female squabs 80; mature cocks had 60 and mature hens 85.

Leg muscles contained 57, 55, 41 and 51; liver contained 108, 107, 115 and 113 respectively.

SYMPTOMS. Diarrhoea, loss of appetite, slow growth, slipped tendons, poor feathering and mouth inflammation are all symptoms of this deficiency. This is the cause of 'black tongue' in dogs, a disease with which some pigeon fanciers are acquainted. When the protein is adequate, the amino acid, *tryptophane*, is used to supplement nicotinic acid when it is present in inadequate amounts.

Deficiency Diseases

TREATMENT. Give yeast tablets, permit the birds to drink skim milk or whey. All pellets so far marketed have had more than adequate amounts.

FOLIC ACID DEFICIENCY

This is another deficiency condition which is not likely to occur among pigeons. There is usually plenty of the element in average pigeon rations. When a lack does occur, however, it causes anaemia, a stiff neck, drooping wings, diarrhoea and early death after symptoms occur. This results, however, from experimentally refined diets. When a pigeon has access to greens and an otherwise wholesome diet, it will synthesize sufficient additional folic acid to meet its requirements.

A. P. FACTOR (ANIMAL PROTEIN OR B_{12})

When you see pigeons picking around a barnyard they may be eating cow or sheep manure for the *animal protein factor*. All poultry species need it. Recent research shows that cobalt is the principal ingredient which makes it essential. Today B_{12} or A.P.F. in the U.S.A. is made from antibiotics. Pigeons unable to forage are at a disadvantage because they are not able to obtain this factor in grains.

In pellets, they will find a sufficient amount if the table states that an antibiotic is used as an ingredient.

Strangely enough, studies show poultry manure to be especially rich in B_{12}, but not until after it has been out of the bird for several days. Perhaps this explains the tendency of pigeons to pick around compost heaps where pigeon manure is dumped. It is a dangerous practice because of the danger of worm contagion. Better to supply B_{12} or antibiotics in their food. This is probably best done by using pellets as part of the diet.

MINERAL DEFICIENCIES

Pigeons, especially pigeons which never field, are subject to the same mineral deficiencies as other species. Fortunately, a vast amount of research has been done on poultry, much of which applies to pigeons.

Every loft should have a well-stocked grit tray as an essential part of its equipment. But it must be remembered that even if we include in it all the minerals which pigeons are known to require, we could not count on its being of service in every case. Most minerals are best utilized in

Deficiency Diseases

their organic forms as we shall see. Others are worthless in certain combinations as we shall also see.

Phosphorus is a mineral so plentiful in grains that we can disregard it.

Calcium, which functions in combination with phosphorus and vitamin D, to prevent rickets and produce sound skeletal development, is of the first importance. It is often lacking in diets but not in those where ground oyster shells are included with the grit, or when ground bone is fed. Pellets all supply adequate amounts. Indeed, some pellet manufacturers advertise that, with their products, no grit or oyster shells need be fed. I notice that my own pigeons, when only half their ration consists of pellets, eat less than half the amount of grit and shells they ordinarily eat when all their ration is grain.

In addition to causing rickets, shortage of calcium in the diet results in soft-shelled eggs and a loss of the blood's ability to clot normally. In poultry about $1\frac{1}{2}$ per cent of the ration is usually calcium, but pigeons eat what they want. Measuring the grit is one way of determining the amount consumed. If the birds are seen picking at loose mortar between bricks, eating ends of plasterboard (which I saw some city pigeons doing on a dump), one can be sure there is a deficiency.

Magnesium deficiency seldom occurs in pigeons. There is generally more than enough in pigeon feeds. Only in synthetic rations is a shortage possible.

Sodium Chloride (Salt) Deficiency. In view of the fact that blood needs salt to function properly, that gastric juice is rich in hydrochloric acid, and that sodium helps regulate heart function, lack of either sodium or chlorine causes upsets in several ways. Birds fail to grow properly, resort to picking one another, even eating dead birds. True salt feeding can be overdone so that it becomes a poison, but if 1 per cent of the ration is salt, pigeons will be healthier than when it is deficient.

Potassium is another chemical almost never deficient in pigeon rations. In experimental synthetic diets, chicks fail to grow and die when it is lacking.

Manganese deficiency results in slipped tendons and leg weakness. Embryos develop much shorter beaks than normal when they have inadequate amounts of this mineral. Squeakers develop a nervous symptom called *ataxia*, where the head either pulls backwards or is bent under the body. Egg shells lose strength, too, because manganese is a principal constituent of the shell. If there are 25 milligrams of manganese in each pound of feed the ration is adequate and no deficiency results.

162

Deficiency Diseases

Iodine deficiency. Whether grains are deficient in this essential depends on the area in which they are grown. Since most mixtures come from widely different areas, there is almost always enough iodine in the mixture. If you decided to feed only peas and beans grown in Michigan, U.S.A., you might find you must use iodized salt for the birds or the squeakers will develop goitre. The old birds must have iodine in their rations to ensure its being found in the eggs. Chicks may die in the shells or, if they hatch, it may be too late to supply it to the squeakers. Pigeons probably need 0·5 mg. per pound of feed, easy to supply in pellets, or in the salt or salt block with iodized salt which you furnish.

Iron deficiency. Iron is a chief component of red blood cells. Therefore, an insufficient amount of it in the diet eventually produces anaemia. Also, we must remember that egg-yolk contains considerable iron, about 0·5 mg., so breeding birds need a little more iron than non-breeders. We know that grains grown on iron-rich soils contain sufficient iron, and that those on iron-deficient soils may not furnish enough. We often think of spinach and other greens as being rich in iron, but actually only a small percentage of iron in vegetables is in an available form. Pellets generally have more than sufficient iron. When a bird is anaemic from parasites or anaemia, it is well to supply iron in the drinking water in tiny amounts. Chemists can weigh you out tiny papers of ferric-and-ammonium citrate which you can dissolve in the drinking water. Five grains per gallon is sufficient. Sometimes pigeons will pick at old iron, seemingly trying to eat the iron rust, but rust (iron-oxide) is almost worthless. Probably the citrate form is most stable in water.

The deficiency of iron, therefore, produces iron-deficient eggs, results in anaemia and makes long-continued flying impossible.

Sulphur deficiency. A bad egg always smells of sulphur dioxide. As we have seen, cystine and methionine are the two amino acids containing sulphur and are absorbed by the body in the form of these acids. It may be inferred that eggs must be especially rich in cystine and methionine. Thiamine and biotin also contain tiny amounts of sulphur but not enough to be of much use in nutrition. Wheat contains about 0·3 per cent methionine and 0·2–0·3 per cent cystine; Indian corn (maize) 0·28 and 0·15 per cent; soy beans 0·78 and 0·66 per cent respectively.

Since we have seen that nearly 1 per cent of methionine and cystine together are necessary in a diet for growing squabs, we cannot rely on a high protein percentage alone to be certain of having this 1 per cent; we must know what the proteins are, for we will not have good growth without them, nor will our birds lay hatchable eggs.

163

Deficiency Diseases

Since some grains are low in cystine and methionine, the pellet has a great advantage because such valuable items as fish meal, meat meal, dried skim milk and other animal proteins can be included to ensure a goodly supply of cystine and methionine.

Since feathers are composed chiefly of protein, and cystine is an important building block, a shortage of cystine with its sulphur content must result in inadequate feathering. Rapidly growing squabs, especially during their early weeks, if fed insufficient cystine and methionine, will grow with inadequate breast feathering.

I had this experience in 1957. A number of nests had squabs with almost bare breasts, but with back and wings well covered. The ration was only 14 per cent protein, which was inadequate. The six-week-old youngsters which I have seen imported from England, Scotland and Belgium have been much better developed than the general run of American youngsters. Europeans feed peas and beans, much higher in protein than the general American mixed diets of 14 per cent.

TRACE MINERALS. *Zinc,* which is found in sufficient quantity in most pigeon feeds, is necessary in hormone and enzyme functioning.

Fluorine in tiny amounts, not over 0·035 per cent in the ration is useful. Fluorine is cumulative, even moderate amounts given consistently eventually will result in poisoning. Bone meal used in pellets almost always contains sufficient amounts of the element so we can dismiss it from consideration if we feed them. *Selenium* deficiency is seldom found in pigeon rations, and, like fluorine, it can be a poison. Sometimes poultry rations are poisoned by including ingredients grown on soils with too much of this element. *Cobalt,* now known to be a component of vitamin B_{12}, is an essential and without it growth is depressed.

11

External Parasites of Pigeons

Scientists call the external parasites infesting pigeons *ectoparasites*. In this classification we find all the animal forms which live on the outside of the pigeon's body, such as mites and lice. There are quite a few, all easily destroyed. The old saying, 'It's no disgrace to get them; it's only a disgrace to keep them', is indeed true here. Unfortunately, their presence is not always suspected on pigeons. If you know the symptoms, you know what to watch for.

LICE

There are four principal kinds of lice which infest our pigeons, although other species have been found in small numbers now and then. The latter are usually insects which the pigeons have contracted from fowls but they do not last long, nor do they trouble pigeons unduly.

Most of the external insects which infest any species are referred to as 'species-specific' by parasitologists. This means the parasites thrive only on the one species which is their natural host; nor can they live long off that host. Three to five days seem to be the limit for lice.

One often hears it said that an old pigeon coop should be fumigated before putting birds back into it, but this is not true. It becomes necessary only if a loft becomes infested with bed-bugs, and as we shall see, the use of modern insecticides makes even that fumigation unnecessary.

Lice have six legs, are wider than they are thick, are brownish in colour, and some are able to move quite quickly. Lice live all their lives on the pigeon, having a life span of several months. Their entire reproductive cycle seldom takes more than three weeks. They attach their eggs to feathers and lay so many that, if not controlled, one pair of lice theoretically could have 120,000 descendants in three months.

External Parasites of Pigeons

It seems scarcely possible that the tiny feather lice one sees on the pigeon could be harmful. Some kinds are not as harmful as others because they eat skin scales and parts of feathers, but other lice actually puncture the softer quills close to the skin and eat the blood and serum which exudes. The body louse chews at the skin until it bleeds and consumes this blood.

We are not certain how much damage lice do to pigeons. Many of the insects are removed when the pigeon preens itself. Studies on egg production in hens, showed that even moderate infestations reduced the number of eggs laid by about 10 per cent. Probably the worst damage lice do is to keep up a constant nerve irritation which makes pigeons restless and prevents sound sleep.

We do not know what part lice play in virus and parasitic infections. Some viruses have been isolated from them, horse encephalitis from a chicken louse, for example.

The more pigeons there are in a given loft area the quicker the spread of lice. A new bird coming in should always be regarded with suspicion and deloused as a precautionary measure; no strays should be allowed to remain in contact with healthy birds in a clean loft.

The four species of lice are as follows: Narrow Body Louse, *Colpocephalum turbinatum*; Slender Pigeon Louse, *Columbicola columbae*; Small Pigeon Louse, *Goniocotes bidentatus*; and the Little Feather Louse, *Goniodes dammicornis*.

Lice are also classified as the sucking kind and the biting kind, and each type is sub-classified into several species. Some are body, some feather, some shaft, but in spite of obvious differences, their life histories are very similar.

LIFE HISTORY. A louse hatches from its egg, called a nit, which the female has fastened to a feather. The newly hatched louse, if it is the sucking type, crawls on to the body of the bird, fastens its mouth in the skin, and sucks the blood. A large number can suck so much blood and give off such a toxin that the host often becomes anaemic and dies. The biting louse, on the other hand, feeds on skin scales and organic matter as well as on blood. The males and females copulate, the female's body fills with eggs, the female lets go of the skin and crawls on to the feathers where she attaches tiny silvery eggs which are large enough to be seen if one looks carefully. The eggs of the biting louse hatch in 5 to 8 days; those of the sucking louse in 10 to 12 days; the young mature in 2 to 3 weeks after hatching. Lice do not drop off their hosts spontaneously. In general, infestation is spread by contact and by close association. Apparently, some lice move from one host to another of a different species quite easily, as can be attested to by persons working with poultry.

The various kinds of lice infest different parts of the pigeon's body.

Columbicola columbae are found regularly on flight feathers and on the head feathers. The larvae are seldom found on the wings but usually on the throat or in the neck or head region. Egg-laying occurs mostly

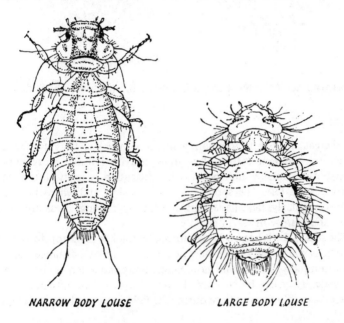

NARROW BODY LOUSE   LARGE BODY LOUSE

on the small feathers on the underside of the wing. Seldom is an egg found on the outermost wing feathers, usually the eggs are found on the outer side of the feathers close to the shaft.

In general, most of the parasites which inhabit a pigeon's body externally will be found most abundant in the areas where the bird cannot reach them with its beak.

As we have mentioned before, anaemia is frequently the result of heavy infestations of the sucking varieties of lice, and all lice cause such annoyance, restlessness, and unthriftiness, as to warrant immediate treatment.

External Parasites of Pigeons

NIT ON FEATHER

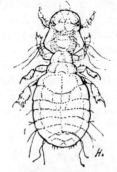

GOLDEN FEATHER LOUSE

CONTROL. See Chapter 4 for descriptions of effective insecticides.

FLEAS

Whereas lice are a common parasite of pigeons, fleas are seldom found in well-kept lofts unless some heavily infested stray enters, spreads the parasites and because its infestation is unsuspected, contaminates the loft. The spread, however, is slow and when the loft is cleaned regularly, fleas have a difficult time increasing. Fleas are found more abundantly in warm climates.

The flea is dark brown in colour and is thicker from top to bottom than he is wide from side to side. Some can jump long distances and all can run rapidly. The female has a longer body and a lighter colour than the male. They live by sucking blood and cause intense itching. Some species suck blood only once during daylight hours and again at night.

LIFE HISTORY. Their life history is interesting: male and female copulate on the pigeon, the female lays several whitish eggs a day which fall off the bird and remain dormant in the sand, on the floor, in cracks of the perches or in the nests. When the weather becomes warm and damp, or in the nests which are warm and damp most of the time, the eggs hatch. Worm-like larvae emerge and eat organic matter, probably consuming a good deal of the adult fleas' excreta which is mostly the residue of the digestion of blood. The larvae grow and shed their skins twice and then construct tiny cocoons in which they pupate and emerge as hard, broad-jumping fleas. They become mature in less than a week after finding their host and sucking blood.

External Parasites of Pigeons

Unlike the louse, the flea, both mature and immature, can live for weeks without food. On the pigeon, fleas may live a year. The duration of their reproductive cycle varies depending upon moisture and temperature.

These are the fleas found on pigeons: the Sticktight Flea, *Echinophaga gallinacea*; the European Chicken Flea, *Ceratophyllus gallinae*; the Western Chicken Flea, *Ceratophyllus niger*.

The Sticktight Flea may be found around the bird's head, sometimes in large numbers, with their mouth parts so deeply embedded in the skin they are difficult to pull loose. Sticktights may infest human beings for short periods. They carry viruses and are such a menace as to demand quick eradication whenever found on pigeons.

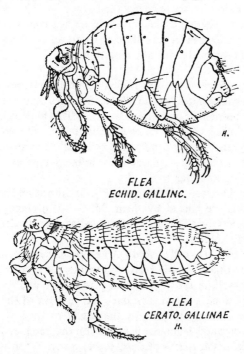

FLEA
ECHID. GALLINC.

FLEA
CERATO. GALLINAE

The European Flea also attacks man. It is frequently found on English sparrows from which it can spread to pigeons. Its effects are like those of the Sticktight but its breeding principally occurs in nests. Its cousin, the Western Chicken Flea, also breeds in nests and feeds on the birds at least once a day.

169

External Parasites of Pigeons

CONTROL. See Chapter 4 for description of effective insecticides.

MITES

Mites, tiny and almost as invisible as they are, probably cause pigeons more misery than fleas or lice. All mites have certain features in common. If a mite is magnified, it will be seen to have a body with chest and abdomen joined in such a way that the mite appears to have no waist. They all have eight legs, some breathe through tubes and some breathe through their skin.

LIFE HISTORY. The mite's life cycle takes anywhere from a week to a month, depending on the climate, the species of mite and finding a hospitable host. The life cycle consists of an egg which hatches into a six-legged larva, which in turn develops into an eight-legged nymph. The nymph becomes the sexually mature adult.

SYMPTOMS. The pigeon sits with ruffled feathers, scratches and picks at itself and, because mites live on blood, becomes anaemic so that the usual bright redness of the mouth is pink. The bird lacks ambition, being more willing to sit than to fly. Naturally, with an inadequate blood quality, there being too few red cells and some toxins which the mites secrete, a heavily or moderately infested bird can scarcely be expected to fly fast or far.

Mites spread disease. Cholera, possibly Ornithosis and several forms of Encephalitis are spread by them. Mites are of many forms and produce a variety of effects as will be noted as we consider each of the more common species.

The *Red Mite*, also called *Roost Mite* (*Dermanysus gallinae*), is the most common of all mites and has world-wide distribution. It breeds in cracks in the wall, in the floor behind perches and attacks the pigeons only at night. I have stood in a dark loft and heard the birds seem almost to be dancing, judging by the sound of their stamping feet. When the owner and I shone a flashlight on the perches, we could see the mites, like small specks of dust, scurry away. When we examined these creatures we found them to be enlarged and red, so we knew they had been fed.

LIFE HISTORY. Only seven days are required for the life cycle, the adult female laying eggs in less than a day after she has had her first meal.

External Parasites of Pigeons

So far as their ability to weaken pigeons is concerned, any experienced breeder or flier must know how much loss the mites cause. When sitting hens have been killed by them, because of the amounts of blood an army of red mites often withdraw, it is obvious that their presence is

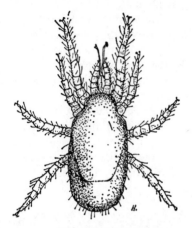

RED OR ROOST MITE

dangerous in any loft. If nests are not cleaned and powdered against mites, squeakers can hardly be expected to thrive. When pigeons seem to want to sleep out of doors in the fly instead of in lofts, when they stamp their feet at night, and when they appear anaemic, examine the perches at night and destroy the mites.

CONTROL. See Chapter 4.

The *Harvest Mite* is also called Chigger, Chigre, and Red Bug, *Entrombicula alfreddugesi.* Almost every human being who lives or has visited the middle-western or southern parts of the United States is well acquainted with chiggers, the insignificant-looking creatures which are picked up out of doors and which raise great welts on the human body, especially in areas where slight pressures are experienced, such as under one's belt or on the ankles. Chiggers are not the adult because adult chiggers are not parasites; those which cause grief to pigeons and to us are the immature form, the larval stage only.

I can well sympathize with the infested bird, for I have experienced hundreds of such chigger bites myself. They leave welts on the skin

171

about an inch across and about one-eighth of an inch high which produce intense itching caused by a toxin which the chiggers inject. This infestation occurs when the pigeons go fielding, but not on birds kept in the loft or permitted outside only to fly, never to walk in grass or bushes where chiggers abound.

Adult Harvest Mites breed on the ground in bushy areas. When the larval form attach themselves to the pigeon's feathers they soon manage to reach the skin and there cause the itching vesicles. Many quail chicks are annually killed by the mites and pigeons can be made sick enough to worry the owner. The ailment is of short duration because the mites drop off after a few days.

Scaly-leg Mite (*Cnemidocoptes mutans*). This is called the itch mite by poultry men who know how it appears on the legs and causes the scales to stand out, but is also found among the feathers. Authorities used to include pigeons among the species of poultry which this mite infests. Today some modern authorities assure us it is never a pigeon

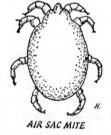

SCALEY LEGGED MITE   AIR SAC MITE

parasite. They say that when the lower legs of our birds appear thickened the ailment is due to some other cause.

Here is an opportunity for pigeon fanciers to assist in determining the truth because poultry scientists may not have had the opportunity of seeing pigeons whose leg scales no longer lie flat.

An easy method of determining whether roughened legs are caused by the scaly-leg mite is to wind a piece of Scotch tape about the leg, then remove it and examine the sticky side with a microscope or powerful reading glass. If you use an 8-power glass you can see the mites but no details. By this method I have found mites on pigeon legs in several lofts, and assumed they were the scaly-leg mites. I may have been wrong. If you find any, send them to the State Poultry Pathologist

External Parasites of Pigeons

in America for diagnosis, or in England consult your veterinary surgeon.

CONTROL. See Chapter 4.

The *Air Sac Mite* (*Cytoleichus nudus*). This is a mite which has become adapted to the respiratory system (windpipe and lungs), and the air sacs.

LIFE HISTORY. The life cycle apparently is not known, although eggs are found in the faeces indicating that they must have been coughed up and swallowed. It is thought that the eggs may be carried on dust particles and inhaled by pigeons, and that they may be transmitted by breeders feeding squabs.

This mite is almost nude, tiny, oval and cream coloured. Its eight legs are equipped with suckers. The amount of damage it does to a pigeon is questionable, even though some bird students report deaths have been caused by them. The mite has been recovered from pigeons, turkeys, chickens, pheasants, and other fowl from the respiratory tract, the air sacs and bone cavities.

SYMPTOMS. Symptoms are a droopy appearance, lack of endurance in flight, coughing. Pigeons heavily infested have symptoms typical of Tuberculosis. Birds lose weight ('go light'), sometimes develop abdominal infection, pneumonia and obstructions of the air passages. Very likely the presence of the mite permits bacteria to gain access to the blood.

DIAGNOSIS. Diagnosis is made by finding the eggs in the faeces or by observing the mites in the air sacs of dead pigeons. The lining of the air sacs is almost transparent and the whitish mites may be seen by those with good eyes, moving slowly about. It is wise to use an 8-power reading glass or a 100-power microscope to make a positive diagnosis.

TREATMENT. It is likely that fumes from a Vapona bar hung in the loft will destroy the mites as it does red mites on perches. The fumes are inhaled in the air and pass to all the air sacs.

The *Flesh Mite* (*Laminosioptes cysticola*). This inhabitant of the skin has been reported in pigeons in nearly all parts of the world. If it remained in the skin it would not be too serious, but it oftens tunnels into the connective tissue underneath and sometimes even into the muscles, the intestine, lungs and abdominal lining. The body often walls them off into nodules which sometimes mislead examiners into diagnosing the case as Tuberculosis. It is not uncommon to find large numbers of these nodules in old pigeons.

The amount of damage Flesh Mites do to flying homers we do not know, but certainly they do some, the amount depending upon the number of mites.

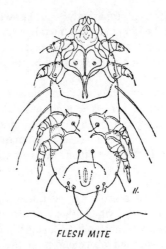

FLESH MITE

The life history is not known, nor is any method of control.

The *Quill Mite* (*Syringophilus columbae*). The Quill Mite of poultry has been long known but the pigeon Quill Mite was first discovered in 1942. It is rare, but occasionally damages pigeon quills. If untreated the mites can denude a bird, leaving only quill stumps in which a powder is found containing mites, easily seen with low-power magnification.

Because the mites live inside the quills, no known means has been discovered to destroy them. They live in the quills of all types of feathers, so pulling feathers is no cure. With the advent of the newer miticides, we can look toward the possibility of a dip being developed which will kill the mites by contact if all the pigeon's feathers are coated, and yet not poison the bird when it preens. Probably perch paints and Vapona will prevent their spread.

The *Barb Mite* (*Falculifer rostratus*). Students differ in their estimates

174

External Parasites of Pigeons

of the amount of damage which the Barb Mite does to feathers. It is a rather common mite in Europe and America. The mite is small, even for mites. It may be found, when present, between the barbs of the flight feathers.

The Barb Mite's life history is not completely known. Some evidence exists that its nymph stage occurs under the skin, which would cause irritation. Perch paint helps greatly as a control measure. Dusting with Derris Powder is also effective, and Vapona should be tried.

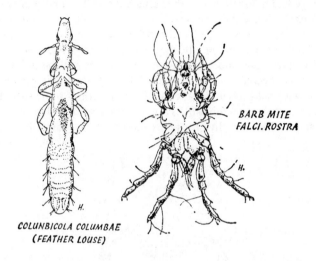

BARB MITE
FALCI.ROSTRA

H.

COLUNBICOLA COLUMBAE
(FEATHER LOUSE)

Neck Mite (*Megninima columbae*). This is a mite which occasionally is found on the body feathers and on the feathers of the neck. Life history has not yet been described.

Nasal Mite (*Neonyssus columbae*). A rare mite first described in Texas. It inhabits the nasal passages. Nothing is known of its life history.

TICKS

Only occasionally do we hear of ticks on a pigeon. But when they do attack the birds of a loft they can do much damage. Ticks are more troublesome in warm climates and seldom are found in cold climates. If you find bean-like bodies attached at one end to your pigeon's skin, you will want to know how to remove them and how to prevent re-

175

infestation. If you find a swarm of insects as large as bed-bugs crawling in your loft, you will also want to eliminate them, and you should, because they can be very troublesome.

The life history of all ticks is similar. All have four stages: egg, larval, nymph, adult. The male is much smaller than the female when she is distended with blood. They copulate, the male dies, the female drops off the pigeon, crawls to a suitable sheltered place and lays from a few hundred to several thousand eggs and then she dies. The eggs hatch and the larvae find a host to which they attach themselves and engorge with blood. At this stage they are tiny. The larvae moult, becoming nymphs with eight legs. They resemble the adult ticks but cannot reproduce. Some kinds of nymphs moult only once; others moult several times before they become adults feeding on blood between the moults. The adult female becomes so large when fully engorged that persons unfamiliar with ticks often mistake one for a growth of some sort. These are what most persons think ticks are, never having heard of the several other stages. Ticks can live for many months, even years, off the host.

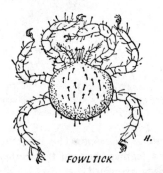

FOWL TICK

In addition to the damage which ticks cause the pigeon from the amount of blood they draw from its body, ticks produce toxins which poison the bird mildly, but worst of all they spread disease. It must be remembered that ticks are not all specific about their hosts. Some even manage to survive on snake blood! There are many instances of wild birds being killed by ticks. Quail are especially susceptible because of their habits and in America pigeons which forage in quail grounds are especially prone to have ticks, too. Rabbit ticks, dog ticks, bird ticks and other kinds have been found on pigeons. But the most troublesome is the Fowl Tick.

The *Fowl Tick* (*Argus persicus*). Found in many parts of the world, this tick goes by several names. The engorged female is about 1/3 inch long and the male about half that size. It is reddish brown, flattened and bean-shaped. Most of the body is bulbous, the legs and head which are attached to the pigeon's skin being small by comparison.

The female lays 200 to 300 eggs at a time, feeding between layings. She usually lays eggs three times, after which she dies. Because we are interested in pigeons, we should note that one of the favourite places for the Fowl Tick to deposit eggs is under bark of tree limbs, where the young can attach themselves to pigeons if they roost in trees.

The nymphs need only to feed a short time during the night after which they hide a week and shed, feed and hide and shed again and then are adults ready to engorge. If no host is found, this tick sometimes lives two years awaiting one.

SYMPTOMS. Symptoms of tick infestation are ruffled feathers, diarrhoea, loss of appetite, and fortunately, bumps which are plainly felt when the bird is handled.

CONTROL. See Chapter 4.

BED-BUGS

No one who has not known the results of a loft infested with Bed-bugs, has any idea what these insects can do in lowering the vitality of a flock of pigeons. There are several species of bed-bugs of which *Cimex*

BEDBUG

External Parasites of Pigeons

leclutarius is the most important. *Haematosphon inodora* are found more often in southern climates, and *Oeciacus vicarius* is also a common parasite of barn swallows.

Bed-bugs are so flat they can crawl into tiny cracks and escape most cleansing methods.

LIFE HISTORY. The female lays her eggs, one or two large ones a day, in cracks. Each female lays about 200 eggs which hatch in 10 days. The bug passes through 5 nymph stages but feeds between each moult. In the nymph stages, bed-bugs can live two months without food and in the adult stage they can live for a year.

It is surprising how quickly a bed-bug can attack a pigeon, drop off filled with blood and scurry away to hide for another 24 hours. Ten minutes or less is required. The danger and damage to the birds come from many bugs attacking and drawing blood. Following the attack, the pigeon itches and swellings develop at the location of the bites.

Unsanitary nest bowls make excellent homes for bed-bugs and squabs are hampered in their growth by the pests. With the development of newer insecticides, bed-bugs should become almost unknown in lofts within a few years.

CONTROL. See Chapter 4.

THE PIGEON FLY

For the creature which is seemingly so unprolific, the Pigeon Fly, *Pseudolynchia canariensis*, can cause a great amount of discomfort and unthriftiness, especially in nesting birds and squabs. It is known to pigeon keepers especially in the warmer sections of the world, such as the southern part of the U.S., Central America, parts of southern Europe and Asia and rarely occurs in Great Britain. The fly is small, the body being less than 1/8 inch long, and is blackish in colour, reminding one of the common Black Fly. The Pigeon Fly, also, bites human beings, making a much more painful and longer lasting wound than the Black Fly does. Sometimes, in handling a pigeon, the flies may be felt moving about under the feathers.

LIFE HISTORY. The flies feed on pigeons, moving about among the feathers and sucking blood. They are especially prone to feed on
178

squabs. Pigeon nests are their chief place of reproduction. The adult female lays only about 5 pupae each in a white case and half as long as the fly, on the squeaker. These roll into the nest and turn black in a few

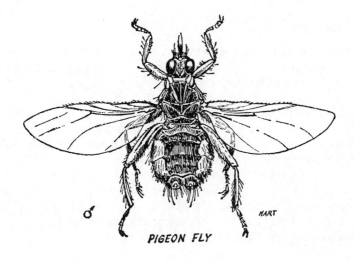

PIGEON FLY

hours. A month later the flies emerge from the cases, live about 45 days, during which time they in turn deposit their 5 pupae.

CONTROL. Changing the nest material after each pair of squeakers has left it and burning it will prevent the flies from increasing. Applications of insecticide powder to nests and in moderation to growing squabs, is also worth while.

BEETLES

There is such a variety among the beetle family that we do not know for certain how many affect pigeons. We do know, however, that some species are hosts for several tapeworms and other parasites of poultry and may be implicated in transmission of diseases. Some species are directly harmful, in their larval form, by feeding on young squabs. These species breed in pigeon droppings and can sometimes be found in nestbowls. The larvae of some are about $\frac{1}{2}$ inch long. When they do eat squab skin, it is not uncommon for the wound to attract flies, which

External Parasites of Pigeons

lay eggs, which soon become maggots. Many a squab has been killed in this way.

Control is effected by keeping nesting material clean and using insecticide powder in it.

MOSQUITOES

Pigeon fanciers—especially in U.S.A.—are well aware of the nuisance mosquitoes can be to their birds, but few realize the damage they do to a flock in the diseases they spread.

Mosquitoes and Malaria have long been studied, using pigeons as hosts. A great deal is known about the effects of one upon the other, and the various species of mosquitoes which can infect pigeons. In addition to Malaria, the diseases which mosquitoes transmit while travelling from pigeon to pigeon make it imperative that every loft be protected in some way against the ravages of these pesty insects.

More than 120 species of mosquitoes are known, but only a small proportion attack our birds. The hum of many is not understood; only the male hums and does not suck blood. The female goes right to work silently. Males live on other fluids such as nectar.

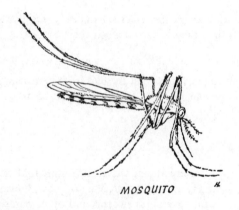

MOSQUITO

LIFE HISTORY. Without water in which they pass most of their lives, there would be no mosquitoes. The females lay eggs on tiny rafts on quiet stagnant pools. The eggs hatch and become wigglers, larvae and pupae, all stages of which are spent under water. From the pupae the mature insects emerge, copulate and seek a host on which to feed.

180

External Parasites of Pigeons

Depending on the species, the temperature and food in the water, the entire life cycle is completed in from 7 to 16 days. Mosquitoes travel miles in a single night and are most active during the night.

SYMPTOMS OF MOSQUITO ATTACKS. When swarms of mosquitoes invade a pigeon loft one may be certain there is anaemia among the birds. In unprotected lofts you may hear your pigeons stamping their feet. A flashlight beam may reveal 8 or 10 on each leg, just above the hock. Its long proboscus enables a mosquito to suck blood through several thicknesses of feathers.

The night-long irritation causes a loss of condition among the birds and anaemia adds to it. More homers are lost while flying because of these insects than is generally known. The ravages of the insects themselves, however, are but a small part of the damage they do.

DISEASES TRANSMITTED BY MOSQUITOES. Malaria comes to mind at once as a mosquito-borne disease. What about Pigeon Pox? It is now certain that they spread Pigeon Pox and are able to infect pigeons for six weeks after they become infected. Pox is more often a summer and autumn disease. One finds the lesions chiefly on the pigeon's legs and head, just the places where mosquitoes feed.

Mosquitoes spread St. Louis Encephalitis, which affects man as well as poultry and also help to spread horse Encephalitis. As yet no certain vector has been incriminated in the spread of Toxoplasmosis, but certainly the mosquito is a likely suspect. Any of the virus diseases might be spread by these insects and probably are.

CONTROL. If you are troubled by them, as many American fanciers are, it is helpful to empty any stagnant bodies of water in the vicinity of the loft. Spreading oil on them completely eliminates such areas as breeding places but does not prevent the wind-blown or flying mosquitoes from finding our birds.

It pays to screen lofts, but when this is impractical, the loft should be sprayed with a repellant, the walls coated with a substance which kills mosquitoes on contact. One U.S. product does both and while it is not the province of this book to recommend proprietary mixtures, this product, Carbola, is such a standby and of such worth in the loft that it can be recommended without reservation to all those who have no objection to putting whitewash on the walls of their lofts. Some persons do object to the use of whitewash since it rubs off on clothing.

181

External Parasites of Pigeons

Spraying with DDT or other insecticides kills many mosquitoes by contact. If any fancier objects to the carbolic odour in whitewash he can add DDT, which will help but not be as effective as a repellant. Carbola contains both.

Phenol in whitewash repels mosquitoes as long as there is any trace of the odour left. When it disappears, another light spraying refreshes it. Four of five sprayings during the mosquito months are needed.

New insect repellants are annually being announced. One, perfected by the U.S. Department of Agriculture, is effective for some hours, but more information is needed as to its permanency when sprayed on to perches, screens and walls. In lofts without too many windows the fumes of Vapona bars act as a repellant and kill any mosquitoes which enter.

DDT, Malathion, Chlordane sprays and others used on the walls and screens will kill insects for many weeks. See Chapter 4 for more details on insecticides.

I 2

Internal Parasites of Pigeons

There is no point in trying to eliminate either external or internal parasites which infest pigeons, without knowing something of their life cycles. Somewhere the cycle must be broken. By a cycle I mean the chain of events from egg to parasite to egg, or from parasite to egg to parasite, whichever you prefer. If we destroy the parasite and then permit pigeons to have access to the eggs of the worm or insect, we cannot eliminate it completely. Somewhere during the cycle we must place a bar; this may be accomplished by as simple a means as sanitation. If, for example, we know that a certain worm never lives longer than nine months and we remove its eggs by frequent loft cleaning, we can be reasonably sure the pigeons cannot become infected during that length of time.

We have often heard of a flier whose birds rated low during one season and then made remarkable showings the following season. We wonder why. A feasible explanation is that through careful sanitation he eliminated worm eggs, so that his birds were free from parasites in the second season. It has been well established that parasites weaken pigeons and make long-continued flying impossible.

As you read the following life histories and the damages each parasite does, you will fully appreciate why this is true.

In this discussion of internal parasites, I have placed the common name of the parasite first, the scientific name second. Perhaps you think the latter is unnecessary. But suppose you wish to study further the life of one of these parasites. You may search in vain through the index of several modern books on parasites and find no common names given. The scientific names given here will help you in your study.

You will note that if a certain parasite infests other species of birds, it is mentioned in order to help you know where your birds may have contracted it and thus prevent them from being contaminated again.

THE LARGE ROUNDWORM (*Ascaridia columbae*).

This is common in pigeons, doves and some other fowl. The full-grown worm is about 1½ to 2 inches long and 1/32nd of an inch thick. One female worm lays hundreds of eggs. A large proportion of pigeons are known to carry them.

SYMPTOMS. Despite their size, ascarids are probably the least serious of any worms and are now easily removed. If a pigeon has a large number in its digestive tract, it will act droopy, certainly lack the ability to sustain long-lasting flights. Pigeons have been known to die from very heavy infestations.

Young pigeons show the effects of roundworms and are more susceptible to them than are birds more than a year old. The better the pigeon's diet the faster the worms grow.

LIFE HISTORY. Eggs pass out of the pigeon in its faeces. In warm weather, or in piles of manure which generate their own heat, the eggs incubate and a larva or tiny worm forms in each in 2 weeks or more, depending upon the time of year. A pigeon swallows the incubated eggs

ROUND WORM

in contaminated food or water. The shells, or coating, are digested off the larvae which then proceed to live in the duodenum for 9 days and then penetrate the lining (mucous membrane) of the intestine, where they live for 17 days. After that period they emerge and live freely in the intestine, becoming mature worms 50 days after the pigeons swallowed the original eggs and the worms, in turn, lay eggs themselves.

184

Internal Parasites of Pigeons

Ascarid eggs are very resistant to cold and also to drugs. Some species of ascarid eggs will live five years in the soil waiting to be eaten by a suitable host. There are no ordinary drugs which can be used to destroy the eggs.

CONTROL. Scrupulous sanitation to prevent reinfestation. Piperazine citrate, used 8 grammes per gallon of drinking water over a period of 60 hours, eliminates most of the large roundworm. The author published a paper showing that this method was used to rid roundworms in more than 1,400 homing pigeons with no harmful effects. Some roundworms were found within four hours after the birds first drank the treated water.

THE STRONGYLE WORM (*Ornithostrongylus quadriradiatus*)

It is taking some scientific liberty to call this little worm with the long name, the Strongyle worm, because scientists repeatedly have written that it has no common name.

It is a small reddish worm measuring from 1/3 of an inch in males to almost an inch in females and is about as thick as a shoe tread. It lives in the small intestine of the pigeons and doves and probably in some other species of birds. It was the most troublesome intestinal parasite in the U.S. Army pigeons.

SYMPTOMS. A pigeon only mildly infested may show no signs. One heavily infested is a sorry sight. The bird usually sits on the ground in the usual puffed-up attitude of a very sick pigeon. The head is pulled in and the chest rests on the ground. If the bird is disturbed it may try to move and topple over frontwards.

A considerable thirst is made evident by frequent drinking. The appetite is maintained, but the bird vomits much of what it eats; hence the appetite which is maintained until the pigeon's system runs out of thiamine. The pigeon loses weight rapidly.

The droppings are liquid and greenish. If a bird is examined after death, the intestine will be found to show haemorrhages and even lumps of the sloughed-off lining of the intestines. Death is caused by haemorrhage in the bowels and by inflammation of the intestines.

LIFE HISTORY. Eggs from these roundworms are passed out with the faeces. They hatch within 20 to 24 hours when the temperature is warm.

Internal Parasites of Pigeons

After changing by moulting, the larvae are infective after 3 days or more, depending on the temperature. If the larvae are swallowed by a bird, the worms mature in the small intestine and in 5 or 6 days begin to lay eggs.

CONTROL. Sanitation is of first importance. Wire-bottom porches are essential and perches and floors must be kept clean, especially when the temperature is above 60 degrees. Cleaning the loft at least twice a week should be the rule. Food and water containers must be kept covered and food must not be placed so that the birds can step on it, tracking stools on to the food and thus becoming infested.

Piperazine citrate, 8 grammes per gallon, is the drug of choice. It must be left in the drinking water for 60 hours, according to the latest findings.

THE CAPILLARIA WORM (*Capillaria columbae*)

The species, found in a large proportion of pigeons and also sometimes found in other farm and wild birds. This is a small roundworm, sometimes called a Hairworm or Threadworm. It is about 5/8 of an

HAIR WORM
(⅗ natural size)

inch long and is so thin it is often overlooked in a post-mortem examination. Capillarias infest grouse, pheasants, quail, guinea-fowl, turkeys, chickens, in addition to pigeons.

SYMPTOMS. Capillaria worms, when abundant in a pigeon, produce symptoms almost identical with those produced by the Strongyle worm. There is often enough diarrhoea to cause balls of faeces to accumulate about the vent. The tissue around the eyes and in the mouth may be pale and anaemic. There is not so much thirst as in the case of infestation by Strongyles, nor the nausea, but both thirst and appetite are depressed. Post-mortem examination may reveal a thickened reddened small intestine with sloughed areas, but only in heavily infested birds.

186

Internal Parasites of Pigeons

LIFE HISTORY. Capillaria worms lay eggs which pass out in the faeces. They must incubate for from 6 to 10 days in a warm temperature before becoming infective. The female will mature sufficiently in 16 to 26 days after the egg has been swallowed to lay eggs herself.

The larvae penetrate into the walls of the small intestine and cause extensive damage to the intestinal lining. It is this first infestation which is especially harmful to our birds, but the presence of the worms and the toxin they secrete keeps the pigeons at a low ebb when the worms are plentiful.

Some interesting facts about the eggs of capillaria should be known: they can live through very low temperatures; they are infestive for at least 7 months when left in droppings; but a helpful fact, when dried thoroughly at room temperature for 24 hours, the eggs fail to be infestive. In summer, the eggs are harmless in thin layers of droppings, but in thicker layers they will develop and live for a long while. Here is one of the best arguments for frequent loft cleaning.

The worm's life is less than 9 months. If no eggs of capillaria worms are swallowed within that time, a bird becomes entirely free of the parasites.

CONTROL. Until recently the only control method was by sanitation. That is still necessary but the worms can now be destroyed by the use of a drug, Mintic (Methyridine). Pigeons do not like the taste of it so it is necessary to fool them by taking advantage of their propensity to drink anything which looks like water when they are very thirsty. Forty (40) cubic centimeters (about 5 tablespoonsful or $1\frac{1}{3}$ ounces) are mixed thoroughly with a gallon of water. All water is removed from the loft at night. Next day at noon the treated water is supplied. The pigeons, being thirsty, will drink. Before they stop they will each get enough to remove the worms. Some may vomit but even these are cleansed of Capillaria worms. (*See footnote on page 197*).

An enterprising British Company now markets a mixture of Piperazine and Mintic which is mixed in drinking water and eliminates both Roundworms and Capillarias at one time.

In the event that Mintic is not available, Piperazine can be purchased in a 16 per cent solution from several pigeon remedy dispensers. By introducing 3 c.c.s of the 16 per cent solution directly into the crop of birds a researcher learned that Capillaria worms could be eliminated. By this method of treatment, every bird must be caught and dosed, whereas, with Mintic in the drinking water the birds dose themselves.

187

Internal Parasites of Pigeons

STOMACH WALL WORM (*Dispharynx nasuta*)

Again we take liberties in giving a worm with only a scientific name, the *Dispharynx nasuta*, a common name. It is about 1/3 of an inch long and slender in proportion. It is always found in the glandular stomach (the proventriculus) of birds and is a common parasite of many, notably game birds. It may be the most important of ruffed grouse, is frequently found in quail, Hungarian partridge, pheasants, and in such domestic fowl as turkeys, guinea-fowl, and chickens. The worm was the cause of many fatalities among U.S. Army pigeons, notably in Texas.

SYMPTOMS. Vomiting is almost a constant factor which causes many fanciers to suspect their birds of having sour crop. The usual symptoms of a sick pigeon are exhibited: ruffled feathers, lack of ambition, diarrhoea, wasting and often death. And no wonder, when we realize that the walls of the stomach are so thickened with ulcers from the worms' heads being buried in the tissues that the mucous membrane almost hides the worms, making it difficult to reach them with worm-killing drugs.

LIFE HISTORY. This worm is not directly infestive. It seems to rely upon either the Sow bug or the Pill bug to be intermediate hosts. The Pill bug is able to roll up into a ball due to the construction of its body which is composed of a number of overlapping plates, like armour, with a pair of legs on each of the larger segments. There are several species, the largest being about $\frac{1}{2}$ inch long and $\frac{1}{4}$ inch wide. All of the Pill bugs of one genera live in California, but the species of another genera are found all over the United States. All are dark grey in colour.

Sow bugs are very common, having two dozen or more species among four families and some are found everywhere in Europe and America. You find them in dark places, under stones, boards, or logs. Many are dark brown or blackish, others are dark grey spotted with white. Some Sow bugs, but not all, are able to roll themselves into a ball.

It is this ability of Pill and Sow bugs to roll into balls which makes them dangerous to pigeons. The birds probably mistake them for seeds. Four days after the bugs have eaten stomach wall worm eggs, the larvae from them may be found in the bugs' bodies where they must live for 26 days to finish developing and become infestive. After the pigeon swallows the bug and digests it, 26 days are required before the worms, which are liberated at that time, are mature and laying eggs.

Internal Parasites of Pigeons

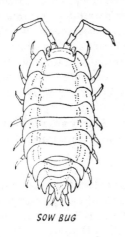

SOW BUG

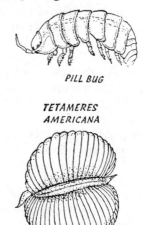

PILL BUG

TETAMERES
AMERICANA

To date, no cure is known. Prevention consists of restricting the flock to their loft which must be cleaned often enough to ensure its being free of Pill or Sow bugs. Keep the birds off the ground. In time pigeons will recover because the worms die of old age.

Tetrameres americana is another stomach wall worm rarely reported in pigeons and much smaller than *Dispharynx nasuta*, being 1/6 of an inch in length and bright red in colour. The female lives within the stomach wall, the male outside. Females are globular, being as wide as long, whereas the male is thread-like.

This worm also requires an intermediate host, the grasshopper and the cockroach being two certain ones and probably there are others, possibly those bugs which curl up into balls.

Tetrameres pissapina has been reported as an infestation in the glandular stomach of a dead pigeon studied in Uruguay, the first such report I have been able to find. The lesions produced caused the stomach to be unable to function properly.

The author of the report states that the outward appearance of the pigeon was 'identical to that produced by *Imeria confusa*'. This is a form of coccidiosis.

THE EYE WORM

On rare occasions pigeons develop an eye disease caused by eye

189

worms. How they acquired the parasite was long a puzzle. But research with chickens showed that larvae of the parasite, *Oxyspirura mansoni*, were often found in the abdominal cavity of cockroaches which lived in chicken coops. The roach, when eaten by the chicken, enters the crop in a crushed condition. The larvae escape, ascend the gullet and reach the eye via the tear duct (naso-lacrimal). Some of the larvae make their exit from the roaches in the chicken's mouth and within 20 minutes have reached the eye.

Since pigeons do have eye worms, how do they acquire them? Surely from eating bugs which have eaten eggs of the eye worm. Do they eat roaches? If not, what bugs?

Is it not now abundantly clear how parasites can weaken our pigeons to the point of making successful breeding or racing an impossibility?

Another analogy is in the effect Hookworms have on human beings, dogs, cats, or any other animal affected. The Hookworm lives by sucking blood. They live on the blood serum. So does *Ornithostrongylus* in our pigeons. The infested human being is listless, lacks ambition, has no endurance, and why not? Our pigeons with the equivalent parasite act much the same. The first impression may not lead us to suspect they are infested. But get them to do something strenuous; let the man chop wood, the dog hunt, the pigeon fly a race and you very soon discover that something is amiss. How could they be normal when they do not have sufficient red blood cells to carry oxygen to the tissues. Without a doubt, these parasites have been the cause of discarding millions of excellent pigeons which have not possessed sufficient speed or stamina, when the real trouble lay in the birds not having sufficient red blood cells or being poisoned by toxins. And that is always the fault of the owner, not the pigeon.

Winter in the north is the period during which time the pigeons seem to improve in physical appearance. I think you will agree that the reason is not to be found in the temperature, but rather in the fact that cold prevents parasite eggs from incubating and thus becoming infestive. If a capillaria egg must remain in a warm environment for 6 days before it becomes infestive and the temperature stays cold, that egg is unable to incubate. But if manure piles are permitted to accumulate under perches, they will become warm in the interior by bacterial action and eggs will incubate in winter. Therefore, reasonable cleanliness is imperative even in cold weather.

By now it must also be apparent, that no pigeon loft should ever be

Internal Parasites of Pigeons

without feeders which prevent stools from touching the food. I have seen many lofts where flat dishes were used and these dishes were kept scrupulously clean, but the floors were neglected. The pigeons have faeces on their feet when they jump into the pans. All the grains they touch become infested. Grains may stick to the bird's feet. When they .jump out they leave this grain among faeces on the floor and there you have Achilles heel again. Just that small neglect may make it impossible to clear up a flock.

Another fact only recently brought to light is the importance of keeping coops as free from dust as possible. The eggs of some intestinal parasites are so small and light that the fanning of pigeons' wings can actually blow them up off the floor. If they adhere to light particles of dust, then all the more are they likely to float. Not that they stay aloft for long, but it is likely that they can blow up into the nostrils and on to food. When lofts are cleaned twice a week or every 5 days at the most, if moist sand is spread on the floor, it will generally be 5 days in drying sufficiently to become dust.

If sand is used and not changed after 5 days, pigeons eating the coarser particles for grit can quite easily eat worm eggs clinging to the grit.

Have you watched your birds when they have been freed from the loft to see what they eat? You will notice they will pick at grass and other green material. Then, have you realized that if pigeons have defaecated on the grass, there will most certainly be worm eggs clinging to the succulent blades? There will be and doubtless this is one minor source of infestation—yet another Achilles heel.

TREMATODES (FLUKES)

In conversations among pigeon fanciers, one hears so little talk about flukes that one would think they were no problem. But they may be. Flukes are leaf-like flatworms not made up of segments as tapeworms are, but consist of a single organism. Adult flukes have suckers or other appendages which enable them to stay in one place, but the immature forms have locomotive structures. Twenty-eight different species have been reported in pigeons. Most of them, however, are of slight importance and only a portion of this number have been found in Europe and North America.

The life history of all flukes is quite complex as they live in more than one host. Fortunately, most of their intermediate hosts are animals

191

which pigeons seldom, if ever, eat. Flukes which infest pigeons are hermaphrodites, having both male and female sex organs.

LIFE HISTORY. Fluke eggs pass from the pigeon in the droppings and must be several days outside the bird to become infestive of the host, while the eggs are embryonating. The eggs must reach water, either by being dropped into it with the faeces or washed in with rain. Eggs hatch in the water. The embryo, called a *miracidium*, swims until it locates a snail. Once inside its host, the embryo goes through changes becoming a *sporocyst*. The sporocyst turns into a *cercaria*. The cercaria has a body which will be the mature fluke and a tail with which it swims. When liberated from the snail it may seek another one, or a tadpole, or fish and bore its way inside where it then becomes a *metacercaria*. If it is in a snail eaten by a pigeon, the fluke is liberated and takes up its residence in the pigeon, growing to maturity in some organ, depending upon the kind of fluke it is.

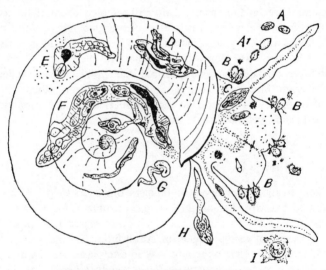

FLUKE STAGES, DIAGRAM OF LIFE-CYCLE

A. Egg . A1. Miracidium escaping from egg B. Miracidium entering snail C. Sporocyst D. Redia, with daughter redia escaping E. Daughter redia. F. Older daughter redia with cercariae G. Cercaria. H. Cercaria escaping from snail. I. Encysted cercariae

Internal Parasites of Pigeons

Echinostoma revolutum. This parasite is about 2/3 inch long and 1/6 inch wide. It lives its adult life in the intestine and cloaca. Generally infection takes place by pigeons eating snails which they probably eat for calcium. This species of fluke can be especially troublesome to pigeons. One investigator removed 5,000 of them from 8 pigeons. Initial infestation causes sickness and the heavily infested birds may die.

SYMPTOMS. Bloody diarrhoea is an early symptom followed by rapid loss of weight. The birds lose appetite, become very weak, develop abnormal thirst due partly to the loss of fluids from the diarrhoea. Pigeons usually die within a week or 10 days. Internally, the breast muscles decrease in size, the liver enlarges, the intestine is congested and a blood-tinged mucous secretion is usually found inside it.

LIFE HISTORY. The life history follows the general life history given above. Snails are the intermediate hosts and pigeons seem very fond of snails.

Hypoderaeum conoideum. This parasite is similar in size, appearance and life history to *E. revolutum*.

Echinopharyphium recurvatum is also similar to the above.

Tamerlania bragai is a tiny fluke only about 1/10 inch long. It is contracted from land snails and lives in the pigeon's liver and urinary tract. It has been reported in Brazil, Puerto Rico and Philippine Islands In small numbers they do little damage, but what they would do to a pigeon flying long distances we can only surmise.

FLUKE - ECHINOSTOMA REVOLUTUM

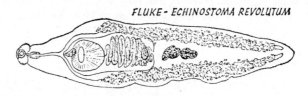

Parasites of this species were found in 19 out of 20 pigeons studied in central Puerto Rico. The kidney walls were enlarged, the kidney pelvis and the collecting tubules were dilated. In Brazil 15·7 per cent of the pigeons studied harboured this fluke, with urinary tracts in the same swollen and enlarged condition.

In addition to the above, there are many other flukes which are known to be capable of infesting pigeons experimentally, but which are never found naturally in the birds because they do not eat their specific

Internal Parasites of Pigeons

intermediate hosts: fish, for example. One study, however, found a severe diarrhoea in pigeons which was caused by the water-fowl fluke, *C. Cornutus*.

TREATMENT. When flukes are known to exist in a flock or in a single bird, tetrachlorethylene is a fairly effective and safe treatment. The dose is 0·2 c.c. for a pigeon, given on an empty stomach.

Carbon tetrachloride, ¼ c.c., in some bland oil given by a syringe inserted into the crop, is recommended by one student.

PREVENTION. The fact that flukes are dependent on snails to be transmitted to pigeons, makes it imperative that we keep our birds away from ponds where snails live. If we have such a pond from which we cannot keep our pigeons, the snails in it can be killed with copper sulphate, which also will kill the fish and the algae. If we use enough copper sulphate to give a concentration of 1 : 500,000 for 24 hours it will suffice.

TAPEWORMS

Pigeons are not immune to tapeworms. Occasionally a bird is reported with a different form, but the common pigeon tapeworm the world over is described in the following discussion; any others are apparently inconsequential.

Apornia delafondi (also called *Tenia delafondi*). This is a worm made up of many segments. You may find it in the small intestine any length, depending upon how old the worm is, up to 5½ inches long.

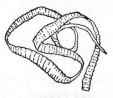

TAPEWORM

Occasionally a report will be found of a student's having discovered other species of tapeworms in pigeons. Thus *Davainea proglottina* and *Raillietina tetragona* have been described. However, the number of other species which might live in pigeons as they do in other bird species has not been determined. If the pigeon were as omnivorous as

194

Internal Parasites of Pigeons

the domestic fowl and ate the tapeworm hosts which these species eat, the picture might be different.

LIFE HISTORY. All species of tapeworms require intermediate hosts in order to be transferred back to the primary host. A few years ago the list of hosts was small, but it is growing annually as more and more insects and other animals are discovered as having eaten worm eggs passed out in the droppings. These intermediate hosts become infested from the eggs which become cysts in their bodies, a process requiring about 3 weeks. When eaten by the primary host, the egg covering is digested. Freed from their cysts, these *scolexes* (heads) attach themselves to the intestine and grow segments which, when sufficiently mature, lay eggs and start the cycle again which requires about 6 weeks in all.

A familiar illustration of the tapeworm and its hosts can be found in the dog. His principal hosts are, for one, the flea; for the other, the rabbit.

No one has as yet determined any specific insect as the intermediate host for the common pigeon tapeworm. It may well be found to be a louse. It must be some living creature which eats droppings and which is eaten in turn by the pigeon. It is possible that pigeons may eat lice when they preen themselves, or they may mistake a Pill bug or some similar creature for a kernel of grain.

SYMPTOMS. Except in the case of a rather heavy infestation, symptoms may be obscure. Droppings are likely to be watery or of a catarrhal diarrhoea nature. Some birds show leg weakness or paralysis. Mild infestation slows race birds, produces unthriftiness.

Occasionally you may find segments of tapeworms in the droppings. Their eggs may be found in faecal examination. Usually, however, they are discovered when a dead pigeon is dissected. The intestine should be laid on a table and split lengthwise, the contents examined for these flat parasites. If you suspect them but find none because of mucus or faeces, lay the opened intestine in a pan of water; the intestine will sink but the worms will tend to float, keeping attached by their heads to the gut wall.

CONTROL. If a flock is found to have tapeworms, it becomes necessary to look for any suspicious intermediate host. Be sure all body insects are eliminated, all bugs which the birds could eat. Frequent cleaning of

Internal Parasites of Pigeons

perches and removal of manure is imperative. Prevention is the first line of defence.

TREATMENT. When you know the flock or any single bird is infested, don't waste time medicating with old-fashioned drugs, such as kamela, which simply cause the worm to drop off a section of its body. Use a drug which makes the head let go. See Chapter 4 for details on the use of drugs.

FILARIA

Filaria worms are long slender creatures which are found in various parts of an animal's body. The best known of these is the heart worm which is spread by mosquitoes and lives in the hearts of dogs.

Pigeons have their filaria worms also, *Eulimdana clava*. This parasite lives in the tissue just under the skin, but fortunately, it is probably not common. From one pigeon 45 worms were removed, each winding about in the sub-cutaneous tissue.

There is no known cure. Prevention is a matter of keeping mosquitoes away from pigeons.

POULTRY PARASITES

There are several important chicken and turkey intestinal parasites which are of no importance to pigeon fanciers, chiefly because the parasites have intermediate hosts which omnivorous poultry eat and pigeons do not. A pigeon fancier reading poultry books may wonder why a book on pigeon diseases makes no mention of, say, gapeworms or certain tapeworms. Gapeworm eggs are eaten by earthworms, which are eaten in turn by chickens; pigeons do not eat earthworms. Fortunately, our pigeons have fewer parasites on this account.

When pigeons lose their feathers under the throat and over the crop, one parasite to suspect is a poultry louse which shears off the feathers close to the skin and leaves only a stub. Many fanciers are certain that the condition is brought about by friction where the birds rub the skin over the edge of a food tray or drinking water holder. To be certain as to whether lice are the cause, examine the feathers on the periphery of the defeathered area and if you see a tiny black speck on a feather close to the skin, use a reading glass and examine it. I have done this for many fanciers, pulled out feathers with the lice on them and

196

upon presenting them to experts, confirmed my own diagnosis in every case, that the creature was a poultry louse.

To destroy them, use perch paint or hang a Vapona bar close to the pigeon. We found that poultry mites do not seem to live in lofts with Vapona bars but that to kill an infestation it is necessary to keep the birds in a small space with one bar in it: at the recommended one bar to 1,000 cubic feet of space, where there is a window in the loft, the dilution is too great for this particular parasite.

Note to page 187.

Another method is to give each, 3 c.c.s of a 10% solution of Piperazine, in a tube and syringe, directly into the crop.

13

Tumours and Cancer

That lump growing under the pigeon's skin which develops slowly, that rapidly growing tumour on the wing, that soft pliant swelling, those lumps in the breast of your bird—what are they? Will they cost his life? Should they be removed? Will they return if they are removed? Many pigeon owners have many misconceptions about growths.

A tumour is a growth of new, useless tissue growing independently of the surrounding tissue but not replacing it. Even canker in the mouth, when it grows as a lump, is a tumour.

In medical terminology the term *malignant* means a virulent growth that tends to go from bad to worse.

A *benign* growth is only a relative term. Compared to a malignant tumour, it stays within itself and does not recur elsewhere. But what growth could really be benign? Canker? Even so small and seemingly innocuous a growth causes discomfort and sometimes pain. No tumour is really benign in the common sense of the word.

Cancer—not to be confused with canker—is a malignant tumour. The word comes from the Latin, meaning *crab*. This implies that it is a growth which invades other tissue by extending crab-like tentacles. But this is an old definition, hardly acceptable in the light of newer knowledge. There is cancer which grows in a lump apparently as benign as any non-malignant tumour. This lump, in the lungs let us say, sends off a bud or cell into the blood stream which is halted in the skin on a pigeon's back, where it grows. Careful miscroscopic examination of the lump after removal discloses that it is tissue characteristic of the lungs, even though it is growing in the skin. This is called a *metastasis*. Surely such a tumour is a cancer. Perhaps a lump will appear in a bird's neck. It shells out easily in the hands of a surgeon. It looks benign. But down the lymph chain, a month after the tumour's removal, another lump

198

grows which is found to be a tumour with the same characteristics as the first. The first growth, then, was definitely malignant, even though it was not invasive in a crab-like sense.

Pigeons are subject to several forms of cancer, some serious, others practically harmless if discovered and treated in time. *Carcinomas* arise in the skin, in the intestinal linings, and in all tissues which develop from the same original embryonic sources. *Sarcomas* are tumours made up of connective tissue—the part of the bird's body which binds it together and supports it.

Under these two classes, carcinomas and sarcomas, fall the various kinds of tumours. If your veterinarian tells you your pigeon has a *malignant melanotic sarcoma*, you know it is a tumour of coloured connective tissue, that it gives off buds or invades the adjacent tissue, or both. A pigment cell must have gone wild.

What causes these growths? The causes of a few kinds are known. Some believe a virus is the initiating agent of certain forms, if not all. Irritation; certain hormones; contact with irritating chemicals—all are known to cause some types of growths; for others there is no explanation. Perhaps mutations or sudden changes in the characteristics of a cell are induced by irritation and once started, simply grow out of control.

When a cut or abrasion occurs in an animal, the body heals it by the growth of surrounding cells. Something in the body applies a brake to this healing growth at the right time. If it didn't, every cut might grow out of all proportion. We are not sure what this brake is. The cancer cells have no brake applied by the body and grow by cell division on and on until they overwhelm the host.

This overpowering growth may kill a bird in several ways: (1) It gives off poisons. Lest this fact be doubted, one has only to remember the cases of pigeons with even small tumours, who became listless and prematurely old. When the tumours were removed, rejuvenation was effected. (2) It may exert pressure on vital organs which prevents their proper functioning. (3) It may create an obstruction, such as a growth within the intestines which prevents passage of food. (4) It may increase the size of a gland, as when a tumour develops in the spleen and inhibits the free passage of blood through it.

Diagnosis of malignant growths is accomplished by removing a section of the growth and preparing it by an elaborate process of slicing and staining, until it can be examined with a microscope by a pathologist who can classify it.

Tumours and Cancer

Tumours in pigeons are less common than in dogs or human beings. In one series of pigeons of all ages which were studied, 1 in 170 was found carrying a tumour. Had all 170 of the birds examined been old, the percentage would doubtless have been much higher.

Cancers of the female sex organs are most common. Carcinomas are less common than sarcomas. Fatty tumours are not infrequent, especially in birds more than seven years of age.

While it is not often seen appearing spontaneously, the *Rous's sarcoma* is one of the most studied of all the bird cancers. It is of virus origin and easily transmitted.

Many may have heard of mouse tumours which are produced by treating their skin with a coal tar product, debenzanthrozene. The same substance failed to produce a like effect in pigeons. It has been found possible to produce a pigeon cancer by *injecting* the chemical dissolved in benzol. In this case, the tumours produced were transplantable and apparently were not of virus origin.

One of the most frequently found growths in pigeons is a deep-red spongy, rapidly growing skin tumour which is currently being studied in several laboratories. There is no telling where it will appear. Because of my interest in pigeon tumours, many birds with these tumours have been brought to me. Some had a large growth on the side of the chest under the wing, some had them on the thighs, some on the back between the wings and several on the wings themselves.

In every case I assured the owner the lumps would dry up and fall off leaving the bird no worse for the experience. They did, and having healed it was difficult to find the area from which the tumours had grown.

Hen pigeons frequently develop ovarian tumours which terminate their productive life. In the last stages the growths are so large they cause the abdomen to bulge. Large cankerous growths within the abdomen produce the same effects. I have removed five of these to date and the pigeons have recovered.

In youngsters canker in the navel produces a swelling. When the bird is treated with canker cure, the lump is reduced in size and finally can be pulled out through the enlarged opening of the navel.

Some hens deposit large amounts of fat under the skin of the abdomen, giving the appearance of a growth. It would seem the lump would interfere with the laying of eggs but it does not. As the breeding season progresses the fat is absorbed.

14

Pigeon Surgery

There are times when the pigeon fancier will need to perform minor operations for the relief of his bird. It is sometimes impossible, inconvenient, or economically unfeasible to call a veterinary surgeon, occasionally there is a minor emergency in the loft which requires immediate attention on the owner's part.

Surgery of any kind is not a pleasant duty, since the person caring for the bird usually fears that he is hurting it and since his own emotions and imagination credit feeling where it often does not exist.

But pigeon owners should know how to attend to abscesses, clean and suture wounds if necessary, relieve birds which are cropbound, remove superficial tumours, set a broken bone, as well as how to take care of such simple things as beak and nail trimming.

Among the instruments, drugs and accessories that may be needed for the minor surgery that an owner will undertake, are the following:

Razor blades	Tincture of Metaphen (Nitromeriol)
Sharp knife	Mineral oil
Sharp shears	Adhesive tape
Nail file	Narrow gauze bandage
Clippers	Needles for suturing
Toothpicks	Silk for suturing
Iodine	Catgut for suturing
Peroxide	Scotch tape

Now for a brief description of common home surgical procedures which, with care, can be performed by any pigeon owner.

WOUNDS

Depending upon their severity, wounds need more or less surgical

201

attention. First the wound must be cleaned thoroughly both of dirt and of shredded tissue, which will die and become gangrenous if it is not removed. Cut or torn muscles should be sutured, or sewn as the layman calls it, with catgut, which is left in. A little antibiotic applied to the area before the skin is brought together often suffices to prevent infection. Feathers should be pulled a ¼ inch back from each edge of the wound, after which, the skin can be sutured with silk, or with mono-filament fish line, its *inside surfaces touching*. The silk can be removed in 5 days. It is a wise precaution to paint the stitches daily with peroxide or tincture of metaphen to prevent stitch infection.

CROPBOUND

This is the term usually applied to a condition in which the bird, having eaten a goodly quantity of roughage—sometimes because of a perverted appetite—over-distends the crop to such an extent that its normal function ceases. Food begins to decompose. Some birds eat queer objects which may stick in the crop, causing pain and often death. Both impactions and foreign objects may be quite easily removed.

The feathers are pulled from the area to be incised. If possible, a tiny amount of local anaesthetic, such as procaine, is injected under the skin, and more into the crop tissue where the incision is to be made. When the anaesthetic has taken effect, the skin and the crop may be opened. The incision should be no longer than is necessary to remove the largest of the impacted particles.

Any blood that is present can be sponged off with wet cotton which has been squeezed out. The crop content is then worked out through the incision with the aid of a rolling motion made with the fingers and thumb grasping the crop on each side. Any food which refuses to work out by this means may be removed with forceps or tweezers. A foreign object can usually be lifted out in this manner without difficulty.

After the area has been disinfected with hydrogen peroxide, the out-side surfaces of the crop are sutured together with gut. The skin is sutured last with silk, or with mono-filament fish line, which can be removed in 4 or 5 days. This skin *must* be sutured with its inside layers touching. Healing will usually be quite uneventful.

To avoid stretching the crop and having the stitches come loose, the bird must be fed only a small portion of its normal food requirement until the healing is complete.

Pigeon Surgery

ABSCESSES AND BUMBLEFOOT

Pigeon keepers sometimes find that after injuries, their birds have abscesses which need attention. The pus forming in birds is not a liquid, such as that found in mammalian abscesses. It is of a cheeselike consistency and must be scraped out.

In 'bumblefoot', for example, the large central pad becomes infected and swells. In this case, or in any other where abscess formation occurs, tincture of iodine seems to serve nicely as an antiseptic. The skin over the abscess is opened with a sharp instrument—scalpel, razor blade, or knife blade—and the edges parted widely enough to expose the cheesy pus, which is then scraped out as completely as possible. The inside is flushed with iodine and the abscess left to heal from the bottom. Bumblefoot had best be covered with a bandage, the bird kept in a clean cage, and the bandage changed with fresh medicated salve every few days until healing is complete.

TUMOUR REMOVAL

Superficial tumours, which are obviously in or under the skin, can be removed by applying a little procaine about the area, pulling the feathers, painting with iodine and cutting a neat line all around the tumour, as close to it as possible without cutting into its substance. When the skin has been incised, the tumour is held up and the tissue under it freed by scraping with the tip of the blade, rather than by cutting it off.

If blood appears, a needle and catgut can be run under the vessel and it can be tied off. The skin is brought together and sutured with silk, or with mono-filament fish line, which can be removed in 5 days.

BONE SETTING

Since one of the most common troubles with pigeons is broken bones, the home veterinarian should know something about bone setting. This is especially true today with so many television aerials on rooftops with which the pigeons collide.

Bone setting usually is successful in simple fractures, especially if the break is recent and the sharp ends have not cut the soft tissue. Of the several ways of setting, the use of splints is simplest. Scotch tape is excellent in bone setting. The leg is pulled out until the fracture is 'reduced' (i.e. set end to end), the feathers are smoothed down tightly against it and the tape is wound around the leg several times and cut off. That may give sufficient support. If the feathers do not give adequate support, then add a few toothpicks or matchsticks for splints as you wind the Scotch tape about the leg.

If the tape is applied too tightly, however, the circulation will be cut off and the bird will lose its leg from gangrene.

Another method preferred by many people makes use of liquid rubber adhesive, such as is used in hospitals. It is available at most chemists. Wipe the leg free from grease by using a little ether. Apply a layer of the adhesive. Before it dries, wind a layer of narrow gauze bandage once around. Then apply more adhesive, lay a toothpick (several for larger birds) in it for a splint and wind the bandage around again and cut it off. It will stick and make a strong, light support.

Still another way to set a fracture is to mix a little plaster of Paris with water, soak a narrow piece of gauze bandage in it, and wind this around the leg, holding the leg in place for 5 to 10 minutes until the plaster has dried.

Most bird bones will set by 15 or 16 days, so that the splint may then be removed—which is not always as easy as it sounds. Adhesive tape may be removed by applying alcohol; rubber adhesive is dissolved by vanishing cream; and plaster of Paris slowly softens in vinegar. Scotch tape can be cut off or unwound with the expectation that many, but not all, of the feathers under it will be pulled out. All of these solvents should, of course, be washed off when the job is finished.

In setting wing fractures, some experts advise clipping or pulling feathers, but good results may often be obtained with the feathers left intact. The bones are set and a splint applied. Then the wings are both folded in place against the body and gently bound with bandage gauze covered with adhesive tape so that the bird cannot move them. Fifteen days later the bandage and splint may be removed. After that it usually takes a week or more for the stiffness to leave the wings sufficiently for the bird to fly.

FEATHER REPAIR

A pigeon's feather is not a dead tissue but very much alive. It is easy enough to pull a broken feather and let a new one grow in. But what if the feather is important to a racing bird? It can be repaired by grafting and will often mend satisfactorily.

Pigeon Surgery

Use a very sharp knife and make a slanting cut on the quill. From another pigeon, pull the corresponding feather and cut it off on a slant to match the cut-off broken quill. Now use a small sewing needle. Push the eye end half-way into the piece to be grafted. Push the sharp end into the stub in the bird's wing and be sure the ends match. Now close the wing carefully and bind both wings to the pigeon's sides. Leave them for three or four days. By then the feathers will usually have grown together and the bandage may be removed.

EGG RETENTION

There are times when hen pigeons form such large eggs that they are unable to pass them. The bird sits on the nest at first, but after a few days she may sit on the floor, showing great discomfort.

Examination shows the bones of the pelvis to be extended sideways, and gentle pressure will generally reveal two eggs. One egg can usually be moved alone by applying some mineral oil with a medicine dropper and massaging with the finger inserted in the cloaca. If this method fails, and the egg can be seen, the end must be punctured, the contents drained out, and the shell cracked and worked out with the finger. The second egg will usually pass out of its own accord.

BEAK TRIMMING

It definitely pays to trim pigeons' beaks when they have grown into abnormal shapes. Sometimes the lower beak grows too fast and pushes the upper to one side giving a scissor effect. Then, too, the upper beak often grows in a downward hook and because there is no wear from the tip of the beak against the feed tray, the tip cannot wear and the pressure causes it to bend more.

At the very start of such abnormalities, a pair of fingernail clippers can be employed to good advantage. If the lower beak is too long it must be trimmed short enough to end just below the tip of the upper beak. The upper beak, if it grows too long, should be trimmed off to look like a normal one. Sometimes, when the tip refuses to grow out straight, a sharp nail file can be used to make a V-shaped groove across the top of the beak and a short distance, 1/16 or 1/8 inch, from the tip.

The initial trimming is merely the start. The beak should be examined at least once a week and trimmed until it eventually is normal and the tips wear off together as is natural. A lot can be done with a nail file in pointing up the beak when it is back almost to normal.

205

Pigeon Surgery

NAIL TRIMMING

Pigeons are probably descendants of the Rock Pigeon which lived on hard surfaces and wore off their nail tips. Our fancied birds, which live on wooden perches, wire netting, sand, shavings, etc., almost never stand on stones which will wear the nails down properly. Sometimes the nails grow so long that the toes are bent backward when the pigeon stands on a flat surface.

A good nail clipper or strong scissors can bring much comfort to a bird with long talons. Observe the length of a four-months-old youngster's nails and clip the nails of old birds off to that length.

15

Sanitation and Disease Prevention

These two subjects, sanitation and disease prevention, are so closely allied that they must be considered together. Sanitation is basic in disease prevention, as basic as isolation. This chapter constitutes a summary of all that has gone before.

Sanitation in the loft helps to prevent virus, bacterial and fungus diseases as well as to keep parasites in check or eliminate them altogether. It is one of the principal bases of health and success in dealing with pigeons. It keeps fancy pigeons in show form, is fundamental in squab production and gives homers a chance to do their best in racing.

Sanitation involves loft care. Ventilation, cleaning, feeding, watering, bathing, even sunlight exposure are all concerned with this subject as well as isolation, disinfection, preventive medication and prevention of fielding.

What constitutes a filthy environment? Many factors, some of which are invisible. A filthy loft is not necessarily one with inch-high droppings under the perches. One of the top English homer fancier cleans his loft only twice a year, according to his own written words; a prominent and successful fancier in Massachusetts, U.S.A., never cleans his until the breeding season. Aesthetically filthy, yes, but perhaps not medically filthy. There are many worse practices than leaving dung on the floors. If successful men do it, perhaps it is in order to ask, might they not be more successful if they removed the droppings frequently? Perhaps these men feed the birds so that their food never comes in contact with droppings.

A filthy loft may be one infested with red mites, one particularly in the U.S.A. without mosquito protection; one with pigeon flies developing in the nest bowls; one with Psittacosis spreaders among the birds; one with bath water older than 36 hours; one with lice on the birds or Para-

207

Sanitation and Disease Prevention

typhoid in many of the pigeons. These things one would not see from a casual observation, but the owner knows, or should know, if he is giving proper attention to his charges.

In disease prevention our aim must be: (1) To prevent our birds from coming into contact with other pigeons, poultry, rodents, or the places these other species have been. (2) To prevent vectors such as sparrows, or mosquitoes, from transporting infection from other species to our birds. (3) To prevent our pigeons from being annoyed and made anaemic by insects. (4) To keep them away from contamination from intestinal parasites. (5) To prevent their being poisoned. (6) To ensure proper ventilation. (7) To prevent overcrowding. (8) To prevent the spread of established diseases within the loft. (9) To keep our birds in such glowing health that those diseases which develop in weakened birds, may never get a chance to develop. (10) To feed sufficient food and no more.

Here are the *whys* and the *hows* of the above points.

1. *Prevent contact with pigeons, poultry, rodents, or other species capable of transmitting diseases*

Why? The answer is obvious. Poultry yards, barn yards, wild pigeons coming to one's loft, are all sources of disease contamination. You have read about the diseases which are transmissible from other species to pigeons, and now you know how important it is to keep the species separated.

How? By not permitting an open loft where one knows his birds can fly to these sources; by preventing wild pigeons from even alighting on the loft, much less coming in and eating or living with our birds; by destroying every wild pigeon as soon after it enters as possible; by quarantining every stray homer; by covering fly pens to prevent droppings of wild pigeons or wild birds from falling in.

And of great importance, as I shall point out in a later chapter, is the trapping of all the wild pigeons in the neighbourhood, even if it entails a concerted effort by combined pigeon fanciers to have city ordinances changed to permit such trappings and eradication.

2. *Prevent vectors from transporting infection from other species or from pigeon to pigeon*

Why? One answer is obvious: Because we want our birds to keep

Sanitation and Disease Prevention

well. A less obvious reason is that we do not want our pigeons blamed for being reservoirs of infection for other species. During one epidemic of sleeping sickness in horses, authorities knowing that the virus had been demonstrated in pigeons, stated that perhaps pigeons were the latent source which kept the virus alive and that mosquitoes transmitted it from them to the horses. Swine erysipelas, too, infects pigeons but we do not want our birds blamed as being the reservoir. If mosquitoes cannot reach our pigeons, then our birds certainly cannot be the reservoir.

How? By not only screening our lofts, making it impossible for a single mosquito to enter, but by spraying with drugs with long residual effects which will stick to walls and screens and kill mosquitoes and flies which light on them. Also by including enough phenol or other mosquito repellant in our indoor sprays or paints to repel insects.

Easiest of all methods is to hang Vapona bars in the lofts so that every flying insect which enters will be killed, as well as external parasites if any are making their home on our birds.

By using wire on the flies and porches with mesh small enough to preclude sparrows and by providing tops to the flies and porches so that bird droppings are prevented from falling in.

3. *Prevent pigeons from being annoyed by insects*

Why? A bird which is kept awake at nights by mosquitoes, lice, red bugs, ticks, bed-bugs, cannot possibly be kept in the same good condition as the ones free from such annoyances. And remember, too, that these pests often cause anaemia as well as nervousness.

How? By studying all the means of insect control and employing them; not by sitting comfortably in an easy chair and planning to do it some day.

4. *Keep pigeons away from internal parasitic contamination*

Why? Because these worms and protozoa weaken our birds so materially. They cause anaemia, poison the blood, and generally weaken the birds. Coccidia even change the blood picture considerably, especially the blood sugar.

How? By cleaning the loft thoroughly once every 5 days during summer and once a week during winter. By changing drinking water once a day. By never leaving bath water available where droppings can fall

Sanitation and Disease Prevention

into it for more than 12 hours. By meticulously preventing any food or grit from any contamination by droppings.

This means that the food must not be thrown down on the floor where there are droppings nor left on the clean floor where birds may soil it. A covered food tray which prevents pigeons from stepping on food is almost essential. Some of the best fliers clean the floor with scrapers and mop with a damp rag before feeding and then give only the amount of food that the birds will eat in a few minutes.

Self-feeders can also be arranged which preclude food contamination and prevent the food from scattering or coming in contact with droppings.

Parasitic contamination can also be prevented by using floor coverings, litter, of absorbent material. Dry sand has been proved satisfactory but it is heavy. Dampened peat moss is favoured by some but it tends to become dusty and blow about. In America dehydrated sugar cane is greatly favoured because it is absorbent and clean and, like peat moss, makes an excellent garden fertilizer when mixed with the droppings. Shavings are also clean, light, and absorbent. Chopped straw, such as the kind used in poultry houses, makes a good litter. Pigeons do not scratch as hens do and spend much less time on the floor than poultry.

The use of wire bottoms on porches and flies wherever possible helps greatly in keeping parasitic worms in check. In a personal communication from a veterinarian in charge of U.S. Signal Corps pigeons during the war, he says in commenting on what I have called the Strongyle worm, 'This worm is the most virulent found in pigeon lofts. As you know, I had a chance to observe many thousands of pigeons during my military service and found that, as long as we changed the litter (sand) on the floor at one-week intervals, and kept the birds on wire porches, we had no difficulty from any of the worm parasites.'

Birds must be restricted from picking about under wire porches, which should be screened to keep them away from the areas.

Open loft must be restricted. We cannot permit pigeons to eat snails and other intermediate hosts of tapeworms and expect to keep them free from these parasites. Nor can we permit them to eat Sow and Pill bugs without paying the penalty of having sickly birds infested with stomach wall worms. Even pigeons which only occasionally light on the ground may find these intermediate hosts coming out from under old boards. Miscellaneous old boards lying around the loft should be removed and, if overturned, the bugs should be scuffed and mashed. Inside the coop, derris sprinkled on the floor and in cracks will kill all such insects and the flapping of wings will also help spread this insect poison, harmless to the birds.

5. Prevent Poisoning

Why? No answer needed.

How? By watching the food, no mould being permitted; by being careful there is no food or water where insect sprays may drift on it and contaminate it.

Fielding should be restricted, especially in spring when agricultural fertilizer is being spread. Often mixtures with tankage, bone meal and other ingredients attractive to pigeons is spread and the birds are poisoned and die after eating it. Caution should be practised when garden sprays are used on nearby foliage so that pigeons do not eat the succulent leaves and become poisoned by the sprays. Rodent poison, left where pigeons can reach it or when it is dragged from a safe place by a rat, can cause deaths. Warfarin mixed with grain is one of the principal rat poisons today and it, as any other, should be well covered to preclude pigeons reaching it.

6. Insure adequate ventilation

Why? No positive answer can be given except that it seems that pigeons given the maximum amount of air, no matter how cold the temperature, are the healthiest. Pigeon fanciers assure us this is true, but there are no published figures to test it that I have been able to find. There are some results showing that birds kept in lofts with no ventilation whatever were a sickly lot. And of course the Bible says that Noah had 7 of nearly all the species of animals in the world in a ship 3 stories high, with the only ventilation being found in a roof opening 22 inches square.

How? Noah's ventilating system, however adequate it was for the birds and animals, would not suffice today. We know that even in climates where the temperature drops to 30 degrees below zero, F., pigeons are kept in lofts completely open on one side. They fluff out their feathers, 'pull in their necks', and thrive. But is this best? For early squab raising it is not, because too many youngsters will freeze. Some protection is necessary. On cold nights a loft that can be completely closed, just for the night, seems somewhat more humane and certainly puts the owner more at ease. A loft arranged to prevent wind from blowing through it is advisable. We are still told that 'draughts are sure to cause disease'. Many persons continue to believe that draughts cause human colds, when recent discoveries show they have little or nothing to do with colds; it is virus contracted from another person having a cold which is responsible.

I know of a loft which is divided so that the front half is completely open and the other section closed except for a 3-ft. square window. Both sections are the same otherwise. The birds all chose the closed section in which to spend the night, using the open section for most of the day.

In damp, badly ventilated lofts, there seems to be much more disease than in airy lofts into which the sun can shine.

7. Do not overcrowd

Why? Some fanciers tell us that so long as there is a perch for every bird the loft is not overcrowded. Others will look into such a loft and tell the owner he has too many birds. If fertility is considered, we may observe that pigeon eggs are more likely to be fertile in under-populated lofts.

How? We can take lessons from the big squab farms where every inch is precious. Long experience has taught them that: so long as all of the other features of sanitation are meticulously cared for; and if every pair of birds has its own nest box; if there is ample opportunity for all the birds to eat at the same time; then there is little cause to be alarmed about the health of the birds even though it may seem that the lofts are crowded.

Homing pigeons, Flights, Tipplers and other breeds spending much time on the wing need less space in the loft than the same birds kept for breeders or as prisoners.

8. Prevent the spread of established diseases in the loft

Why? To avoid disappointment, save money, keep the birds healthy.
How? This is where quarantine and medication are most important. Every loft or breeding establishment needs a quarantine cage and preferably two. Flying lofts obviously can do well with two: one in which to keep strays until their owners are found; another in which to put ailing birds either for diagnosis or treatment.

When I was a boy, if our pigeons got Sour Crop many of them died.

Sanitation and Disease Prevention

We isolated them, but often the infection had been started and we were too late. Today, when it starts in the U.S.A., we dose the entire flock with an antibiotic in the drinking water and the disease is conquered in a day or two. So it is with many diseases: instead of quarantining or letting the bird die, we simply dose them as a flock, or individually, with the proper drug, either by mouth or by injection, and stop the disease. Sanitation involves keeping droppings or nasal discharge off the food and in dosing drinking water to kill the germs left by sick birds. Disease control involves medicating the sick and keeping the spread to a minimum. Coccidiosis is a good example. Assuming that all pigeons will have it, as we have seen, our object should be to keep the attack as light as possible. This involves preventing re-infection as far as possible, so we are especially careful with all sanitary measures.

If some of the birds develop blood poisoning which apparently is the cause of their sick appearance, we inject those birds and try to sterilize their blood.

Here I want to add a further note on the disposition of strays and quarantine. Stray pigeons are bound to see your birds and either enter your loft or try to. If you breed fancy pigeons, you do not want strays sitting on the fly top leaving droppings where your birds can contact them. And if you fly or race pigeons, you do not want strays coming into the loft.

There are men and boys in big cities who make considerable money trapping strays and these men are willing to risk disease. The rest of us whose birds these persons catch want to keep strays out or dispose of them. Occasionally valuable birds drop in. Even they should be quarantined. Homers which are exhausted more than likely quit because they are sick. Every strange pigeon should be looked upon with suspicion.

Naturally you will try to find the owner if the bird is ringed. Keep it quarantined until you do.

9. Keep the pigeons in glowing health

Why? Because healthy pigeons, when they become infected, are able to recover from many diseases easier than those in run-down condition.

How? By proper diet, by sanitation which prevents the spread of disease.

Sanitation and Disease Prevention

10. *Feed only sufficient food*

Why? Because too much food is a health menace when it becomes soiled from droppings. When birds are overfed they become choosey, picking out only certain grains and ignoring others which might offer better nourishment.

How? By watching until the birds show they are no longer hungry and then removing all uneaten food. At the next feeding give the amount they *ate* at the previous feeding.

Pigeons feeding squabs need more and more food as the youngsters grow older, so one must feed them oftener, giving the old birds all they will eat without leaving a grain or a pellet.

An occasional complaint of neighbours against pigeon fanciers is, that their compost heaps or manure piles in the backyards breed flies to infest the neighbourhood. Occasionally the decomposing manure odours are wafted by breezes where they are not appreciated. Aside from the aesthetic objections, there are other important health considerations.

Flies carry parasite eggs and are notorious spreaders of coccidiosis. Unscreened and uncovered piles of manure treasured for garden fertilizer may be reservoirs of parasite eggs. Every fancier knows how the birds seem to enjoy picking around on such piles. We keep a large compost pile for our garden where we put leaves, sheep manure, pigeon manure and anything else which will rot and make fertilizer. The pigeons have often flown to it upon alighting from their period of exercise instead of going through the loft trap. It became such a nuisance in trying to keep the birds away that it had to be screened.

If you have such a pile and can shield it from the pigeons and have no intention of using it for fertilizer, simply spread a thin layer of borax over it every time you add new cleanings to the pile and flies will not be able to breed there.

16

Poisons

Although there are a great many substances which would poison pigeons if the birds ate them, there is probably less poisoning among this species than among any others. It is rare indeed for pigeons in squab farms and those in flying flocks to be poisoned. When they are, my experience indicates the poisoning is either maliciousness or is due to carelessness on the part of the owner.

Most of the poisoned pigeons which I have been called upon to diagnose were homers, which had been permitted open loft and came home poisoned and died. In one instance, ten birds in one flock died within 48 hours and some did not return. It was never determined where they had been, but the crops of those which returned and died contained arsenic-poisoned grain, possibly grain set out in some freight yard to poison sparrows.

We must declare that if pigeons are not permitted open loft, poisoning would be cut to a fraction of what it is when they can come and go at will.

Fertilizer Poisons. Judging from reports in European and American books and magazines, more pigeons are lost from this type of poisoning than from any other. Most of the damage occurs in the spring when farmers are sowing commercial fertilizers or seed dressings. Pigeons alight on freshly ploughed fields and pick up particles of chemical and organic material. The poisons contained in such material can be chemical or organic; that is, the compounds of phosphorus, potash and nitrogen may contain substantial amounts of other more toxic chemicals. Pigeons starved for salt will eat nitrate of soda which may taste like sodium chloride to them but does not have the same effect. Others attempting to obtain animal protein may eat particles of tankage which has become moist and infested with salmonella germs, the toxins of

215

Poisons

which are responsible for much human food poisoning, and botulism toxin too.

Some pigeons will vomit the toxic substances but many die slowly from the poisoning. If they are saved these birds may have less value as fliers but can be kept for breeders. The kidneys may be permanently damaged, as will be evidenced by the pigeons showing a much greater thirst than before the poisoning.

If you wish to try to save a poisoned bird, probably the best treatment, is to give into the crop by syringe or medicine dropper, about a teaspoonful of glucose solution every 3 or 4 hours for the first day. Not knowing what poison you are trying to combat, you are trying a substance which helps protect the bird's liver and kidneys and has considerable detoxifying power.

Botulism. A disease in wild ducks is called 'limber neck'. Dead or dying ducks are often found along the shores of lakes or ponds. The head is generally stretched out and many of the feathers may be blown off. This is due to the ducks having eaten dead sea life, snails, etc., which have been killed by *Clostridum botulinum*, which produces one of the deadliest poisons known. Pigeons, also, have been found dead in this condition and there is excellent reason to conclude they visited the seashore and ate snails, too.

Unless the poisoned bird is reasonably near home, it will fail to reach it, so deadly is this poison. Even if the pigeon does reach home there is little that can be done to save it. The symptoms are chiefly a paralysis of the entire body. Glucose will help as much as anything and a recovered bird may be as good as new.

Salt Poison. A very thirsty pigeon may be flying over inlets from the sea, see the water and drop down to drink. He may have a good part of a cropful before he finds it is toxic. The bird may vomit the water or fly again, only to have a far worse thirst. This is a great handicap to homing pigeons and may account for heavy losses for loft owners whose birds fly along the coast or over bodies of salt water.

There is little likelihood of death from salt-water poisoning because the birds drink fresh water copiously and finally eliminate the salt from their bodies.

Road Tar. Speaking of water, the glistening surface of freshly tarred roads must look like water to thirsty birds because so many of them return from races with tar on their feet and feathers. Realizing their mistake, the pigeons may manage to get home but many cannot fly well after the sticky substance has gummed their feathers. In my first season

Poisons

of recent racing, three kind persons wrote me they had birds of ours which could not fly because of being tarred.

To clean feathers of tar, soap and detergents are useless. A solvent must be used. Paraffin is generally used and this washed out with soap and water. A milder and effective treatment is light mineral oil which will dissolve the tar and can be washed out of the feathers with soap or detergent.

Contaminated Food. Birds in many lofts have been made sick or killed by the food which they regularly eat, when a batch comes along which has been contaminated. In rare instances poisonous substances have dripped into bags of grain, or the bags have been set into fluids which worked by capillarity up into the grain.

One of the most common instances of this type of poisoning is mouldy food. The container gets wet, the atmosphere may be damp, the weather warm and moulds grow. The moulds may be invisible, or you may notice a change of the colour of the food or smell a musty odour. Some moulds are benign, penicillin, for example, but many are extremely poisonous. Throw out all mouldy food, never take a chance on feeding it. And be sure to bury it where the birds cannot find it.

Treated Grain. It is often possible to buy pea seed or beans from commercial seed houses, which have been treated to kill weevils or to prevent insect and mildew attacks on the seed after it is planted. Such seed can be mighty expensive in terms of mistaken use for pigeons. Be sure to inquire whether any seed you buy has been treated. There are anti-weevil drugs with which even food for human consumption has been treated. But this evaporates and leaves no poisonous residue. The poisons used to treat seed which is to be planted, however, may be particularly poisonous.

Arsenic and Lead. Should pigeons eat lead, calcium arsenate or Paris Green which has been sprayed on foliage, you may save them before the poison has been absorbed, by giving a large pinch of Epsom salts in a little water.

Phosphorus. Should a rat drag poisoned bait out where pigeons can eat it, and if phosphorus is the poison used, give each bird a teaspoonful of hydrogen peroxide and water (50–50). Peroxide is the best antidote for phosphorus.

Thallium. This poison which was so commonly used for bugs is counteracted best by table salt.

DDT amd Other Insect Poisons. These are usually taken into the system when they have been accidentally sprayed on food or into drink-

217

Poisons

ing or bath water. For these, follow the directions on the package as to antidotes. First and foremost the bird should be made to vomit and empty its crop. This can be done by giving a tablespoonful of salt and water with a syringe. There is little absorption from the crop which may prove a life-saver if you act in time. After the crop is empty, give the antidote.

A grain sold under the name of *Arueja sativa* some years ago was found to contain a glucocide and was poisonous to pigeons. *Vicia sativa* is its botanical name.

17

Pigeon Enemies

In addition to having diseases and parasites, pigeons have enemies in the form of birds and mammals. Some kill and some terrorize. To have healthy pigeons and birds eager to home or, in the case of flying types, to drop quickly, one must keep them calm and contented. The following are some of the common enemies.

Cats. Unless the fancier knows the owner of a cat, he should not hesitate to trap it and dispose of it humanely. Every country is overrun with feral cats. Once these tame cats, or kittens from tame cats, go wild, they are well able to shift for themselves. They eat chiefly rodents, but enjoy birds too. In one game-breeding establishment of my acquaintance, which is a considerable distance back in the country, more than 500 feral cats have been trapped. I have seen some of these cats and they are fat and sleek. All were trying to steal the young of pheasants, ruffed grouse or wild duck.

No one can say how many thousands of pigeons cats have been known to kill. When a cat gets into a loft, if it knows it can get out, it may kill many pigeons. But if it tries and finds it cannot get out, it will generally not kill.

Nevertheless, it does great harm by the panic it causes, and a wise fancier of flying breeds knows not to permit his birds freedom for several days after the cat has left.

Cats are easy animals to trap. Nearly every cat will go to a fish bait and if you use a box trap or a catch-'em-alive device of any kind, fish for bait will draw them in.

Rats. The Norwegian rat may be the greatest mammalian enemy of pigeons. They kill in lofts, chew through shipping crates and kill birds inside, frighten others and when sufficiently hungry, they commit their depredations even in the daytime.

219

Pigeon Enemies

Rats are easily controlled today. There are many poisons but Warfarin which can be mixed with food is seldom rejected by rats, which bleed to death internally after 3 or 4 meals. When rats are known to be around, set some tasty food, such as dog food, in a pan and see how much they eat during a night. Do this for 3 or 4 nights until you have trained them to expect this food to be in a certain place, which should be where pigeons or pets cannot reach it. When the rats have learned where to eat, mix the Warfarin in the food in an amount according to the directions on the Warfarin container (it is sold in several dilutions) and each day you will find less and less food eaten and fewer rats to plague you. Four days is generally enough time to dispose of them.

Warfarin is safer than most rat poisons because one meal of it will not kill a pigeon or a pet; several are required. Red Squill is another fairly safe rat poison. It is a violent emetic and kills rats and mice because they cannot vomit, whereas most other species can.

Phosphorus is still sold but is too dangerous to leave around. Rats often drag the poisoned bait out from places where it has been hidden and pigeons eating it will die.

Raccoons. Not infrequently, raccoons have destroyed many pigeons in lofts in the U.S.A. They prowl at night; are exceedingly adept climbers; can crawl through bob-wires and kill. Sometimes when they find the exits barred, they generally can pull back the bob-wire and get out. Having such excellent night vision, raccoons can see pigeons and catch them with their paws. Usually a raccoon will hold a pigeon down while he bites it through the head. Raccoons are mischievous and one will have a wonderful time in a pigeon loft before he makes his exit, often dragging a pigeon away with him.

Coons are easy to trap and, like cats, love fish. They will enter any trap to eat fish. A jump trap with a small minnow tied to the pan will be almost sure to catch a marauding coon. Wire traps to take them alive will be effective baited with fish or with a mirror hanging in the middle suspended by a string.

Opossums. These night-prowling marsupials are an American problem. This once southern mammal which carries its young in a pouch, has migrated north and has spread over thousands of miles of new territory. It is such an excellent climber that it can get into any loft through holes even smaller than pigeons can enter. It will seemingly kill for the joy of killing. Anyone observing it when it is frightened, might wonder how such a sluggish creature could ever kill anything. But such an impression

Pigeon Enemies

is pure sham: it is as quick as a flash. Pigeons are left in a highly nervous state after an opossum has done its work.

Kill every opossum you catch in or around your coop. If it is liberated it will try to enter again.

Stoats (called *Weasels* in Ireland and America, although the true weasel does not occur in Ireland or America). A stoat generally makes the fancier aware that it has been in a loft by the musky odour it leaves. After it has killed, one generally finds fang-marks in the back of the pigeon's neck close to the head. Stoats are small but deadly. They are fair climbers but tend to enter through openings close to the ground. In summer stoats are brown: in winter they are white, in northerly climes. They create panic among the birds even though they always stalk at night. Weasels, although smaller than stoats, can also do damage in pigeon lofts.

Weasels. See *Stoats*.

Grey Squirrels. Just why a squirrel will create panic in a flock of pigeons one time and not at another is difficult to explain. Squirrels show no interest in harming the birds but enter a loft only to eat the grain and sometimes eggs. The pigeons may even get used to them. On the other hand, for no obvious reason, one squirrel will panic a flock so badly it is not safe to let them out to fly. I had two such experiences. In one case the birds were shut in. A squirrel got into the loft through the bob-wires and soon the birds were flying around wildly. One pigeon broke its neck in the mêlée. It took several days to calm them down. Another time the birds had alighted and were about to enter the coop through the trap. At this moment a big grey squirrel darted out. The pigeons panicked. It was three-thirty in the afternoon and they were still flying over the loft at eleven-thirty that night when I went to bed. Fortunately the moon was almost full. One out of thirty was lost, but the last bird to come home arrived after noon the next day.

Such bold squirrels should be destroyed.

Snakes. I have been told that snakes will sometimes enter lofts through coarse wire screening and eat pigeon eggs. The remedy, of course, consists in screening with finer-mesh wire.

Hawks. Some hawks are definitely enemies of pigeons, but not all, as so many persons think. This was brought clearly to my attention by the fact that within 200 yards of one of the Speedome Lofts, a pair of huge hawks raise their brood every year. They fly and soar about over the loft and, while the pigeons are terrorized by their presence at first, they soon lose fear and seem to want to include the hawks in the flock. Nor

Pigeon Enemies

are the birds afraid of the frequent hawk calls. Upon climbing the tree and studying the contents of the big hawk nest, I found no pigeon rings in it.

I have consulted a well-known American authority, E. H. Forbush, who left us his monumental *Birds of Massachusetts*. In Volume II, 90 pages are devoted to hawks and birds of that general nature.

In the Forbush treatise, there is a table of injurious and beneficial hawks compiled by E. H. Eaton. Of the several species in America, 4 are beneficial, 2 are borderline and 5 are injurious. This was based upon the examination of the stomachs of 2,700 hawks.

The following table is a condensed version of the Eaton table:

TABLE X

PERCENTAGE OF STOMACHS EXAMINED CONTAINING
VARIOUS KINDS OF FOOD

Species of Hawk	Poultry and Game	Other birds	Snakes Frogs, etc., Crayfish	Mice	Other Mammals	Insects	Empty
BENEFICIAL							
Rough-Legged	0	0	2	81	10	2	8
Broad-Winged	0	3	43	22	19	45	10
Red-Shouldered	1	6	32	50	20	45	7
Sparrow	1/3	17	13	28	4	7	9
BORDERLINE							
Red-Tailed	10	9	7	50	24	8	19
Marsh	6	27	8	46	18	10	7
INJURIOUS							
Goshawk	36	8	—	—	40	12	32
Cooper	23	49	3	—	8	2	30
Sharp-Skinned	4	66	—	4	—	4	35
Duck	35	45	—	5	—	10	20
Pigeon	4	80	—	4	—	32	9

Of all the hawks, the American Duck Hawk, very similar to the Peregrine Falcon of Great Britain, doubtlessly kills more pigeons than any other. These birds nest on cliffs and palisades in city buildings, and thousands of them live on pigeons. They learn the flying routes of

Pigeon Enemies

homers, and because they are among the fastest flying birds alive, find weary homers or confused pigeons easy prey. There are many accounts of persons who have discovered and studied hawk nests. Large numbers of homing pigeon bands are often found in them. City Duck Hawks may have as many as 50 bands in a single nest; one Massachusetts nest contained 78.

Pigeon hawks are about the size of a pigeon and derive their name from the size comparison, not because they kill pigeons. They sometimes dive at a flying pigeon or one sitting on a tree and knock it down, sometimes following the stunned victim, and while they may not kill it, they often tear at the skin. I have seen two such attacks upon my own birds.

Most of the hawks are clumsy and are unable to catch flying pigeons, but some are adept at dropping on them when they are on roofs or even on their own lofts.

There are laws protecting certain species of hawks, but the laws vary from nation to nation, state or province. In general, the beneficial hawks are protected and the injurious are not.

How is one to distinguish these types? Some, to most of us, are too similar to take the time to distinguish. If we see a hawk lurking about our loft and we live where we can use a gun, we shoot. The pictures on the next page will help you in the future. If you live in the American suburbs or in the country, a hawk trap on a tall straight pole or sawed-off sapling is permissible.

If a hawk attacks our pigeons once, it is almost certain to return. Anyone will be excused for shooting such a bird whether it was legally protected or not.

One fact has been established which few pigeon men realize: some hawks migrate in the autumn: they start going south in August and some stay part-way between north and south until the first part of November. There are few species which spend the winter in the north. Some Sharp-Skinned Hawks do, however, winter in New England and when they do they become so hungry they will attack very boldly. Some have been known to fly through loft windows to capture pigeons.

The Cooper's Hawk remains in the south until March, which accounts for its great numbers there in winter. This hawk is shy and seldom seen, and for this reason is seldom shot. It darts out, takes a pigeon and flies away. As a result, the large soaring Red-Shouldered or the Red-Tailed species are blamed because they are so conspicuous although they seldom trouble pigeons.

223

Pigeon Enemies

ERNEST H. HART

(1) Red-tailed Hawk, (2) Marsh Hawk, (3) Cooper's Hawk, (4) Red-shouldered Hawk, (5) Goshawk, (6) Sharp-Skinned Hawk, (7) Duck Hawk, (8) Pigeon Hawk, (9) Sparrow Hawk, (10) White Gyrfalcon.

18

Pigeons and Public Health

The question: 'Are our birds a menace to health?' is one which must be faced with honesty. Most fanciers prefer not to have the question asked. And some categorically deny the charge.

It seems to me, however, that we should frankly admit that under certain circumstances they can be a health menace. Because so many persons have been educated to believe they *always* are, ordinances are rapidly being passed forbidding pigeon lofts in many localities. New housing developments are being built and the homes sold with restrictions many of which contain a provision against the keeping of pigeons. Wrong impressions are often made on parents who have read of persons being sick with 'parrot fever' which had been traced to pigeons. Then, too, disastrous diseases on chicken farms have been blamed on pigeons without determining what or whose pigeons—epizootics, which destroyed thousands of chickens causing large money losses to the poultry owners.

The greatest concern of every pigeon fancier should be, not the health of his pigeons, important as that is, but whether the public will permit him to keep pigeons at all. His first thought should be, "can my pigeons be a public health menace?" Can they spread any disease to human beings? Can they be a reservoir of diseases which vectors (mosquitoes for example) can spread to people?

There is no use pretending that there is no way in which pigeons can be responsible for human illness because we all know that there are ways. Pigeons, yes. But our racing homers and our well cared for fancy breeds? That is the crux of the matter.

Through newspaper and magazine stories the public is fast being educated to believe that *pigeons* are filthy, destructive, disease-spreading creatures which should be eliminated. There is no distinction between

225

the wild pigeons and those we fancy. This is not only unfair but manifestly dishonest.

We have here an almost perfect parallel between the public's concern for rats and that of the scientist. Wild rats are filthy, disease spreading mammals which cause several billion dollars worth of damage annually. Rats kept as pets and the millions used by scientists could also be public health menaces were they not properly cared for. But they are properly cared for and no one objects to that kind of rats. Why then do they object to well cared for pigeons?

Every scientist objects to wild rats which carry many human diseases, and every pigeon fancier objects to wild pigeons. In fact he objects more vociferously than any scientist because the wild pigeons can fly into his loft and spread pigeon diseases to his disease-free birds. Wild rats seldom get into colonies of rats used in science. No one objects to well-kept rats in cages. We pigeon fanciers often refer to wild pigeons as rats.

Having had the opportunity of testifying at a number of hearings at which attempts were made to outlaw pigeon lofts, or to pass ordinances which would relegate pigeons to the country, I have kept notes on all the objections heard from those who testified for the opponents of pigeons. In some hearings considerable money was spent bringing experts to testify while in others the objections were entirely on the basis of the damage from pigeon droppings or carelessness of individual loft owners who deserve to lose their pigeons, but whose slovenliness brought enmity toward all fanciers.

Here are the objections and the answers to them as presented by those of us who tried to set the record straight.

"PIGEONS SPREAD PSITTICOSIS."

It is possible for them to do so. We think it is remarkable that no human cases have been reported for several years however, as contracted from pigeons, because we know that probably one-third of all the wild and park pigeons are carriers. Since the discovery that tetracyclines cure the disease and even eliminate the carrier stage in pigeons, we who own pigeons dose them once or twice a year with Auromycin or Terramycin and thus have eliminated all danger in our flocks. We wish the wild pigeons were eliminated because they are an ever present threat to our well cared for birds.

Pigeons and Public Health

All bird manure affords a splendid medium for the growth of fungus organisms. What are they and what is their danger?

Cryptococcus neoformans is one fungus which grows readily in any bird manure—sparrow, starling, pigeon, poultry, etc. When the manure dries and becomes dust, it can, if inhaled, produce a human disease called Cryptococcosis. Two deaths from it among New York City's 8-million persons created a furore but no one knows whether the dust they inhaled came from starling or pigeon manure. A total of 20 cases are reported annually. The scientists who studied the cases took droppings from pigeons in a pet store and found the organisms. They could as well have found them in a Kosher poultry market, but pigeons took the onus.

Do pigeon fanciers permit droppings to accumulate and remain until they become dust? That there is dust from feathers and skin scales in every loft no one can dispute but not dust from droppings. One expert raised the objection that some loft owners permit droppings to accumulate until they become dust several inches thick on the floor which is kept raked and dry. This, he said, caused dust when the pigeons flew. He is right. There is no defence against this system which may constitute a public health menace. All we who testified for the pigeon fanciers could state was that only a small fraction of the fanciers use this system and that health authorities could outlaw it.

A few cases of cryptococcosis have been reported in other cities but it is a rare disease.

Coccidiomycosis is caused by a fungus (Coccidioides immitis). It produces, in man, pulmonary symptoms and nodules in the skin. This is another disease which, to be contracted, depends on the inhaling of the dust from bird manure. Extremely rare.

Histplasmosis, caused by another fungus, *Histoplasma capsulatum*. It causes fever, anaemia, leucopenia and emaciation. An article in the American Legion Magazine called it, "Our Unknown Lung Disease". While the author did not incriminate pigeons as the sole source of the infection which occurs all over the world, enough was said about pigeon manure so that those who would outlaw all pigeons, used the article to prove the danger. The author tells of ten men who were made sick from digging worms in a swamp where blackbirds had lived. In another area, starlings were definitely the reservoir. In still another area 77 per cent of the residents were infected by the fungus when trees which had been the home of many species of wild birds were chopped down and the dust had blown all over town. More than 10,000 of the 30,000 residents developed the curious lung disease.

It is estimated that over 30 million Americans have had the disease yet never knew they had it. Possibly as many as 1,000 persons die every year from it. All of the 30 million recovered persons have life-long immunity.

Does this mean that our well cared for pigeons are the source of the infection? They couldn't be unless the owners left the piles of droppings about until they turned to dust. Any fancier who does that can't succeed as a racer or as a producer of show birds. So we can practically rule out our pigeons as a public health source. But wild pigeons can be and definitely are a menace when they accumulate in such numbers that droppings pile up and eventually turn to dust.

Pigeon Keepers Disease. This is still another disease caused by fungi and it is making medical news. It causes pneumonia-like symptoms and so far as I can learn has been reported only in owner's of lofts. One pathologist suggest it is much like the old "Farmer's Lung" disease so often reported in farmers who breathed dust from mouldy hay. Pigeon Keeper's Disease is an interstitial pneumonia of a mild type. Like Histoplasmosis most of those whose blood tests reacted positively to the disease were not aware they had been sick. Since the disease is one of pigeon keepers, and rare, it can hardly be considered a public health problem but rather represents a personal risk, surely one well worth taking, considering the fun to be had from the pigeon hobby.

We have been discussing fungus diseases. Now we must consider the development of fungus. In most of the areas where pigeons are kept, there is only a short space of the year when fungus can grow and dust can be blown about. In winter, only in deep piles of manure will there be sufficient warmth from bacterial decomposition to provide a climate for fungal growth. If manure piles under porches are so solidly frozen that they can't be removed, surely fungus cannot grow.

During the times when there is much moisture in the air, droppings will take up the moisture because they are deliquescent and surely not become dust. This leaves only dry, hot times which are dangerous because such times can produce dust in lofts where droppings are not removed regularly. But well kept lofts are scraped daily in order to keep parasites to a minimum.

So far as our birds are concerned, the only way in which they can be

228

a health menace is when dust accumulates inside or when droppings are piled up outside where they may turn to dust. And who leaves the manure piles uncovered? They would smell and become a nuisance so that the neighbours would object. A person with such slovenly habits should be told by health officials to cease and desist.

"PIGEONS SPREAD PARATYPHOID."

Another frequently cited menace which, some say, pigeons provide is *Salmonellosis*. They suggest that human beings can contract food poisoning, paratyphoid and other diseases caused by bacteria of this great class of organisms. But they do not realize that the one form of Salmonellosis which pigeons have almost exclusively is so specific for pigeons that very few other species can be infected with it. Pigeons rarely are found with one of the poultry paratyphoids but human beings are resistant to the pigeon disease.

So much for diseases. There are other objections which must be answered. One is the claim that parasites of pigeons cause diseases in other species, including man. They are said to be the repository of horse encephylitis; wild pigeons like most of the species of birds probably have been. But our domestic birds are kept pretty much protected in their lofts from mosquitoes. As for fleas, lice and ticks leaving pigeons to live on human beings, such a claim is absurd; pigeon parasites are all choosy about living on pigeons. Even if one did bite a human being, what chance is there it would communicate a disease? Extremely little!

The testimony of one of America's greatest pathologists, which he presented in the Patterson, New Jersey hearing, should weigh heavily in every consideration of this subject by public health officials. Dr. Harry S. N. Greene is head of Yale University Department of Pathology and chief of the pathology divisions of eight Connecticut hospitals. In reply to a question as to how many deaths he had known of from any of the diseases we have considered, he replied that such cases would have been almost certain to have come to his attention because they are so unusual, but that he had never seen one in any of the hospitals where he has charge. It was his opinion that well-kept pigeons are not a threat to public health.

The best answer to those who would outlaw pigeons because of the danger from fungus diseases appeared in Science Magazine (February 7, 1964). It was written by Dr. John D. Schneidau, Jr. of the Tulane

Pigeons and Public Health

University Department of Mycology. A mycologist is one who specializes in the subject of fungous organisms.

PIGEONS AND CRYPTOCOCCOSIS.

The furore in New York City regarding the possibility that pigeons may spread human cryptococcosis is a good example of the hysteria generated by premature or ill-considered pronouncements of public officials. The numerous articles on the subject that have appeared in newspapers throughout the country and in *Time* and *Newsweek* contain many incorrect and misleading statements, and the time and effort already spent in ballyhoo borders on the ridiculous. Before all this leads to a possible warranted expenditure of considerable sums on pigeon extermination, a more critical and unbiased review of the evidence should be presented to the public.

"The finding of *Cryptococcus neoformans* in pigeon droppings is nothing new. As long ago as 1955, this organism (which is never referred to in scientific circles as CN, as some articles have stated) was shown to be present in the excreta of pigeons in Washington, D.C. by investigators at the National Institutes of Health. There is no question of the validity of these findings, but there is no clear-cut evidence that the incidence of human cryptococcosis in a city is significantly increased by the number of pigeons. The birds are not infected, nor is the organism present in their digestive tracts; the pigeons do not actually spread the organism around in the environment in their droppings. The fungus cannot be isolated from fresh droppings, but only from old, dried excreta. It is known the *C. neoformans* is widely distributed in nature, and it has been isolated from a variety of natural substances, including soil, fruit juices, and milk, so that it seems most probable that the fungus gets into the pigeon droppings from the surrounding environment and grows there because the droppings furnish a rich culture medium. Thus humans are constantly exposed to the fungus whether pigeons are present or not. It is true that there have been documented outbreaks of cryptococcosis following such operations as the cleaning of a pigeon roost, and undoubtedly such an operation presents a hazard to the health of the individual engaging in it by exposing him to an unusually high concentration of the infective agent in the dust. The simple solution to this particular problem would be the use of a respirator to prevent inhalation of the dust. However, in the case of isolated infections occurring in the community, it is practically impossible to prove a relationship between the presence of pigeons and the initiation of the disease; the mere fact that the patient had previous contact with pigeons is no proof at all that they were the source of his infection.

"In the case of another fungus disease of man, histoplasmosis, it has been demonstrated that the causative agent, *Histoplasma capsulatum*, can readily be isolated from chicken droppings and from soils around chicken houses, and some fatal cases have been linked with a close association with chickens. Histoplasmosis is a much greater public health problem than cryptococcosis; it is estimated that between 20 and 30 million persons have had the primary, usually mild and self-limited, respiratory form of the disease. Yet no one has seriously advocated the mass extermination of chickens.

"It should also be pointed out that *C. neoformans* is not found exclusively in the excreta of pigeons, but can be isolated from the droppings of quite a number of species of birds, including the canary.

"The incidence of 20 cases per year reported in New York City is slightly less than two cases per year per million inhabitants, and is not likely to be significantly different from the incidence that might be found in almost any U.S. city, with or without pigeons".

Another objection to our racing homers which has been repeatedly voiced is that our lost homers constitute the principle source of the wild pigeons. This appeared to be a valid claim. It did until we counted bands on wild pigeons killed or caught in cities. Anyone who will study the problem must conclude that the banded pigeons in wild flocks caught or killed are usually birds temporarily lost. They are thin and tired.

Of over 6,000 caught in one city only 14 banded birds were found. Of 420 living in barns on the outskirts of a city, 6 had bands. In another city where over 7,000 were trapped, 22 were banded. In the tower of a church 125 were caught one night. Eighteen had bands. The next day, the 18 were fed and released. That night the tower was examined and not one of the 18 could be found in it. They were obviously a part of a flock on the way home and had sought a stopping place when night overtook them.

One cannot honestly conclude that lost racers constitute the source of wild pigeons. Just the difference in appearance should convince one that wild pigeons are a different breed of bird.

Pigeons are indeed a public health problem, mild in contrast to other sources but enough that we would be better off without them.

Pigeons and Public Health

So our efforts should be, as nearly as possible, to eliminate the wild. And this should be a concern of pigeon fanciers more than of any class of persons because wild pigeons bring diseases to our well-kept flocks.

Another objection to our lofts which seemed to hold considerable weight was that our birds attract wild ones to a community. Indeed there are instances which proved to be coincidences, where the objection seemed valid. Just at the time a new loft came to a community, buildings in another part of the city were torn down in urban renewal projects. The pigeons living in them had to find new abodes and did, under eaves in homes.

The real objections, however, are almost always found to be due to wild pigeons; but for which homers are blamed. For example, it has been claimed that the birds sit on houses and soil them or soil clothes on lines, that they increase populations. In both cases wild ones are to blame. People toss scraps out for wild pigeons and rats eat the surplus.

Then there is the usual debate about whether a flock of pigeons flying drop excreta as they fly. Pigeon fanciers claim that they never do. But they must, otherwise pigeons which start a race with full crops, would have full crops when they arrive home. True the legs and feet of a flying bird do cover the vent, but they can be moved to permit droppings to be passed. However, the objection cannot be serious. Behind Speedome Lofts is a large Club with an Olympic size swimming pool. I have asked persons sitting about the pool to let me know if any one has ever seen a dropping fall from my flock which frequently passes over the pool and in five years no one has ever seen a dropping fall.

There is an important distinction which must be decided in several States and Provinces of America, namely as to whether pigeons should be classed as poultry or as pets. Ordinances in some areas permit pets but not poultry to be kept within city or suburban boundaries. And here the important considerations of taxes must be thought of. Food for pets is taxable, but poultry food is not. The dilemma has to be resolved.

Only in America is the health danger seriously used to try to force fanciers to give up their pigeons. In many other countries of the world public health authorities are certainly as well trained and alert as those in the U.S.A. In England the Queen Mother attends pigeon shows, the Queen owns her own racing pigeon loft and takes pleasure in the hobby.

In Belgium 95 per cent of the pigeon lofts are in the top stories of homes. And that is the best argument I know that well-kept pigeons are

232

Pigeons and Public Health

safe. The 160,000 fanciers and their families and neighbours are surely as healthy, as free from lung diseases, as the Yankees.

Compared to other pets kept by the public, pigeons surely rate close to the bottom of the list so far as their being a potential danger to us. Dogs probably stand at the top and constantly spread diseases, yet what health authorities would dare to attempt to outlaw dogs? If they want to protect the public from diseases communicable from pets, let them start at the top.

Properly cared for, pigeons are almost never a health menace. It is safer to keep pigeons than it is to kiss your sweetheart or your own mother. It is far more dangerous to go to church, or ride on a bus, or attend a political rally, or even to attend a hearing on whether pigeons should be permitted in your locality.

Who and what then is to blame for the bad name some localities give the pigeon?

1. The irresponsible person who gives his birds too much liberty.

2. The person who believes in open loft and lets his birds annoy his locality, alighting in poultry farms, and when there is an epizootic, being responsible for the poultrymen putting the onus on *pigeons*, not his pigeons, not the wild pigeons, but pigeons generally. True, the wild pigeons may be found harbouring the same organism or virus which is killing his chickens, but he won't ask whether the chickens gave it to the pigeons, he will be sure it is vice versa.

3. The careless person who permits a loft to become filthy enough to smell. Naturally neighbours object, and they claim flies are breeding in the loft: 'Never had so many flies until Mr. Blank started keeping pigeons. How do we know the flies are not carrying disease to us?'

In each instance, the persons described above are undeserving of public consideration and it would be better for careful fanciers if health authorities forced them to dispose of their pigeons.

Occasionally neighbours object to cooing in backyard lofts, a sound that can harm no one and soothes many. Persons who find fault with such mild, and to many, pleasant sounds, are generally troublemakers. They may live on a truck route where trucks thundering past make a thousand times the noise and this, they say, they no longer hear. They can, if they want, cease to hear cooing.

It seems to me that there is a simple way to overcome most of the public opposition to the keeping of pigeons on the basis of their being a health menace: let every club start a campaign in its community to exterminate wild pigeons. Let them tell the public that *wild* pigeons are

233

a health menace and that well-kept loft birds are not, and that we want to keep the wild pigeons from carrying diseases to our birds as well as to keep buildings clean. We want to change the ordinances to permit trapping the sacred pigeons which so many communities protect. The *wild* pigeons are a menace. We want the public health authorities to co-operate!

This approach is the proper start in public education for the control of wild pigeons as a health menace. If we fanciers take the aggressive attitude and not the negative in fighting for our rights, we will soon have most of our communities on our side. It will mean a running fight, never to be relaxed. But it will do the pigeon hobby a world of good.

Pigeons can be a health menace, but our well-kept birds are not; let's get rid of the wild ones, they are the health hazard.

Over 100 years has gone into making the racing homer what it is today—a powerful, beautiful pigeon as different from the wild pigeon as a Greyhound is different from a Fox Terrier or a thorough-bred race horse is different from a range pony. For thousands of years, the fancy breeds have been evolving away from the original rock dove and into such exotic forms as we know them today. It would help the pigeon hobby greatly if every club, combine or concourse would devote some of its funds towards educating the public to realize that there is this difference. Suppose a booth were rented at a hobby show or exposition where cages of beautiful pigeons were shown and a large sign displayed which urged the public to

"HELP US DESTROY THE WILD PIGEONS—

THEY ARE A MENACE TO OUR BIRDS."

Circulars could be distributed which tell why we pigeon fanciers want to eliminate the disease carrying pigeon rats. With such actions we would be in the opposite position from that which many fanciers now find themselves. We'd be on the offensive, not having to defend ourselves.

How to Catch Wild Pigeons.

When the Health Commissioner of Bridgeport, Connecticut, enlisted the services of a local fancier to eradicate the wild pigeon nuisance, the two men asked your author to study the best means of accomplishing the purpose.

We investigated traps, nets, night capturing, baits, drugs and so on, but the most effective means proved to be drugs. Every drug from poisons to tranquillizers was considered and tested. A large group of unwanted pigeons was maintained.

It was easy to poison the birds but poisoned grain was too dangerous to have about and song birds were destroyed by it. Moreover, the local Humane Society objected. We had to hit upon a method which would only anaesthetize the birds which, at their insistence, would be turned over to the Humane Society for disposal.

The drug of choice finally proved to be Pentobarbital sodium. The amount to use and the kind of grain to treat next came in for study. We found that the soft grains with husks were least desirable, also that whole corn was of little use because the birds filled up so quickly that many flew away before the anaesthetic took effect. Cracked corn, wheat, milo proved excellent and inexpensive.

The amount of the drug used varied from one ounce to six pounds of food, which usually killed the birds, to one ounce to eight pounds of food which was satisfactory, provided no disturbance frightened the pigeons for 20 minutes. Those which went to sleep on this amount usually were back to normal in 24 hours. A dilution of one ounce to seven pounds of food was satisfactory.

The food is prepared by dissolving the Pentobarbital powder in a little water and thoroughly mixing the solution with the grain.

The birds are baited in a quiet location for four days until they expect to find food there, and on the fifth the treated grain is put out. A pan of water should be available. Those which drink go to sleep quicker than those which do not. The food is placed on a flat surface where any surplus can be swept up and used again. This should be done to prevent song birds from eating it.

We find it best to wait until all the pigeons have gone to sleep before we gather them up. Should any desirable bird be found among them, we insert a tube in its crop and flush it out, thus lessening the amount of the drug which would be absorbed.

Pentobarbital is a prescription drug. It must be handled only by responsible persons. It is preferable to let the local Health Commissioner obtain it and let him or a subordinate mix it with the grain. The Police Chief can be counted on to keep traffic off the area where the birds are being caught.

Pigeons and Public Health

Best time to do the job is soon after daylight when the city is asleep and no one is liable to create a disturbance which might cause partially anaesthetized birds to fly away. In a city they may break windows or cause car accidents by their blind flying.

The person who has had more experience than any man alive when it comes to eradication of wild pigeons is Thomas J. Dalton, R.S., who does his work for the New York City Department of Health. It is reliably reported that he has disposed of three quarters of a million. He tells me that very few have been banded pigeons.

He uses Tribromoethanol, which can be obtained from Winthrop Laboratories, Special Chemicals Department, 1450 Broadway, New York, New York 10018. In London, their address is Winthrop Products Co., Winthrop House, Surbiton-upon-Thames, Surrey.

This drug does not keep the pigeons asleep as long as Pentobarbital.

19

Conclusion

You have noticed in reading this book the great similarity of the symptoms caused by several diseases. By now you realize why I was so emphatic at the beginning in saying there was no disease called 'going light', that it is merely a symptom of many diseases. If an owner is content to say his pigeons have been 'going light' and let it go at that, he will learn precious little about the ailments of his birds. In the diagnostic table on page 231 of the book you have seen many of the diseases of which 'going light' is a symptom. And by now you realize how difficult it may be even for a poultry pathologist to diagnose the disease which is giving you cause for concern.

What steps should you take to ease your mind, when you are not certain which disease your birds have, or to be certain that your diagnosis is correct? In all countries, the nation, state, province, or commonwealth maintain diagnostic laboratories. This is done to save money for the farmers and to protect the health of the community. These laboratories are especially interested in pigeon health because pigeons can be spreaders of certain poultry diseases. Only those who take excellent care of their flocks will be interested in pigeon health and diagnostic laboratories know it. They realize that a fancier of the fancy breeds keeps his birds confined, that homing pigeon men do not permit open lofts where the birds can contract disease from poultry runs, so when you consult the pathologist you will receive a welcome reception; you will not be looked upon as a criminal, nor as a nuisance.

When you are uncertain, therefore, of the sickness which is weakening or killing your birds, take a dead bird and a sick one to your nearest 'lab', and let the experts help you.

Veterinarians who sometimes take little interest in poultry diseases, because that work is done free by the Government agencies, will

Conclusion

nevertheless be of great help to you, especially in the diagnosis of internal parasites. If you consult your local veterinarian, be sure to take with you a small quantity of droppings from each sick bird, a $\frac{1}{2}$ teaspoonful will suffice, and have faecal examinations made.

Take this book with you to help him recognize the parasite eggs. He should not object because as this book is written, there is no book of which I know which shows the eggs of pigeon parasites, and the illustrations of the eggs with comparative sizes will be useful to him.

In the commercial squab section of the pigeon field, breeders have systemized their business, until now, it is as substantial and efficient as almost any part of the whole poultry industry. In the fancy pigeon part of it there is small loss, but considerable room for improvement. In the flock flying sector, the inefficiency is quite glaring, but in the homing pigeon area the inefficiency is truly awful. I doubt that in the entire field of pets and farm animals is there as much needless loss as there is in the field of homing pigeons, unless it is in the overfeeding which annually kills so many millions of aquarium fishes.

There has been too much unnecessary impatience with pigeons which through no fault of their own fall below par in health.

The more I study the problem, the more I am convinced, that most of the birds lost in training are actually not lost at all but are unintentionally *thrown away*.

I consider myself fortunate that my principal experience in veterinary medicine has been with dogs. And I am glad of my unique opportunity of almost living with the thousands of dogs I have raised and of having hunted extensively with them. When one hunts with dogs, one can see at once what an infection of any disease will do to a dog's hunting passion, his endurance, and his ability. The dog is a large animal; if pigeons were larger their ailments would probably become more apparent.

There are parallels to be drawn between hunting dogs and racing pigeons, and here are some of the lessons I have learned.

Consider Carre's Disease, one of the virus diseases, and its effect. We used to call it 'Distemper'. Compare it with Psittacosis, so common among wild pigeons. A dog runs a fever, he acts droopy, he wants to curl up and be left alone, and he has loose watery stools indicating bowel infection. His breathing apparatus is affected. Take him a mile from home and expect him to hunt. What would happen? He wouldn't; he couldn't. Leave him in the woods, would he try to find his way home? He might, in stages, but more than likely he would 'shack up' at the first house or farm he came to.

Conclusion

The pigeon's symptoms and the effect of Psittacosis on its body and functions are much the same. Take it off on a training fly, what happens? The pigeons feels as sick as the dog felt, of that we may be reasonably sure. Why should we expect it to try to reach home? More than likely the virus and the fever have upset its homing mechanism. Certainly the bird's vitality is sapped, it has little endurance, it finds breathing difficult and probably the whole air passage system throughout the body is not functioning properly.

I maintain that training a bird that is sick in this manner is simply throwing it away.

As a further means of comparison, consider a pigeon sick with coccidiosis and a dog with the same disease. Probably every dog during his life contracts at least one of the four forms of the infecting organisms and many dogs have all four, sometimes three at a time. Once over the 4-weeks' illness, the dog is immune for life to that form or those forms. Most dogs have the disease while still in the puppy stage and they are really sick pups. Older dogs, although not as sick as puppies are with the disease, are none the less badly incapacitated. The obvious symptoms are watery, often bloody stools, unthrifty coats, fever, lack of ambition, loss of weight. The symptoms are often mistaken, even by veterinarians, and the disease is diagnosed as 'distemper'. Would anyone in his right mind expect a dog sick in this way to hunt? Surely not. All the dog wants to do is curl up and be left alone. He couldn't hunt if he wanted to, not for long.

And what of the pigeon? Almost all pigeons, like dogs, contract coccidiosis. They lose weight, sit fluffed up, are lazy. Driven out to fly, they want to alight soon, pant from exertion, drop watery stools and often their blood is infected with one or more forms of bacteria, which the mechanical damage of the coccidia to the walls of the intestine have let in. They are sick birds, most of which recover by themselves and are immune for life.

Again, is it good judgment to train such sick birds? No, you say. Yet actually the very time when the disease strikes pigeons the hardest is about the time when we start to train them. To anyone who has seen what the disease can do to young pups, it is a marvel that a homer can or will even try to fly home. One would expect it to drop down after a few miles of flying. Probably many of them do.

As a third comparison, how about worms, intestinal parasites? What does the Whipworm do to dogs? In a study which my son and I published in *Veterinary Medicine* magazine, we showed what a high per-

Conclusion

centage of dogs are infested with this parasite. And what does another worm, the Hookworm, do to dogs?

The Whipworm produces a toxin which takes the ambition out of any dog. The Hookworm does also, but in addition, this parasite lives on blood and makes the dog anaemic. Any hunting dog infested with either parasite had better be left home. He may start out and show mental keenness but it lasts a short time only. The difference between his ability when he is in this half-sick condition and his ability after he has been dewormed is remarkable. I have suspected worms in the case of dogs' 'playing out' almost before the hunts got underway and have made faecal examinations to confirm my suspicions. A week later, after the dogs had been dewormed, they were rejuvenated; acting like different dogs; dogs to be prized.

And again, what about the pigeon? I find many pigeons are infested with Capillaria worms which look and produce symptoms much like the Whipworms of dogs, even lay eggs of a similar appearance. The Hookworm of the dog has a comparative pigeon worm, Strongyle, which also sucks blood. Pigeons so infested can scarcely be counted on to race; they must have trouble staying aloft for any length of time. Is it right to train them?

No, liberating such pigeons at a distance from home is not losing them, it is throwing them away.

These are but three examples of afflictions which can be compared between pigeons and larger species. Yes, if the pigeons were larger we could see the signs of sickness more easily; they would be more apparent. And yet there *are* signs which any careful observer can use as a guide to know whether his birds are sick or well. If you train your birds while they are sick, why bother? Kill them at home and save the expense. Why go through all the bother of raising squeakers? Surely it is better to delay training and racing until the bird is in sound robust health and certainly it is more humane.

You have read in this book the consequences and effects of the ailments of pigeons and how to diagnose some diseases. You must agree that there *are* signs for those with eyes to see and that it is an insane waste, and inhumane as well, to train or race any but homers in exuberant health. Try to observe the signs of illness. Train and race only those birds which are thoroughly healthy.

The feel of the bird in your hands tells you something of its condition, the way is takes off and its desire to fly also indicate its state of health. Does it fly exuberantly with powerful wing-beats, or is its flight slow

Conclusion

and wavering? Does it want to leave the flock and alight early? Does it seek a roof-top or tree? When it alights, does it land soundly, or does it tip forward out of balance? Does it pant with beak open when the other birds land and keep their beaks shut? Does the bird sit hunched up when others are lively? Is its appetite all it should be? Are its droppings normal, or are they green and watery?

Do you ship your pigeon youngsters when they show disease symptoms? Or do you put them aside until they have regained their health and *then* train or race them? Most pigeon diseases run a course of from 2 to 3 weeks. In some, convalescence takes 6 weeks and manifestly, only birds of considerable value are worth that much attention for so long. But the symptoms of short-term diseases, such as coccidiosis, are over in 2 weeks. In the case of external parasites, some may have caused anaemia for which 2 weeks are needed to bring the blood up to normal. In the case of internal parasites which have produced toxins or anaemia, time is required to rid the system of the pests and longer to rid it of the toxic substances.

Sometimes all the birds in a loft may become droopy on the same day. As we have seen, the initial effect of intestinal worms is the worst. After the first impact of the toxins, the bird learns to live with the parasites in a state of sub-par health. Such an overall effect on the loft is easily explained by the possibility that all the birds drank from a puddle of water in an outdoor fly, or from a puddle in which pigeon droppings had accumulated.

Such a puddle may have had thousands of incubated worm eggs in it which, when swallowed, would start an infestation in all the birds simultaneously. The birds would all show the symptoms the same day, because the parasites would all develop to the point of doing damage at the same time.

Necessary patience often pays. One of the most famous and successful fliers in America showed me several birds which he had decided to eliminate in 1956 because they were out of condition. They flew poorly and came in days late. But he procrastinated and let them live. In 1957 these same birds were glowingly healthy and as yearlings, they *won* several of the major combine and concourse races in severe competition.

This same story is repeated the world over. I have heard of similar incidents from Belgians, Germans, Englishmen, and Americans. Of course we cannot afford to keep useless boarders, but we can save ourselves effort and expense by patience. As we have previously stated, there are those who maintain that once a pigeon has been sick it is per-

Conclusion

manently ruined. The obvious answer is that almost every pigeon has been sick several times during its life and we owners have missed the symptoms.

By sharpness of eye to detect the signs, with the knowledge of the many new drugs specific against many serious diseases, with the up-to-date information concerning the life cycles of parasites and how to eliminate them, you as a pigeon fancier have entered a new era. I trust that this book will help you to enjoy it.

Diagnostic Table

The table on the next four pages is designed to help you use this book to the best advantage. It should make it possible for you to identify more easily the common pigeon diseases, and then tell you where to read further about them.

If your pigeons are sick they will exhibit several symptoms. In the table these symptoms are shown in small capitals: under each there is a list of ailments, diseases or conditions with which they are most commonly associated. You will find in the book a detailed discussion of the symptoms, causes, prevention and treatment of each of these diseases.

Here is a suggestion of the way the table may be used: Suppose your pigeon or several pigeons are passing watery droppings, lose their appetites, are gradually losing flesh. In short, showing symptoms of what used to be called *going light*. Diarrhoea, Loss of Appetite, Wasting are all shown in the table as symptoms. The diseases listed under each of these symptoms vary greatly, but *Paratyphoid* appears under all. Look up *Paratyphoid* in the index, read the discussion and you may be able to determine whether the disease is infecting your birds and what you can do about it.

ANAEMIA
Fleas
Haemorrhage
Haemoproteus
Iron deficiency
Lice
Malaria
Mites
Mosquitoes
Parasites

Toxoplasmosis

APPETITE, LOSS OF
Anaemia
Aspergillosis
Canker
Change of feed
Coccidiosis
Diseases
Erysipelas

243

Diagnostic Table

Mineral deficiency
Newcastle disease
Overfeeding
Parasites
Poisoning

APPETITE, RAVENOUS
Hunger
Undernourishment

BLINDNESS
Encephalitis
Eye worm
One-eye cold
Pantothenic acid deficiency
Pigeon Pox
Vitamin A deficiency

BREATHING, ABNORMAL
Air sac mites
Anaemia
Aspergillosis
Erysipelas
Heart ailments
Haemoproteus
Infectious coryza
Malaria
Overheating
Pneumonia
Toxoplasmosis
Vitamin deficiency

CONVULSIONS
Encephalitis
Meningo-encephalitis
Newcastle disease
Paratyphoid
Poisoning
Uraemia

COUGHING, SNEEZING
Air sac mites
Canker
Dust
Infectious coryza
One-eye cold

DEVELOPMENT, IMPROPER
Amino-acid deficiency
Hunger
Mineral deficiency
Nutritional deficiency
Vitamin deficiency

DIARRHOEA
Aspergillosis
Canker
Cholera
Coccidiosis
Erysipelas
Flukes
Food
Hexamita
Newcastle disease
Nicotinic acid deficiency
Ornithosis
Parasites, internal
Paratyphoid
Poisoning
Pseudotuberculosis
Pullorum
Thiamine deficiency
Toxoplasmosis

DIZZINESS
Accidents
Anæmia
Brain Tumours
Encephalitis
Magnesium deficiency

Diagnostic Table

Meningo-encephalitis
Paratyphoid
Thiamine deficiency

EATING, DIFFICULTY IN
Beak abnormalities
Canker
Foreign bodies in crop
Tumours

EGGS, FAILURE TO HATCH
Canker
Chilling
Food
Infertility
Iodine deficiency
Paratyphoid
Vermin
Vitamin deficiency

EGGS, SOFT-SHELLED
Calcium deficiency
Magnesium deficiency

EYES, INFLAMMATION OF
Eye worm
Infectious coryza
One-eye cold

FEATHERS, ABNORMAL MOULTING
OF
Light conditions
Parasites, external
Parasites, internal
Poisoning

FEATHERS, RUFFLING OF
Cold
Diseases, all
Parasites, external

Parasites, internal
Weather, inclement

JOINTS, SWOLLEN
Paratyphoid

LUMPS
Canker
Hernias
Paratyphoid
Pox
Tumours
Wounds

NERVOUS MOVEMENTS
Aneurin deficiency
Encephalitis
Erysipelas
Meningo-encephalitis
Newcastle disease
Paratyphoid
Puffinosis
Poisoning
Uraemia

NOSE, DISCHARGE FROM
Eye worm
Infectious coryza
One-eye cold

PARALYSIS
Broken bones
Encephalitis
Paratyphoid
Poisoning

THIRST
Aspergillosis
Diarrhoea
Kidney disease
Poisoning

Diagnostic Table

Pullorum disease
Strongyle worms
Water supply inadequate

TUMOURS
Abscesses
Canker
Paratyphoid
Pox

VOMITING
Canker
Pigeon milk
Poisoning
Sour crop
Stomach-wall worm
Thrush

WASTING
Air sac mites
Aspergillosis
Canker

Kidney disease
Parasites, external
Parasites, internal
Paratyphoid
Poisoning
Pseudotuberculosis
Pullorum disease
Thiamine deficiency
Toxoplasmosis
Tuberculosis
Tumours
Undernourishment

WATTLES, DISCOLOURATION OF
   Infectious coryza
   Feeding youngsters

WHEEZING
Asthma
Coryza
Newcastle disease
Roup

Index

Index

248

Index

Ethyl-alcohol, 88
European chicken flea, 169
Excretory system, 39–40
Eye, 48–50; troubles affecting, 99, 245
Eye worm, 189-90

Faecal examinations, 109–10
Falcons, 222, 224
Fat-high foods, 79, 80; fats, 57–8, 59
Feathers, 22; cystine in, 56; lengths of, 23–4; repair of, 204–5; *see also* Moulting
Fertilizers as poisons, 215–16
Field peas, 70, 71, 81
Filaria worm, 196
Flax seed, 76–7, 81
Fleas,165–6; three kinds of, 166, 168–9,
Flies as vectors, 107, 108, 149–51, 214
Flint maize, 74
Flukes, 188–90, 191–94
Fluorine deficiency, 164
Folic acid deficiency, 161
Follicles, and 'fluffing', 22
Foods, 52–67; contaminated, 217; home-made mixtures, 83–4; ingredients, 68–84; in month before laying, 84; of old birds, during breeding season, 43, 62; of racers, 79–82; textures of, 34, 35
Forbush, E. H., 222
Foster parents, 46
Fowl-pest, 125
Fowl tick, 176–7
Fumigation, 165
Fungicides, 95–6; fungi as infecting organisms, 104
Furazolidone, 115

Gapeworms, in poultry, 196
Garden peas, 72, 83
Gawks, 119, 138
Gelatine, sources of, 54
Germicides, 95–6
Gizzard, function of, 36; gizzard erosion factor deficiency, 160
Glandular system, 40–6
Glucose, 37, 38, 101
Glycogen storage, 38–9
'Going light', 15, 102, 125, 146
Goshawks, 222, 224
Gramicidin, 100
Grass in feed, 78

Green leaves, *see under* Deficiency diseases
Greenstick and other fractures, 28
Grey squirrels, 221
Grit trays, 161
Groats, 75
Ground bone, 155
Gyrfacons, 224

Hair worm, *see* Capillaria
Halibut oil, 154; *see also* Cod liver oil
Harkanka, 101, 147
Harvest mite, 171–2
Hawks, 221–24
Heart worm (of dogs), 196
Hemoprotins, 149–51
Hemp seed, 35, 74, 77, 81; fat content of, 59
Hermaphrodites, 45
Hexamita, 152
Hookworms (analogy), 190, 240
Hormones: and crop milk, 35–6; and fertility, 89; and glycogen control, 39; *see also* Prolactin; ovarian-secreted, 44, 45
Horse-beans, 72, 81
Hydrogen peroxide, use of, 96
Hypoderaeum conoideum, 193

Immunity to disease, 105–6
Indian corn, 73, 81, 89; *see also* Maize
Infectious coryza, 119–20
I.N.I. (disease), 135–6
Insecticides, Ch. 4 *passim*, 182
Insulin and glucose, 38
'Intermediate hosts', in disease, 108
Intestines, 37
Iodine, use of, 95–6, 135; as essential mineral, 108; deficiency of, 163
Iridescence of plumage, 23
Iron deficiency, 163
Irradiated ergosterol, against rickets, 155

Jaundice, 15

Kafir grain, 75, 81; 'texture' experiment with, 35
Kamela, 196
Keratin, sources of, 54
Kidneys, ailments of, 120–1; excretion by, 39, 40

249

Index

Index

251

Index